# PEOPLE AND FOREST
UNFOLDING THE PARTICIPATION MYSTIQUE

## About the Author

**Himadri Sinha** is Associate Professor in the Faculty of Rural Development, at Xavier Institute of Social Service, Ranchi. Currently he is also associated with the Department of Research and Consultancy in the same institute. He did his masters in Agronomy from Allahabad Agricultural Institute, Allahabad University and obtained his Ph. D. from Indian Institute of Technology, Kharagpur.

He has been teaching Natural Resource Management and Agribusiness at postgraduate level for past 14 years. He has published several papers in leading national and international journals.

His research interests include Forest management, Land and water use management, Leadership and conflict resolution in commons, Livelihood promotional activities, Self Help Groups and Micro-credit. He has conducted numerous Management Development Programmes. He is a member of IASCP (International Association for Study of Common Property) and presented several papers in national and international conferences.

# PEOPLE AND FOREST
## UNFOLDING THE PARTICIPATION MYSTIQUE

**HIMADRI SINHA**
Associate Professor
Xavier Institute of Social Service
Purulia Road, Ranchi, (Jharkhand)

**CONCEPT PUBLISHING COMPANY, NEW DELHI-110059**

**Cataloging in Publication Data—DK**
*Courtesy:* D.K. Agencies (P) Ltd. <docinfo@dkagencies.com>

**Sinha, Himadri,** 1965-
People and forest : unfolding the participation mystique / Himadri Sinha.
p. cm.
With reference to India and South East Asia.
Includes bibliographical references (p. )
ISBN 8180692469

1. Community forestry—India. 2. Community forestry—Asia, Southeastern. 3. Forest management—India—Citizen participation. 4. Forest management—Asia, Southeastern— Citizen participation. I. Title.

DDC 333.750 954 21



ISBN-81-8069-246-9

First Published 2006



*Published and Printed by*
Ashok Kumar Mittal
**Concept Publishing Company**
A/15-16, Commercial Block, Mohan Garden
NEW DELHI-110059 (India)

*Phones* : 25351460, 25351794
*Fax* : 091-11-25357103
*E-mail* : publishing@conceptpub.com

*This book is dedicated to my parents, wife Praveena, son Arpan Enoch, and daughter Ipshita Keren who have renounced so many hours of my company to let this book come to fruition*

# Foreword

What makes people to protect the forest existing in their vicinity has long been debated both in academics and forest protectors' parlance. In this book, the author has not only analysed why and when people protect the forest but also offered some insightful approaches for forest conservation. The book blends a wide range of theories with real life situations to draw pragmatic policies for forest conservation.

The first section of the book discusses the objectives of forest management in India and their consequences. It explains that the 'colonial forest policy' has disrupted the complementary association between people and forest. Consequently, people have tuned from conservators of forest to its destroyers. It highlights the efforts recently emerged participatory forest management policies and practices to restore the lost association between people and forest.

Effective forest management requires collective action. Just change in policy is not sufficient. It calls for an institutional arrangement of people working together whose economic interests often vary. Collective identity of people with the forest can help developing an appropriate institutional set up. Such identity can be promoted by transferring ownership from government's hand to people's hand, democratic institutional set up, participatory leadership, and communities' social capital. The author proves these points studying and drawing evidence from three forms of community forestry— Joint Forest Management (JFM, a government initiated), Crafted Community Forest Management (CCFM, initiated mostly by NGOs), Indigenous Community forest Management (ICFM, a village/community initiated forest management regimes)— in India through qualitative and quantitative research.

The second section of the book explains policies and practices related to forest management in India and South East Asia. It offers plenty of policy information and cases of centralised and decentralised participatory forest management. Earlier points and counterpoints are once again validated here.

Lastly, evidences are put together for building a framework. It depicts the process for eliciting people's participation for sustainable use and conservation of forest resources. The framework can recharge the minds of practitioners, activists and academicians. This work fills a niche and does so very well. It will be of immense help to students, teachers, NGOs, activists and donors who are interested in forest management.

**Damodar Suar,** Ph. D.
*Professor*
Indian Institute of Technology, Kharagpur

# Preface

*'Wisdom is better than strength.*
*Nevertheless poor man's wisdom is despised,*
*And his words are not heard.'*
—— Biblical Proverb

The political, social, economic and technological changes of the last three centuries have seriously challenged the long tradition in common property, the use and management of common-pool resources (CPRs) in general and forest in particular. Forest management practices in South and South East Asian nations were radically altered by their colonial rulers. Such policies alienated forest dwellers from their habitat and replaced their ways of forest management that with a centralised system. Centralised forest management systems primarily focussed on to meet colonial demands viz. timber need of railways, ship building, and defence ventures. It paid little interest to community welfare on one hand and to understand the existing practices of forest protection of communities on the other. As a result large-scale depletion of forest resources began. The above quoted proverb perhaps aptly describes the reasons for consecutive ecological degradation.

Acrid experience of the centralised forest management compelled governments of India and South East Asian nations to adopt a policy to involve people in forest protection and regeneration in a collaborative manner. Under this policy approach, forest communities were offered rights to collect non-timber forest produce from reserved forest and a partial share of the final timber harvest as a token of appreciation for their contribution. Such effort began with the concept of social forestry. Later on in India, the social forestry movement was modified to attract more participation by offering more power to local communities over forest. This movement later on was popularised as Joint Forest Management (JFM). JFM is probably first government initiated programme that has the flavour of community based forest management (CBFM). Apart from JFM, Indian forest protection movement has witnessed two other kinds of CBFM. The first type of CBFM emerged out of local initiatives and another emerged with the active sponsorship of local government and NGOs.

People's participation is considered as indispensable factor for the efficient CBFM. Efficient management requires rule-ordered behaviour of the community members geared towards sustainability of natural resources. Institutional governance provides framework for such rule-ordered behaviour. Institutional governance with wide acceptability among resource users promotes prolific people's involvement in resource conservation, inculcates mutual sharing of responsibility and accountability, lessens conflicts, and reduces free riding. Similarly, local leadership plays pivotal role for the involvement of people in collective action like forest management, cooperatives, water user's association etc. by changing the mindset of people and imbibing conservation values in members of community. Evidences also suggest that people's participation, commitment, job satisfaction, and performance increase if individual values match with the organisational values. The book dealt with the questions how participation is influenced by (a) different forms of forest management system - that is related to the policies; (b) composition, type, and quality of institutional governance - that is related to institutional framework; (c) style of leadership; and (d) value identification both at organisational and individual level.

Book is divided into two parts. Including the introduction first part has five chapters that deal with ' Understanding Participation Mystique in CBFM'. In Chapter II, we have discussed how social identity approach can help in eliciting people's participation. While Chapter III discusses how institutional governance influences people's participation, Chapter IV analyses how leadership and congruence of institutional and individual values influence level of people's participation in forest management. Chapter V focuses on role of social capital in natural resource management and attempts to unfold the link between social capital and people's participation in managing the commons.

Second part of the book focuses on 'Policy and Practices of CBFM'. It has four chapters. Chapter VI elaborates the policies and practices of Joint Forest Management in India and some successful cases of JFM. Chapter VII analyses few cases of forest management systems of South East Asia. Chapter VIII discusses cases of self-initiated as well as NGO initiated crafted community based forest management. Finally in Chapter IX, we present a conceptual framework for eliciting people's participation in grassroots commons and offer suggestions for policy implications.

Book will enable the readers to comprehend and appreciate the participation dynamics in CBFM specifically. This will help students of Forest Management, Rural Management, Research Scholar working on environmental issues, NGOs and Social Activist working on forest and natural resource conservation to work in CBFM with better understanding of complexity of people's oriented forest management. The book may also generate interest among Sociologist, Anthropologist, and Behavioural Scientist from theoretical perspective.

**Himadri Sinha**
Xavier Institute of Social Service, Ranchi

# Acknowledgements

First of all, let me exalt Almighty God, author and perfecter of all creation, from whom flows all blessings and wisdom for without His grace this work could not have been accomplished. I would like to express my appreciation and gratitude to many individuals who have helped me to understand rural realities as well as contributed to the development of this book. First, I would like to extend my sincere thanks to Dr. Damodar Suar, Professor, IIT Kharagpur who not only encouraged me to publish this book but also provided stimulating ideas, and guidance. It is because of his sustained assistance in every step, this work could be moulded into a concrete shape. I am also thankful to the people of Concept Publishing Company for being kind to publish this book. I am thankful to Prof. Anil Gupta, IIM Ahmedabad who instilled a deep inquisitiveness in me for the study of commons and also to Prof. Anup Sarkar and many practitioners of PLA for imbibing a deep appreciation within me for people's focussed developmental approaches.

I am grateful to the authorities of National Tree Growers Cooperative Federation Limited (NTGCF), Anand, Gujarat, Mr. Jagdeesh Rao, Executive Director (NTGCF), Indian Institute of Bio-social Research and Development (IBRAD), Kharagpur, and Forest Departments of Jharkhand, Madhya Pradesh, Orissa, and West Bengal for permitting me to collect information from their forest protection units. Above all, I am highly indebted to all villagers who spontaneously spared their most valuable time and provided all the required information for various empirical studies included in this book. I cannot forget their warm hospitality and how readily they accepted this unknown sojourner, provided accommodation, and shared their meals with me. I am especially thankful to Mr. Subrata Singh, Mr. Sisir Pradhan, Ms. Meena Das

Mahapatra of NTGCF Angul Team, Mrs. D. Mukhopadhya of IBRAD, and individuals viz. Manas Haldar, Dipankar Sengupta, Victor Soreng, Pankaj Sahoo, and Shanti Mardi for assisting me in data collection. I am much indebted to Dr. (Fr.) C. Lakra s.j., Chairman of Governing Body and Dr. (Fr.) B. A. Ekka s. j., Director, Xavier Institute of Social Service (XISS), Ranchi, for providing all financial and administrative support to carry out my empirical studies. I extend my sincere thanks to Fr. L. Francken s.j., former Director, XISS, Dr. A. Prasad, HOD Publications, XISS and Dr. M. H. Ansari, HOD-Rural Development, XISS for their valuable suggestions on the first draft. I wish to extend my heartfelt thanks to Dr. Rachel Selvaraj, Ms. Ruplekha Khuntia and Ms. Amrita Basu for painstakingly editing the draft and providing valuable suggestions. I am thankful to Ms. Sabina Bara for typing some part of the manuscript.

Last but not the least, I wish to express my heartiest thanks to my parents, and wife for their unceasing encouragement and the sacrifice during the entire study. My son Arpan Enoch, and daughter Ipshita Keren whose company I often missed since their birth owing to this work, deserve special thanks from the core of my heart.

# Contents

# List of Tables

# List of Figures

# List of Boxes

# List of Abbreviations

| | |
|---|---|
| CALC | Certificate of Ancestral Land Claim |
| CBFM | Community Based Forest Management |
| CCFM | Crafted Community Forest Management |
| CCFS | Certificate of Community Forest Stewardship |
| CCR | Corporate Contract Reforestation |
| CFMA | Community Forestry Management Agreement |
| CPR | Common Pool Resources |
| CSC | Certificate of Stewardship Contract |
| DENR | Department of Environment and Natural Resources |
| DFO | Divisional Forest Officer |
| FCR | Family Contract Reforestation |
| FD | Forest Department |
| FLMA | Forest Lease Management Agreement |
| FPC | Forest Protection Committee |
| GB | Governing Body |
| ICFM | Indigenous Community Forest Management |
| ISFP | Integrated Social Forestry Program |
| JFM | Joint Forest Management |
| KTH | Kelompok Tani Hutan |
| MC | Managing Committee |
| NCA | National Commission on Agriculture |
| MFPP | Minor Forest Product Permit |
| NFP | National Forestation Program |
| NGO | Nongovernmental Organisation |
| NTFP | Non Timber Forest Produce |
| PVO | Private Voluntary Organizations |
| SFC | State Forest Corporation |
| TF-AD | Ancestral Land Delineation Task Force |
| VFPC | Village Forest Protection Committee |

# List of Plant's Name Used in the Book

| Local Name | Botanical Name |
|---|---|
| Aakashmani | *Acacia auriculiformis* |
| Acacia | *Acacia catechu* |
| Ankula | *Alangium salvifolium* |
| Arjun | *Terminalia arjuna* |
| Asan | *Termenalia tormentosa* |
| Asana | *Terminalia alata* |
| Attendi | *Combretum annulatum* |
| Babul | *Acacia arabica* |
| Bahada/ Bahuda | *Terminalia belerica* |
| Bamboo | *Bambusa arundinacea* |
| Bandhana | *Ougeinia oojeinesis* |
| Bhadara | *Gmelina hystrix & G. asiatica* |
| Bhadavadaha | *Opila mentaceae* |
| Bija | *Pterocarpus marsupium* |
| Brinjal | *Solanum melongena* |
| Black gram | *Vigna mungo* |
| Cashew | *Anacardium occidentale* |
| Deva Kanchan | *Bahunia purpuria* |
| Eucalyptus | *Eucalyptus globules & E. citriodora* |
| Gambhari | *Gmelina arborea* |
| Groundnut | *Arachis hypogea* |
| Guava | *Psidium guajava* |
| Halda | *Diospyros montana* |
| Himalayan Lilac | *Syringa emodi* |
| Imli | *Tamarind indica* |
| Indian spinach | *Amaranthus spp.* |
| Kanso | *Himenodictyon excelsum* |
| Kantalu | *Dioscorea belophyla* |
| Karada | *Cleistanthus collinus* |
| Karanj | *Pongamia pinnata* |

| | |
|---|---|
| Kathal (Jack fruit) | *Artocarpus integrifolia* |
| Kendu | *Diospyrus melanoxylon* |
| Khakada | *Casearia elliptica* |
| Khukundi | *Calicopteris floribunda (climber)* |
| Kumbhi | *Careya arborea* |
| Kuruma | *Ardina cordifolia* |
| Lady's finger | *Abelmoschus esculentus* |
| Mahua | *Madhuca indica* |
| Maize | *Zea mays* |
| Mandua/Ragi | *Eleusine coracana* |
| Mango | *Mangifera indica* |
| Mehisaalu | *Dioscorea bulbifera* |
| Nahalbelli | *Cipadessa baccifera* |
| Neem | *Azadirachta indica* |
| Palash | *Butea monosperma & B. frondosa* |
| Panialu | *Dioscorea oppositifolia* |
| Patuli | *Steriospermum chelonoides* |
| Pine | *Ficus(Pinus) roxburghii* |
| Potato | *Solanum tuberosum* |
| Prosopis | *Prosopis juliflora* |
| Rambaans | *Agave angustifola var. variegata* |
| Rhododendron | *Rhododendron arboreum* |
| Sabai grass | *Eulaliopsis binata* |
| Sal | *Shorea robusta* |
| Seedha | *Lagerstromea parviflora* |
| Sesame | *Dalbergia sissoo* |
| Sindwar | *Vitex negundo* |
| Siris | *Albizzia lebbek* |
| Sondal | *Cassia fistula* |
| Subabul | *Leucaena lucocephala* |
| Teak (Sagwan) | *Teetona grandis* |
| Willow Leaf | *Ficus nerifolii* |

# PART-I

## Understanding Participation Mystique in Community Based Forest Management

# INTRODUCTION

The term 'commons' or 'common pool resources' refers to diverse resources or facilities which have some joint ownership or access. Under joint ownership, a group of individuals use the benefits generated by a particular resource by excluding non-group members and putting some restrictions on individual member's behaviour. The exclusion is necessary because such resources are subtractible or reduced after every use and, therefore, may be congested, over harvested, degraded or even destroyed otherwise. Furthermore, management of member's opportunistic behaviour is another crucial challenge for commons. Rational human beings always try to increase personal wealth in a finite world by extracting additional benefit (Hardin, 1968). Individuals try to do this either by free riding (by taking benefits without contributing to its generation) or by overusing the resources. Such phenomena cause the break down of common pool resource management (Hardin, 1968).

Management of commons or common pool resources primarily deals with these problems by setting-up institutional mechanisms. Institutions are the rules that people develop to specify the ' do's and don'ts' related to a particular situation. Rules define who has the access to resources, what can be harvested from, dumped into, or engineered within a resource. It also specifies who can participate in key decision-making about the above issues and the transfer rights and duties to others. Dispute regarding distribution of common pool resources among members/villagers has often stimulated changes in institutional arrangement. Multiple types of institutional arrangements have been devised for reducing the problems of overuse, free riding and conflict over distribution of resources.

## Will Commons Survive?

Substantial number of people often questions the researchers and activists of common pool resources, 'Why are you wasting your time with the study of small, unimportant, local resources and outdated institutions? Don't you know that local resources are boring? Common property institutions are a thing of the past. Common property institutions will fade away within the next few decades.' The basic message of the challengers is that common pool resources are insignificant in modern times and that common-property institutions are not worth studying because they will not survive. On the other hand, it is certainly the case that common pool resources will continue to be a core type of resource of major theoretical and policy significance for as long as humans continue to rely on water, air, and the atmosphere. It is a myth that common-pool resources are all small. In addition to the prototypic local resources, the oceans, the gene pool, and the atmosphere are all common pool resources. No one-to-one relationship exists, of course, between and kind of good or resource and the type of institutions that are used to govern and manage that resources. Thus, common-pool resources might continue for a very long time and be governed entirely by national governments or private property. Will common property institutions survive in the era of globalisation?

Our answer is an emphatic yes! Further, besides the existing, robust common property institutions, new forms of common property are frequently created. For example, some views the modern corporation as the epitome of private property. But a publicly held corporation, however, is more properly thought of as common property than as strictly private property. A large number of shareholders, managers, employees, and customers hold identifiable rights in the corporation, but no one person or family holds all of the relevant property rights. To make decisions related to the allocation of resources from a corporation treasury, multiple institutional arrangements must be evoked for each and every kind of decision. No single decision-maker can make all of these decisions based entirely on his or her own preference or values.

The impact of decisions made for one set of actors affects all of the others who have an economic interest in the profitability of the production processes adopted by the corporation. Besides the modern corporation, many urban families now live in condominiums - a combination of private and common property as well as owning rights to use a vacation residence with ten or twenty other families. The number of common-property institutions appears to be growing rather than diminishing over time.

On the resource side, we are also creating new common-pool resources. The Internet and the multiplicity of servers providing accessing to website, and too large a number of users at a given time can result in collapse of the server. Difficulties that the Indian Railways faces at busiest Railway Stations in Mumbai and Kolkata while allocating platforms for arriving trains illustrates how challenging it is to allocate a common pool resource when the demand for the resource grossly exceeds supply. These are only a few of the modern common pool resources with many difficult and unresolved governance structures.

An important challenge in governing common-pool resources lies in the fact that stocks and flows of these resources are often difficult to define with great precision. These resources can be fugitive (e.g., fisheries and wild line) and often cannot be stored. They are often used at different geographic scales, and these uses are often in conflict: local forest users accrue benefits when the forest is used for timber production, for example, whereas global users of forests benefit from standing trees as they sequester a major global pollutant (Young, 1999). Further, the use of common-pool resources often presents negative externalities to those who do not necessarily benefit from such use. For example, harvesting timber may lead to the deterioration of water quality downstream from the location where the timber is harvested (Bruce, 1999). Most traditional common pool resources have already been governed by one regime or another. These regimes have performed with various levels of success. The challenge in managing such resources is to devise more effective institutions when the remnants of the previous regimes are still present. For example, many policy-makers have acted in accordance with the assertion of policy analysts that two alternative 'Solutions' exits to the presumed ever-present 'tragedy of the commons': common pool resources, according to these analysts, were either to be privatised or to be appropriated by the national government and managed by a governmental agency. After decades of poor management and deterioration of common-pool resources, regimes developed in accordance with this dichotomous thinking are being changed. The challenge now is to devise institutions that reallocate the common-pool resource in the presence of political action by those who would lose in the process of reallocation.

Protecting a common-pool resource from overuse requires that users or external authorities create rules that regulate its use. Devising such rules requires the joint effort of a large proportion of the resource users. Given that it is costly and that all resource users will benefit from new rules protecting the resource, creating such rules itself requires that the users overcome collective-action dilemmas. Groups with longer traditions of mutual trust and close-knit communities that enable resource users to reciprocate in behaviour are more likely than other groups to succeed in devising and sustaining successful institution (Lam, 1998).

Common pool resources and their users are not only found in isolated communities lacking connections to the external world. On the contrary, today most users of common pool resources interact with other people in an institutional environment that is external to the one regulating the common pool resource and imposes constraints on the regime governing it. They are forced to seek external legal authorities to protect the institutions governing the common-pool resource. An external political process determines how much support such users will receive from their national government in enforcing a self-organized regime. This is particularly important when 'outsiders' begin to use a common-pool resource illegally or would like to gain access to it.

The questions raised in the preceding paragraphs are addressed in this volume from the perspectives of forest management in India. One task of this first chapter is, therefore, to provide a common vocabulary for the enterprise. Consequently, in the next section of this chapter, we will be addressing the following issues: What are the core meanings of terms such as 'common-pool resources' and 'common-property institutions'? And what vocabulary term we will use in this volume for our purpose?

**Problem of a Common Vocabulary**

Significant confusion exists in the research literatures about terms such as 'common property institutions', 'common pool resources', 'the commons', and 'commoners' as well as many terms related to these. In this book by common pool resources, we mean those resources that share two fundamental characteristics with other resources. The first shared characteristic is subtractability or rivalness. This means when one person harvests from or deposits in a resource subtracts from the ability of others to do the same. The acre-feet of water withdrawn from a particular water resource by one user are no longer available to others using the same resource. Similarly, if some forest produce from a particular forest patch is used, it reduces the availability of the same to other users. It is this characteristic that can lead to the overuse, congestion, or even destruction of a common pool resources (Ostrom, Gardner, and Walker, 1994).

The second shared characteristic is related to the cost of excluding potential beneficiaries from access to the resource. This characteristic of common pool resources tempts potential beneficiaries to be a free rider. They may be able to gain benefits without contributing to the costs of providing, maintaining, and regulating the resource involved. The institutions that individuals craft to govern any common pool resource must, therefore, deal with the threats of overuse and of free riding. With well-designed institutions, it is possible to implement ways of excluding potential users from any common pool resource or public resource. Mechanisms of exclusion do not come without a cost. Nonetheless, regimes for governance of common pool resources must deal with these costs in some manner.

Besides these two shared attributes, common pool resources may differ from one another in regard to a wide variety of other attributes, such as their size, resource type, production over time and space, etc. For instance, mobile common pool resources like water bodies along with their produce or wildlife vary substantially from stable resources like a forest stand, pasture land and production pattern also varies over time and space (Schlager, Blomquist, and Tang, 1994). Thus, any analysis of common pool problems needs to focus both on the commonalities and on the differences among common pool resources.

Purpose of crafting institutions is to increase the efficiency and sustainability of common pool resources. Institution can be regarded as set of "dos and don'ts" in regard to the entry, harvesting and management of a resource and how individuals acquire or transfer rights to use a resource (Bromley et al., 1992; Schlager and Ostrom, 1992; McCay and Acheson, 1987). Three broad forms of ownership can govern a common pool resource: government, private, or common-property ownership. Many variants of these three broad types of ownership regimes exist. Furthermore, there is no consistent evidence that any one of these regimes is best suited for all types of common pool resources (Dietz et al. 2002), even though, considerable debate about the relative advantages of one regime or the other exists in the academic literature.

In recent times, one frequently recommended solution to the tragedy of the commons is to privatize the resource. Even though a common property regime also is a form of private property, 'privatisation' usually refers to the case in which the rights to a resource are allocated to individuals rather than groups and individuals are free to sell these rights to others. Privatisation is, however, hardly ever complete; individual users or firms are not assigned all rights, but only the right to access and use the resource and to transfer their right to another party (Cole, 1999). Many common pool resources have been privatised, some more successfully than others. The challenge in privatisation of common pool resources is to devise an institutional design that ensures sustainability and efficiency in managing resources with specific characteristics in a given external legal and regulatory environment. We cannot simply transfer an institutional design that worked well for managing one type of common pool resource in one region of the world to another type of resource in another region and expect to repeat the success. Similarly, resource management under an identifiable group also presents its own set of problems. Many of these problems are dynamic in nature and demands considerable flexibility in the institutional framework for their management. Some institutions have successful in handling the problems than others. Several researchers have tried to enlist the characteristics of successful common property institutions for the wider appreciation. Let us now look into those works in order to develop our own conceptual framework.

## Institutional Perspectives of Common Pool Resources

During past decades, several theoretical and empirical researches have demonstrated that users of commons can organise themselves to achieve relatively efficient outcomes from the continued use of resources (Bromley et al., 1992; Balland and Platteau, 1996; Ostrom, 1990; Wade, 1988). Attempts have been made to analyse the comparative efficacy of such institutions. Of the comparative studies, analytical frameworks given by Wade (1988), Ostrom (1990), and Balland and Platteau (1996) are found to have wider applicability. These authors have shown that under some combinations of frequently occurring conditions, members of small groups can design institutional arrangements for sustainable resource management. These conditions are: (a) resources, (b) resource users, (c) local institutional practices, and (d) external environment.

Wade's (1988) work was based on commons' managed irrigation systems of South India in 31 villages. He found 14 conditions as important in facilitating successful management of the commons. Most of the conditions are general statements about the local context, users groups, and the resource systems, but some of them are about the relationship between users and resources. Only one of his conditions pertains to external relationship of the group or of other local factors (Table 1.1). Some of these factors are also used by others which include small group size, well-defined boundary, ease in monitoring and enforcement of institutional rules, and closeness between location of users and the resources. Ostrom (1990) in her design principles while using the above factors also included nesting or federating opportunity for complex institutional systems. However, like Wade, she also reiterated that State policies should not undermine the decision of local people. Balland and Platteau (1996) follow a similar strategy, as does Ostrom. They argue that privatisation of common pool or regulation by central authorities tends to eliminate the implicit entitlements and thereby impair efficiency and undermine the rights of traditional users. However, they also opined that none of the common pool regimes appear intrinsically efficient. They suggested supportive role of central authority in managing the common pool and unlike Wade and Ostrom, they paid greater attention to external forces, external aid, enforcement, and leadership with experience in management of commons (Table 1.1).

The conditions identified above by Wade, Ostrom, and Balland and Platteau have focussed less on external institutional environment, demographic issues, and market related demands that make local demands trivial. Individual's perception and decision are often influenced by socio-demographic factors, external environment, and arrival of new market opportunities. These factors may also change local power relationship by increasing the manoeuvring power of some subgroups within the group using common pool regimes. In many cases, change in individual perceptions may promote new types of associations and alliances. Institutional sustainability depends largely on individual's decision to adhere to and abide by the institutional norms and values. Such decisions are expressed in the form of individual's spontaneous support to institutional causes and participation in its activities. The above three frameworks, although effectively assess group choices, limit the scope of individual perception about existing institutional affairs. This inadequacy can be overcome by assessing individuals' perception about institutional affairs and their impact on management of common pool regimes such as water, pasture, forest resources, etc.

**Table 1.1 : Conditions Required for Successful Governance of Commons**

| Factors | Framework | | |
|---|---|---|---|
| | Wade | Ostrom | Balland and Platteau |
| Resource system characteristics | 1. Small size<br>2. Well-defined boundaries | Well-defined boundaries | None presented as important |
| Group characteristics | 1. Small size<br>2. Clearly defined boundaries<br>3. Past successful experiences social capital<br>4. Inter-dependence among group members | Well-defined boundaries | 1. Small size<br>2. Shared norms<br>3. Past successful experiences – social capital<br>4. Appropriate leadership<br>5. Inter-dependence among group members<br>6. Heterogeneity of endowments, homogeneity of identities and interests. |
| Institutional arrangements | 1. Locally devised access and management rules<br>2. Ease in enforcement of rules<br>3. Graduated sanctions | 1. Locally devised access and management rules<br>2. Ease in enforcement of rules<br>3. Graduated sanctions<br>4. Availability of low-cost adjudication<br>5. Accountabilities of monitors and other officials to users | 1. Rules are simple and easy to understand<br>2. Locally devised access and management rules<br>3. Ease in enforcement of rules<br>4. Accountaibility of monitors and other officials to users |
| External environment | 1. Technology : Low-cost exclusion technology<br>2. State : Central governments should not undermine local authorities | 1. Technology : None presented as important<br>2. State :<br>(a) Central governments should not undermine local authorities | 1. Technology : None presented as important<br>2. State :<br>(a) Supportive external sanctioning institutions<br>(b) Appropriate levels of external aid to compensate local users for conservation activities |

*Sources* : Wade (1988); Ostrom (1990); Balland and Platteau (1996).

**Common Pool Resources in India**

In India, common pool resources include community pastures, community forests, wastelands, common dumping, and threshing grounds, watershed drainages, village ponds, rivers, rivulets, their banks and beds. Even when the legal ownership of some of these resources rests with another agency, such as wastelands belonging to the Revenue department of the State, in a *de facto* sense they belong to the village communities and continue to be a significant component of the land resource base of rural communities. These resources contribute to the production and consumption needs of rural communities in some critical ways.

In general, the rural poor obtain bulk of their fuel supplies and fodder from common pool resources (CPR). CPR product collection is an important source of employment and income, especially during the periods when other opportunities are almost non-existent. Furthermore, CPR income, despite being likely to be under-estimated, accounts for 14 to 23% of household income from all other sources (Jodha, 1994, Sarin, 1996).

Forest resources are one of the most important CPR that contribute to the survival needs of majority of tribal and other disadvanged communities. In general, forest resources provide 50% of household income for 20-30 percent rural population particularly the tribal. Despite their importance to the poor households, by 1995, out of total 76.52 million hectares forest coverage, 30.98 million hectares forest area of the country became degraded (Forest Report, 1995). Such rapid depletion of forest resources raised general apprehension about state of forest affairs in the country.

Rapid decline of forest in India has occurred as a result of centralised bureaucratic management of forest department, failure of grassroots forest management institutions, and lack of community participation in forest protection (Gadgil and Guha, 1992; Malhotra, 1995; Raju, 1998; Sarin, 1996). Prior to British Forest Act (1878), Indian forests used to be managed by forest communities under the leadership of local elders but the Forest Act barred these communities from enjoying both property and usufruct rights (Guha, 1983). This turned forest communities from guardians to encroachers and destroyers of forest. During the past few decades, both governmental and non-governmental efforts have been made to involve forest communities in the all-round affairs of forest management. This has yielded positive results in stopping illegal forest felling and regenerating the degraded forests (Deb and Malhotra, 1993; Poffenberger, 1990; Raju, 1998). This book, therefore, focuses on forest conservation from people's perspectives.

## Indian Forest Management in Retrospect

System of forest management in India can be divided into four phases: (a) Pre-colonial period, (b) Colonial period, (c) Post-colonial period after independence, 1947-1988, and (d) Introduction of participatory forest management.

*(a) Pre-colonial period :* Pre-colonial period (before the enforcement of Forest Act by colonial administration in 1878) is often referred to as the 'golden age' of forests. Local people had unrestricted access and usufruct rights over forests. Forests were protected by ethno-religious values, cultural pride, community identification with the forest, inter-community non-interference, and community restrictions on users (Guha, 1983).

*(b) Colonial period :* During the British period, the use of timber multiplied due to railway construction, ship building, and military purposes. This caused a fast decline in forest reserve and the need for forest conservation was strongly felt. Hence, the first Forest Act was introduced in 1878. The aim of the act was to promote 'scientific forest management' all over the country to meet the growing needs for timber. The act divided the forestlands into four categories: (a) Reserved forest, (b) Protected forest, (c) Private forest, and (d) Village forest. Villagers were given free access only to village forests. In protected forests, these rights were limited only to collection of non-timber forest produce. The act also led to the formation of Forest Department (FD) as a custodian body for forest protection. The earlier role of forest community as conservator of forest was, thus, completely undermined. Colonial

forest policy severely disrupted the lives of forest communities particularly the tribal. Tribal livelihood was primarily dependent on agriculture and forest resources. They were stripped off their usufruct rights and lost the major source of livelihood. FD also reserved the rights to convert village forests into reserved or protected forests. Lack of legitimacy caused violent peasant movements (Guha, 1983) and forest communities gradually lost their interest in forest conservation.

*(c) Post-colonial period (1947- 1988) :* After independence, it was expected that the Indian forest policy would rectify the discrepancies of the colonial Forest Act and make it more people friendly. Unfortunately, the Indian Forest Act (1952), incorporated policies to pursue the colonial legacy. FD assumed the role of sole collector and seller of all timber and other forest produce. FD, therefore, caused the erosion of remaining common pool resources even after independence (Jodha, 1986). As a compensatory measure, FD provided timber at subsidised rate and occasional wage employment to the forest communities. However, such inducement could not ameliorate forest communities' growing disenchantment with the forest. They resorted to illegal encroachment and tree felling. Furthermore, FD's authoritarian role continued to weaken the local community institutions by denying their rights over the forest. By the 1960s, the conflict-ridden relationship between FD and the forest community seriously damaged the forest reserve.

*(d) Introduction of participatory forest management:* Bitter experience of the first two decades after independence impelled FD of West Bengal to adopt a policy to involve people in forest protection and regeneration in a collaborative manner. Under this policy approach, forest communities were offered rights to collect non-timber forest produce from protected forest and a partial share of the final timber harvest as a token of appreciation for their contribution. This movement, later on, was popularised as Joint Forest Management (JFM). A pilot project was started at Arabari in West Bengal. People helped FD to regenerate 1,250 hectares of Sal (*Shorea robusta*) forest. Encouraged by the Arabari experiment

and many such experiences from states like West Bengal, Haryana, and Orissa, the Government of India gave formal recognition to JFM in the Forest Policy of 1988. However, earlier conflicts and distrust between FD and forest communities continues to haunt both the parties in many places. Further, differential benefit sharing system existing in different states prevented JFM from achieving the desirable impact in many places.

Likewise, people's movements like Chipko (embracing the trees) in Uttar Pradesh hills, Orans in Rajasthan, Sacred groves in Western Ghat hills, Shamliyat (Common) forest in Punjab, and Safety forest in Mizoram showed great potentiality of community managed forest (Chakravorty-Kaul, 1993; Gadgil, 1989). NGOs had also started promoting community based forest management from the mid-seventies. The strength of these non-governmental forest movements was that the communities had ownership and usufruct rights.

## Emergence of Community Based Forest Management

Indian forest protection movement witnessed the emergence of three distinct types of community based forest management (CBFM). The first type of community based forest management emerged out of local initiatives as a result of growing stress owing to rapid degradation of forest. Charismatic local leaders, enthusiastic youth groups, concerned outsiders like FD, and NGOs gave moral fillip to communities for consolidating their forest protection initiatives in an organised manner. These groups were confined to those areas where communities had either strong economic dependency on forest or had unbroken tradition of communal resource management. In eastern Indian states of Jharkhand and Orissa alone, an estimated 200,000 hectares of forest were protected by thousands of community organisations (Singh and Singh, 1993). Such forest management was also reported from Rajasthan, Gujarat, Karnataka, and Punjab. While some of these units were small and informal, others were large and formal with well-defined rules and regulations. These community institutions had broad diversity in organisational structure, age, leadership style and governance of the commons.

These community based forest management units are referred to as Indigenous Community Forest Management (ICFM).

The second type of community based forest management emerged with the active sponsorship of local government and NGOs. Village *panchayats*[1], women organisations (*Mahila Mandals*), Tree growers' co-operatives and other NGOs who gave high priority to forest protection, took the lead to motivate and educate people to develop their community based forest management. The effectiveness of these units varied widely depending upon their common interest, functional capabilities, and leadership pattern. During the past two decades, the number of such units has multiplied. This type of community based forest management is popularly known as Crafted Community Forest Management (CCFM).

FD promoted the third type of community based forest management. During the 1930s, such units were first formed in Himachal Pradesh and were popularly known as Forest Co-operative Societies and in Uttar Pradesh they were called *Van Panchayat*. These initiatives generated wide scale people's involvement. However, the state revenue agencies reserved their rights to control the revenue flow from timber and thereby, often deprived the villagers from their legitimate share. More recently, co-operation of villagers was solicited through JFM programme. It started from West Bengal and spread to Orissa, Gujarat, Rajasthan, Haryana, Jammu and Kashmir, Madhya Pradesh, Uttar Pradesh, Bihar, and Andhra Pradesh. Unlike Forest Co-operative Societies and *Van Panchayat*, JFM offered greater opportunities in sharing responsibilities to the villagers. Villagers were given a substantial share of non-timber forest produce along with a certain portion of the timber harvested, which varied from state to state. Forest executives as per the policy of the state FD framed the JFM rules. Villagers had little or no role to play in formulation of rules and

1. *Gram* (village) panchayat is the lowest strata of governance in India consist of 5,000 populations belonging to one or several adjacent villages popularly known as *Panchayati Raj* Institution. *Mukhiya* is the elected representative of village panchayat

regulations for their JFM unit. In West Bengal, JFM became popular owing to a strong felt need rather than a fascination with the rules (Poffenberger and McGean, 1996; Sarin, 1996).

**Box 1.1 Joint Forest Management Movement**

The National Forest Policy 1988, made a significant departure while overhauling the national forest policy of 1952. Impressed by the success of the West Bengal experiment of involving people in forest management, it recognised the need for involving the people around the forest in the development, protection and management of forest. Later on in June 1990, the Ministry of Environment, Government of India, issued guidelines concerning the involvement of village communities and voluntary agencies in the protection, development and management of forests and named it as Joint Forest Management. Till 2000, 19 states had issued resolutions/notifications besides West Bengal and Orissa who played the pioneer role. By 1999, approximately 1.5 million hectares of degraded forest land were protected and managed by 15,000 forest protection committees in 16 states.

In the state of West Bengal, the total number of FPC was 3289 and 3,71,790 members were involved in the protection of 4,493 sq. km. of forest land. In West Bengal, 3023 hectares of Sal (*Shorea robusta*) forests were harvested since 1995 and 25% of the revenue (after deducting Rs. 1.48 crores from gross revenue Rs. 6.09 crores) amounting Rs. 1.15 crores were distributed among the FPC members.

JFM units can be formed with a hamlet, or a village, or a cluster of villages in which each household has single membership. Each JFM unit consists of two bodies, (a) general body which includes all the member households, and (b) managing/executive committee which consists of elected representatives from among the general body members along with few nominated members. Managing committee elects its president and the local forester acts as its convenor secretary. The general body meets once a year whereas the managing committee's meetings are expected to be held once in three months.

(*Source:* Joint Forest Management update 1998)

## Do People Participate in CBFM Spontaneously?

What elicits participation of a rational individual in CBFMs in uncertain situations has always been a serious concern to environmentalists and FD. Individual choice behaviour depends on how individuals learn about, view, and weigh the benefits and cost of actions and their perceived linkage to outcomes that involve the benefits and cost, and social restrictions and risk. Participation means an individual's conscious decision to cooperate with certain activity or organisation. This may be inhibited when individual fails to be convinced about the outcome of an activity. In CBFMs, when people are not confident about the outcome or the eventuality of final benefit flow, they become indifferent about the forest management.

Organising forest users for collective forest management is an uncertain and complex undertaking. Uncertainty has many sources in the Indian forest management context: crop failure due to untimely erratic rainfall in rainfed farming areas, lack of market opportunities for alternative livelihood, absence of legal rights over forest produce, tenure security, transparency and accountability of institutional leadership, conflict resolution mechanism due to political interference, etc. It has been observed that besides the economic factor, seven other factors may act as constraint for people's participation in Indian forest management :

(a) Formation of forest committee with heterogeneous interest groups;
(b) Absence of favourable socio-political environment that promotes participation;
(c) Incompatibility of governing rules with the local socio-cultural concept;
(d) Absence of transparent, and accountable managing committee;
(e) Absence of participatory leadership with idealised behaviour in forest management;
(f) Inappropriate inter- and intra-community conflict resolution mechanism;
(g) Lack of awareness regarding environmental protection leading towards incongruent; value system between leaders and other users.

Collective action problems related to the provision of CPR and appropriation from CPR extend over time. Individuals give less value to benefits that they expect to receive in the distant future, and more value to those expected in the immediate future. In forest management, rapid returns are not quite possible. Hence, immediate benefits have to be sacrificed at the altar of sustainable future return. For this reason, the rational individual seeks assurances in the form of stable institution for safeguarding the future return either to her/him or to her/his offspring. Therefore, institution must try to remove constraining factors that restrain people's from actively participation. The seven constraints of participation in CBFM are discussed below.

**Constraint 1 : Formation of forest committee with heterogeneous interest groups**

In general, community in forest management implies a village or a hamlet (Poffenberger et al.1996; Raju et al. 1993). The 1990 JFM resolution retained village community in title. But the resolution has its own complications. The resolution specifies that the 'village community' must be organised into a village institution specifically for forest regeneration and protection. This could be the *panchayat* covering one or more revenue villages or a cooperative of a village with no restrictions to membership, or it could be a forest committee. In no case, any access or tree *pattas* (exclusive tree ownership rights) should be given to individuals (Ministry of Environment and Forest 1990: Section 3.i). Section 3.vi also notes that the area to be selected for protection and sharing of usufructs rights should be selected such that no non-beneficiaries can have claims, and conversely, no existing user is denied the chance of being a beneficiary. Furthermore, JFM envisages 'village community' not as an individual or collection of individuals but as a corporate body willing to take responsibility.

Community evolution is a historical process and each community is constructed for a specific purpose (Appadurai,1995). Breman (1997) pointed out that the village had acquired a new importance as a result of administrative and economic interventions by the state which treats it as a unit. He also pointed out that breaking down of community within a village is possible during implementation of external government programme. However, such community is fragile in nature and may exist only during the programme phases. How far such communities can be useful for long-term activities like forest management is anybody's guess. JFM programme is likely to suffer from instability if a new kind of community is promoted for the sake of programme alone. In ICFM understanding of community is comparatively easier because it evolves within a village or hamlet and establishes autonomous identity without breaking the existing village community. Different groups and castes find it convenient to come to common understanding due to their historical interaction. Lynch and Talbot (1995) argued that people must have the primary responsibility of defining their own community or communities. However, loopholes of such arrangement could be that powerful sections may attempt to have an upper hand in defining the communities. It happened in some CCFMs of Gujarat where upper class people continued to exclude *Dalits* (the marginalized sections) even after a decade of establishment of forest cooperative.

Other kind of uncertainties occur both in JFM and CCFM due to inclusion of uncompromising interest groups (pastorals, shifting cultivators, migrants, etc.) under a single organising forest protection committee (FPC), male linked married household membership, indifference toward women's role, non inclusion of offspring as member, etc. If different contrasting interest groups are arbitrarily brought under common management forum without defining their usufruct zone, it may give rise to suspicion and victim blaming attitude within newly formed community. It happened in Jamtoli FPC of Hijli range in West Bengal. Here tribal and non-tribal communities were brought under the suzerainty of the same FPC. Owing to higher educational status, non-tribals maintained an upper hand in the managing committee. They missed no opportunity to put the blame on the tribal for every incidence of violation of rules. This calls for setting up of community specific identifiable relationship to an identifiable resource in order to minimise such incidence of nurtured suspicion. Saxena and Sarin (1999) had identified that male linked membership in ICFM, CCFM and JFM was not only a symbol of discrimination but also a practice that imbibes a sense of indifference among women. In most of the ICFM,

CCFM and in all of the JFM membership is restricted to single member per married household at the time of formation of forest management activities. Future generations may turn indifferent if they do not enjoy any additional incentives for participating in such activities.

### Constraint 2 : Absence of favourable socio-political environment that promotes participation

Sarin (1996) has observed that the fundamental objective of CBFM is to elicit people's participation through a favourable socio-political environment. Creation of a favourable socio-political environment requires (a) freedom of expression, and (b) recognition of this expression at the proper forum (Chambers, 1983). During 1878 to 1988, Indian forests were strictly governed by the forest bureaucracies. Forest communities had no opportunity to participate in forest management and their views and expectations were not given any importance. This caused gross alienation of people from forest management activities. A welcome change took place in 1988 when the FD resolved to involve people in forest management officially with a offer of partial stake holding rights under the JFM programme (see Box 1.1). This evoked wide appreciation and many JFM committees were formed in different states. However, after a decade of experience with JFM, it has been observed that initial enchantment is waning in several JFM areas. The reason could be many but some reasons which directly work against the sustenance of conducive socio-political environment are as follows :

(a) Managing committee elections can only be held in the presence of Divisional Forest Officer (DFO) and such elections are not regularly held. This has promoted domination of the personalities in the managing committee when they are disliked by other members.

(b) Elections are often influenced by local political personalities of state assemblies and/or *gram panchayats*. This prevents general body members from electing competent persons into the managing committee.

(c) Meeting between the general body[1] and the managing committee is held annually in a half hearted manner. This has caused the problem of recognition of the stakeholder's view and expectations.

(d) President of JFM unit is selected or elected by the members of the managing committee and often elected persons are not introduced to other stakeholders. For this reason, elected president tries to please the managing committee members rather than the general body members.

In the case of indigenous and crafted CBFM, the above lacunae are taken care of. These are always created at the village level and constitution of rules and managing committee are exclusively decided by stakeholders. Meeting between managing committee and general body are frequent and president and secretary are well known to all. Individual recognition is apparently higher in these CBFMs. However, non involvement of *panchayat* members at times invites unexpected inter-village conflicts. In such cases, *panchayat* politics extracts undue advantage while resolving (or fiddling with) the conflicts. Another major lacuna of ICFM and CCFMs is their limited orientation and fewer number of units. Since 95% forest belong to the government, more acceptable form of JFM can only elicit mass involvement in forest protection. ICFM has shown how participation dilemma can be minimised through a conducive socio-political environment but it is through JFM that a wider mass can be addressed.

### Constraint 3 : Incompatibility of governing rules with the local socio-cultural concept

Principles of institutional governance can help in constituting an equitable management system. Institution governance covers a wide range of issues such as eligibility criteria for general membership, participation of women in decision making, constitution of managing committee, monitoring and sanction system, benefit

1. General body in JFM and CBFM is the body that includes all stakeholders.

sharing norms, and inter- and intra- community conflict resolution mechanism. Uncertainty occurs :

(a) if governing rules fail to ensure equity in access to resources and benefit sharing process;
(b) if governing rules fail to safe guard participation of all sections in decision making process. Disenchantment brews when voices of different sections are suppressed;
(c) if governing rules do not ensure appropriate monitoring and graduated (as per the gravity of violation) sanction. Uniform way of weighing different kinds of violation and imposition of similar type of punishment dilute the purpose of sanction (Ostrum, 1989) and fail to imbibe any attitude of repentance and rectification in the mind of the offender (Gupta, 1985) (see box 1.2);
(d) if governing rules contradict with traditional or existing system of community governance. Social acceptability of governing rules increases when such rules are found to be more compatible with local situations; and
(e) if governing rules do not provide scope of modifications/ amendments in the existing rules as a response to changed circumstances and demand of sustenance.

In JFM enforcement of uniform governing rules (except some minor day to day operational rules) irrespective of local or regional variations resulted in an incompatible coexistence of different institutions out of compulsion. JFM often failed to reduce uncertainties adequately due to bureaucratic interference and standard style of functioning specially in election of managing committee, monitoring, and sanction. Political interference often could not be negated by forest bureaucrats, and prevented weaker sections in voicing their opinion. ICFM apparently has an edge in these matters. Since the governing rules were evolved from the communities in ICFM, local compatibility of these rules were found to be higher. However, in some ICFM powerful sections did manipulate governing rules in their favour.

**Box 1.2 Culture Bound Creative Institutional Management of Village Forest**

A village *panchayat* (assembly of elderly men) in Rajasthan devised a unique way of punishing a person who cut off some branches of trees from the village forest where such poaching was prohibited. The offence was discussed by the village assembly of elders. Hours of discussion about various issues follow such as: when did such an offence take place last; what were the choices considered then: did the culprit commit any similar offence earlier; etc. The elders then decided that the person would be asked to stand barefoot under the sun in the hot summer and feed the birds two and a half kilograms of grain from morning to evening.

This was done perhaps to make the culprit realize: what would be the consequence of deforestation during summer particularly in an arid region like Rajasthan: what would happen to other animals like birds, etc. if the forests were cut: and eventually through this repentance and penance the person might receive God's blessing.

(*Source:* Gupta, 1985)

## Constraint 4 : Absence of transparent, and accountable managing committee

Managing committee's accountability to the general body is another key determinants of effectiveness and stability of forest management institution. There is some debate over the need of a separate managing committee, which wields greater decision-making authority than the general body members. Traditional community organisations have evolved over a long period of time, and many have developed responsibilities and codes of conduct for their leaders. In some cases, the leader's primary role is to function as facilitator in helping the community reach a consensus regarding management decisions. While these roles and codes of conduct may not have been formalised, they often effectively serve to guide the leader's actions. Certain community organisations, particularly the older, and traditional types tend to operate with high levels of accountability and mostly take decisions by consensus (Sarin,1996). In other small and homogenous traditional communities, a single strong leader who enjoys the trust of others may perform daily operational decision-making.

In newer community forest management institutions, when membership expands beyond a certain size, it becomes necessary to delegate power for day to day decision making to a more formalised structure of management or executive body. Members of these bodies are selected or elected by non office bearing members. Interestingly, many of the self initiated community institutions in Bihar and Orissa had evolved their own rules for constituting such management committees (Kant et al. 1991). In other cases, the roles and responsibilities of both general body members and their managing committee need to be clearly defined. Uncertainties occur if managing committee does not take general members into confidence in all major decision making, does not maintain proper financial accounts, does not take care of monitoring of forest resources, does not try to impose sanction to imbibe a sense of repentance and urge for rectification within the mind of the offender; fails to motivate non office bearing members toward forest protection. Transparent and accountable managing committee not only reduces participation dilemma but also enhances active participation of the community simultaneously.

### Constraint 5 : Absence of participatory leadership with idealised behaviour in forest management

Leadership is the art of influencing people so that they strive willingly and enthusiastically to achieve the forest institutional goals. JFM and CFM societies are flatter without division of labour and hierarchy in position. Shah (1991) analysing the leaders in co-operatives found that the leader has to be a role model, dedicated, frugal, good organiser, and personally able to monitor every activity. The style of co-operative leadership may not be replicable in JFM and CFM because the financial investments in forest projects are not required as compared to co-operatives. However, for forest protection and regeneration, the leader has to posses idealised behaviour (honesty, integrity, sacrifice, impartiality etc.) so that the members of the forest community can accept her/him as a role model and can be influenced by her/him. The leader also needs to have the capacity to understand and mobilise people, have vision to articulate ideas in simple ways for future action, sensitivity to the members' needs, have ability to negotiate with external agencies, courage to enforce rules with the involvement and assurance to the general members, and monitor the activities of members and allocate responsibilities to others for the achievement of the objectives of JFM or CFM. Thus the leader can function in participatory style with idealised behaviour in the context of forest management (see Box 1.3).

Suspicion occurs if members of JFM/CFM do not have direct interaction with the leader, or leader fails to be a role model, or the leader is selected/elected by managing committee or FD. This is quite prevalent in many JFMs in West Bengal. Frustration occurs when the leader fails to act as a role model, fails to enforce rules, does not show concern to members' needs, and is unable to expand livelihood opportunities for stakeholders. Such suspicion and frustration leads to participation dilemma.

**Box 1.3 Participatory Leadership with Idealised Behaviour at Khaksi Toli**

Khakshi Toli is a hamlet of Ambatoli village in Bero Block of Ranchi district in the newly formed Jharkhand state, India. The village is situated in Chhotanagpur plateau, and its topography is highly undulated. In late fifties, villagers under the leadership of Mr. Simon Oraon (Minj) started protecting the forest on forty hectares of land. But soon Simon felt that the villagers had very few alternative livelihood opportunities and mere forest protection may not offer any viable alternatives. Agriculture, being completely rainfed and subsistence in nature, barely could meet the growing consumption demand. Simon took up watershed based water harvesting work. A small dam was constructed to store water at higher elevation which was then connected with three tanks in a series at the downstream. Dam water was used both for ground water recharge and surface irrigation. Agriculture production was increased and multiple cropping became possible. Villagers also took up fisheries in all the tanks. Later on Simon pursued the district administration and with their help a village co-operative was formed. This co-operative received various assistance under tribal sub plan programme. Today, Khaksi Toli stands out as one of the most progressive villages with a model watershed and forest protection body.

### Constraint 6 : Inappropriate inter- and intra-community conflict resolution mechanism

Conflict in the community organisations arises when members

refuse to forgo some individual benefits in favour of achieving the common goal. In forest management, conflicts can be classified into four categories: within the membership of local institutions, with neighbouring non-members, with external commercial or industrial interest groups, and with the state or FD. Every local institution has to evolve effective conflict resolution mechanisms for its sustainability. In older and established institutions with trusted leaderships, it is often possible to resolve local conflicts internally, but for conflicts with external interests or agencies, mediation by a neutral third party may be required. In newly promoted local institutions like JFM or CCFM, intervention by FD or NGO is required to resolve even the intra-village/community conflicts.

Intra -community conflicts are more common in heterogeneous JFM/CCFM owing to caste differentiation and different types of forest dependencies. Intra-community conflict can also occur due to the perceived inequity in the distribution of cost and benefits of forest protection, suspicions over mishandling of funds, obstinacy of some members in accepting common rules, and partiality of leader favouring her/his own people. Clash of interest between grazer sub-group desiring grazing access and others desiring closure of grazing for facilitating regeneration of forest often causes conflict.

Conflicts with neighbouring villages arise over unmarked boundaries, denial of collection access to non timber forest produce, non reciprocations of neighbouring villages co-operation, and free-riding attitude of neighbouring villages. Conflicts between FD and villagers are caused when FD tries to sell timber arbitrarily, FD does not honour its own commitment, supports industrial body's interest, and refuses to understand communities' problem and priorities. In the Shamliyat (ICFM) forests of Punjab forest communities had sympathetically considered the needs of nomadic pastorals at the time of settling inter-village boundary disputes (Chakravorty-Kaul, 1993). The goal of many self-initiated protection groups in Bihar and Orissa. was to protect their forests from forest department. In Orissa and Maharashtra FD still sells bamboo to paper mills at a price much lower than the prevailing market price a policy disliked by the forest communities.

Intra-community conflicts are effectively resolved through

frequent and regular general body or *gram-sabha*[2] meetings in areas having strong traditions of community organisations. Most autonomous forest protection groups in Bihar organise such meetings with all members being bound to attend them. Penalty for habitual absenteeism runs from denial of benefits to loss of membership. In such meetings collective community leadership first tries resolve the dispute. If the collective leadership is unable to come up with a satisfactory decision, the responsibility passes over to one or more respected individuals whose decision would be binding. Conflicts generated by the initial rules introduced by such local institutions have led to their progressive improvement or modification through discussions at such meetings.

Uncertainty occurs if inter- or intra-village/community conflicts are not resolved through discussions and negotiations among leaders of the concerned villages, particularly where forest department or other governmental presence has been weak. In areas where villagers are taking up forest management with the encouragement from FD or NGOs, FD/NGO's representatives are often called upon to play a neutral facilitative role. If they fail to resolve, it may evoke greater participation dilemma.

**Constraint 7 : Lack of awareness regarding environmental protection leading toward incongruent value system between leadership and other users**

Values are desirable ideals located centrally within one's belief system (Rokeach, 1971, 1973). They determine what one ought to or ought not to behave or act. The inward possession of values guides our outer activities. Values develop from early childhood through socialising agencies of family, school and a host of other institutions. Being a member of the community institution, institutional socialisation takes place. The member imbibes the values incorporated in vision statements, complies with the rules and regulations of the institution, interacts with similar others. She/he

2. Gram sabha is general meeting of all villagers. This assumes greater role in community decision making.

tries to establish a congruency between institutional values— mutual help, sacrificing present benefit for future gain, obeying common norms of forest management, and avoidance of free riding— and individual values. First, if the leader or managing committee does not change the values of its members through awareness or conscientization, and enforce institutional rules, members may not participate in institution's activities, and institution will gradually fade away (Roy, 1995). Second, if the members do not receive any intrinsic (praise, appreciation, etc.) or extrinsic (tangible benefits) rewards, they will not internalise the institutional values.

## Conclusion

Having discussed the challenges of common pool resources, how institutional mechanism of common pool resources is relevant in forest management and seven constraints that prevent people from participating in forest management, we will now look into how people's participation can be brought forth in common property resourcc management in general and forest management in particular. Book is divided into two parts. Including the introduction first part has five chapters that deal with 'Understanding Participation Mystique in Community Based Forest Management'. In Chapter II, we have discussed how social identity approach can help in eliciting people's participation. While Chapter III discusses how institutional governance influences people's participation, Chapter IV analyses how leadership and congruence of institutional and individual values influence level of people's participation in forest management. Chapter V focuses on role of social capital in natural resource management and attempts to unfold the link between social capital and people's participation in managing the commons.

Second part of the book focuses on 'Policy and Practices of Community Based Forest Management'. It has four chapters. Chapter VI elaborates the policies and practices of Joint Forest Management in India and some successful cases of JFM. Chapter VII analyses few cases of forest management systems of South

East Asia. Chapter VIII discusses cases of self-initiated as well as NGO crafted community based forest management. Finally in Chapter IX, we present a conceptual framework for eliciting people's participation in grassroots commons and its policy implications.

# 2

# SOCIAL IDENTITY AND PEOPLE'S PARTICIPATION IN CBFM

In this chapter, we will attempt to explore how people's participation in in-group activity can be comprehended with the help of social identity approach. Let us begin with the most baffling question what actually elicit people's participation in community based forest management (CBFM). The question has set of practical as well as theoretical agenda for all social scientist. Among broad array of responses, most influential one has centred on people's need approach. This suggests that people's behaviour is primarily driven by the demand to satisfy as yet unsatisfied needs. Further, the motivation to work increases to the extent that any work provides a vehicle for need satisfaction (Landy, 1989). This approach primarily has three main focuses (a) to identify various needs that relate to work performance, (b) to explain how these needs stand in relation to one another, and (c) to identify the processes that lead one need to gain precedence over another in driving work behaviour. Here we will present a process based analysis of need structure and need salience derived from the social identity approach to organisational behaviour. Then we will establish a relation between social identity approach and people's participation in group activities in the context of forest management. Following self-categorisation theory (Turner, Hogg, Oakes, Reicher, and Wetherell, 1987), we argue that people's sense of self-how they see themselves, and who they think they are-encompasses self-categorisation defined at different levels of abstraction. This suggests that people can categorise themselves either as individuals or as members of social group. This relative salience of a particular self-category has distinct implications on their behaviour in in-group context. As a result, it can be suggested that those associated with the advancement of collective interests are more likely to be achieved where the workplace serves as a vehicle for the satisfaction of social needs. In this backdrop, we will examine how social identity approach can help in understanding factors contributing to people's participation in CBFM.

## Social Identity Approach

Research claims suggest that the social identity approach to organizational psychology can explain how individual decides about his role in in-group activities. As an elaboration of ideas in social identity theory, self-categorisation theory suggests that a person's subjective sense of self -who they think they are- can be defined at varying levels of abstraction (Turner, 1985). These definitions take the form of *'self-categories'* that range from conceptions of the self as a unique individual, through to more inclusive definitions in terms of significant group memberships, and then to even more abstract representations of self as a human being (or at an even higher level as an animal).

Theoretically, the first two of these levels are particularly important. The first level serves to define an individual in terms of a *personal identity* that is different from other members of a group (Turner, 1982). The second level defines the individual in terms of a *social identity* that is shared with other members of an in-group but not with members of an out-group. Social identification thus reflects depersonalised self-categorisation, such that individuals perceive their motivations and perspective to be psychologically interchangeable with those of others who share the same *social identity*. Importantly, this leads to behaviours that are qualitatively distinct from that which is predicated on *personal identity* -because it is shaped by, and oriented towards, the interests of the group as a whole.

Social identities too, can be defined at a more or less abstract level. Thus a (male) organizational psychologist can define himself in terms of (a) a distinctive *personal identity* (as Paulus Lakra different from other members of a relevant in-group; e.g. other members of forest protection group), or (b) in terms of *social identities* defined at increasingly more abstract level: as a forest protectionist (different from other resource conservationist viz. water conservationist). Building upon this framework, a major contribution of self-categorisation theory is to provide an analysis of '*social identity salience*' (Oakes, 1987; Turner, 1985). This specifies the processes that dictate whether people define themselves in terms of personal or social identity and, when social identity is salient, which particular group membership serves to guide behaviour. But the basic question remains that in any given organization, when will group member see and act as individuals, rather than in terms of the department or team or caste to which they belong, or in terms of the organization as a whole?

Following the work of Bruner (1957), Oakes (1987) and Oakes, Turner, and Haslam (1991) have argued that one crucial determinant of social category salience is 'fit'. This is the degree to which a social categorization matches subjectively relevant features of reality - so that the category appears to be a sensible way of organizing and making sense of social stimuli (i.e. people and things associated with them). It has two components: comparative and normative.

'Comparative fit' is defined by the principle of meta-contrast (Turner, 1985). This predicts that people will define themselves in terms of a particular self-category to the extent that the difference between members of that category on a given dimension of judgment are perceived to be smaller than the differences between members of that category and others that are salient in a particular context. If a forester is surrounded by other forester and agriculturists, she or he would tend to define herself or himself as a forester only if the differences between the two groups appeared to be larger than the differences within them (foresters). This is more likely to be the case at a social science conference than at a football match, which is one reason why people are more likely to classify the people at an interdisciplinary conference than the people in a sporting crowd in terms of their occupational category.

One broad implication of the meta-contrast principle is that people will be more likely to categorise themselves as group members in inter-group than intra-group contexts (Haslam, Oakes, Turner, and McGarty, 1996; Turner 1985). For example, employees of Company X should be more likely to define themselves in terms of their membership of Company X if the company as a whole is focused on external rather than internal competition.

"Normative fit" arises from the content of the match between category specifications and the stimuli being represented. In order to represent sets of people (including the self) as members of distinct social categories, the differences between those sets must not only appear to be larger than the differences within them (comparative fit), but the nature of these differences must also be consistent with the perceiver's expectations about the categories. If these content-related expectations are not met, the social categorization will not be invoked to make sense of events and define the person's own action. Our forester at the social development conference will be unlikely to classify participants as social worker and forester (or to act as a forester herself or himself) if the members of these two groups are seen to differ from each other in ways that are unexpected - perhaps if the social workers are concerned only with people's well-being and the forester only with forest conservation.

One general implication of the normative fit hypothesis is that because people are motivated to represent the self positively (Tajfel and Turner, 1979), the normative fit of a social self- category should generally be higher to the extent that it allows for positive self-definition. This means, for example, that employees of Company X should be more likely to define themselves as Company X members in situations where they might be proud of the company (perhaps because it has high status and is performing well), and where they feel respected by those who are representative of the organization (perhaps because those people comment positively on their performance; Smith and Tyler, 1997; Tyler, 1999).

The above ideas have been supported by a large body of empirical research which confirms the predictable role that context plays in changing a person's representation of both themselves and others. The details of this research are complex (Oakes, Haslam, and Turner, 1994; Turner et al., 1987), but applied to the organizational domain its simple message is that as context changes, employees and the organization as a whole redefine their place in the world, what they are about and where they are going.

Importantly too, the principles of fit also determine category salience in interaction with 'perceiver readiness' or 'accessibility' (Oakes, 1987; Oakes et al ., 1994). So as well as being determined by the subjectively perceived features of a stimulus array, categorization also depends on the prior expectations, goals, and theories of perceivers - many of which derive from their group membership and group encounters. We organize and construe the world in ways prescribed by the groups to which we belong and in the way our social histories lend stability and predictability to experience (Oakes et al., 1994; Turner, 1999). Identification with a group — the extent to which it is already valued and ego-involving for any given individual— therefore interacts with fit to shape people's willingness to use a given social category to define themselves in any particular context (e.g. Doosje, Ellemers, and Spears, 1995; Kramer, 1993). Amongst other things, this means that when people identify strongly with a given organization, they more readily interpret the world, and their own place within it, in a manner consistent with that organization's values, ideology, and culture. Social identification is thus one individual difference that can impact upon social identity salience, but it is important to emphasise that this reflects the personal experience of the individual (which will typically be shaped by his or her group membership) rather than a personality variable (Turner, 1999; Turner and Onorato, 1999).

*The self and motivation*

The above arguments summarise some of the key faction that dictate whether, and to what extent, people categorise themselves as members of a particular social group. But how exactly are they relevant to the analysis of work motivation and needs? The answer to this question follows from previous observations by, amongst others, Handy (1976), Shamir (1991), and Brunstein and Gollwitzer (1996) puts it: 'this problem of the self, of the self-concept, of the ego-ideal and how it is formed underlies all the work on motivation'.

The reason for this is that one important way of thinking about needs and motivation is *as aspirations for the self.* In this way, they can be seen to arise from a commitment to norms and goals associated with a salient self-categorisation (along lines suggested by Brunstein and Gollwitzer, 1996). More specifically, when a particular self-categorisation is salient this creates needs and motivation to (a) embody norms associated with the category, (b) be perceived as embodying those norms by other members of the category, and (c) engage in activities which promote or maintain the interests of the category. If we define ourselves as academics, for example, then we should want to (a) live up to academic ideals (e.g. to be good teachers and researchers), (b) be perceived as good academics by other academics, and (c) do things which increase the stature and status of academics relative to other groups (e.g. to argue for the value of academia relative to other professions). In this regard, a critical feature of the social identity approach is that the model of self it embraces is very different to those which prevail in psychology as a whole. Two differences are particularly important. The first is that the self is considered to be context sensitive and variable. Specifically, it follows from principles of fit that the way we think about ourselves will change in both level and content depending on who we compare ourselves to and in what context. In the context of intra-organisational competition for funds and resources, we may think of ourselves in terms of a departmental identify and see someone from another department as an out group rival, but in the context of inter organizational competition we may think of ourselves in terms of an organisational identity and see that same person as an in-group ally (Haslam, Oakes, et al., 1996; Haslam and Turner. 1992).

Secondly though; self-categories at all levels of abstraction are seen to be equally 'real' and just as much a reflection of a person's 'true' self. No one level of self-categorisation is inherently more appropriate or useful than another and hence none is in any sense more fundamental to who or what the person is. This proposition is at odds with a general tendency for psychological and motivational theorizing to give privileged status to personal identity -believing that a person's true self is defined by their individuality (e.g. Herzberg, 1966; McClelland, 1987; Oakes et al., 1994; Turner et al., 1987).

When these ideas about (a) the nature of the self and (b) the nature of the link between the self and motivation are combined, this leads to the view that the nature of needs and motivation will itself change predictably and meaningfully in response to changes in social and organizational context. In particular, when people categorise themselves at a personal level they should be motivated to satisfy personal needs that promote their personal identity as individuals, but when they categorise themselves at a social level, they should be motivated to satisfy social needs that promote their social identity as group members. In this way, the needs associated with a salient personal identity should be more specialized and idiosyncratic than those associated with a social identity, which in turn should be more specialized and group specific than those associated with a human or animal identity.

The content of the needs associated with different levels of self-definition should correspond closely to the different categories of needs identified within established needs hierarchies (e.g. those of Maslow, Alderfer, McClelland, McGregor, and Herzberg). So, when personal identity is salient this should be associated with needs to self-actualise and to enhance personal self-esteem through personal advancement and growth. On the other hand, when social identity is salient this should be associated with the need to enhance group-based self-esteem through a sense of relatedness, respect, peer recognition, and achievement of group goals (Smith and Tyler, 1997; Tyler, 1999). Yet when human or animal identities are salient, needs should be more existence, security-and safety-related.

Self-categorisation theory's answer to Landy's (1989, p. 379) question 'Why are needs arranged in one hierarchy rather than another?' thus points to the fact that they all map onto this underlying hierarchy of self. However, it also follows from the theory's assertion that no level of self is any more real or essential than any other, that 'higher-level' needs are inherently no more important, superior, valuable, or valid than 'lower-level' needs. Contrary to the view of many needs theorists, there is nothing special about personal self- actualisation that makes it - independent of contextual considerations - a better motivator than the need to stand well with one's peers or to collectively self-actualise.

## People's Participation : Theoretical Perspectives

### *Meaning and types*

Participation in a group at its narrowest sense is defined in terms of nominal membership (Chopra, Kadekodi, and Murty, 1990; Molinas, 1998), and at broadest sense it is defined as dynamic process in which the disadvantaged have voice and influence in decision-making (Narayan, 1996; White, 1996). Participation has two dimensions (a) direct, and (b) indirect participation. Direct participation includes the involvement of stakeholders in activities like attending meetings concerning forest protection, taking active part in meetings, contributing labour towards forest management, monitoring, patrolling, etc. Indirect participation refers to individuals' obedience to forest protection rules, motivating others as well as own family members for forest protection, providing moral support to community for ensuring equity, justice, and transparency in forest management (Ostrom, 1990; Raju, Vaghela, and Raju, 1993; Sarin, 1996; Silwal, 1986).

From a project perspective, participation can mean informing people about a project either through (a) consulting them, or (b) by delegating managerial power over the project to them (Nuitjen, 1992). While the former type stresses on sharing of responsibilities, accountabilities jointly by project planners and the members of the community, the latter talks about total community ownership. Individual's decision to cooperate with the community vis-à-vis project planners depends on level of personal acceptance and conviction about the forestry project, favourable evaluation of institutional rules, and accrued benefits (Ostrom, 1990; Sarin, 1996).

**Social Identity and People's Participation - The Link**

Individual participation in collective action is a product of individual's self-categorisation within the organization (collective domain), psychological attachment with organizational pride and respect, and identification as organizational citizen (Haslam, Powell, and Turner, 2000; Ouwerkerk, Ellemers, and de Gilder, 1999; Tyler, 1999). Self-categorisation refers to one's social or personal identity in an organizational set up as member. Any person will give higher preference to social (organizational) identity over personal identity if the difference among members of the organization is low in terms of status, access to benefit, and opportunity to share the personal knowledge and experiences in decision-making arena (Turner, 1985). In a homogeneous community or group, the above differentiation is likely to be low and, therefore, self-categorisation would likely to lean towards social identity. Social identity promotes group based pride and respect where individuals take pride in organizational achievement. The process is augmented when organizational objectives matches with local priorities and organization tries to establish local self-governance thereby safe guards the members' rights over resources, territory, and institutional management (Pimbert and Pretty, 1998). Feelings of group based pride and respect promotes the organizational citizenship behaviour - (a) greater loyalty to the organisation; (b) enhanced compliance with organizational rules; and (c) an increased incidence of extra-role behaviour (supporting the organisational cause by motivating others, putting extra labour etc.) (Tyler, 1999). The above process is reinforced through the assurance of realization of social and economic needs both at collective and individual level. Individual needs are associated with (a) immediate survival, (b) security of resources in short as well as in long term, and (c) freedom of choices (Chambers, 1983; Smith and Tyler, 1997, Tyler, 1999). Meeting of these needs acts as source of motivation and enhances group-based self-esteem through a sense of relatedness, respect, peer recognition, and achievement of group goals. All these factors - social identity as self-categorisation, group-based pride and respect, organizational citizenship, and self-motivation through organizational achievement directly influence people's participation in organizational set up as well as activities (Fig. 2.1).

Fig. 2.1: The Relationship between Social Identity, Self-Categorisation, Organizational Behaviour, Source of Motivation and Participation.

## Methodology

### *Sample*

Forest management in the three eastern states of India — Jharkhand, Orissa, and West Bengal — was studied. Seven JFM units — two each from Jharkhand and Orissa, and three from West Bengal; six ICFM units — four from Jharkhand and two from Orissa; and four CCFM units from Orissa were selected for the study. JFM units were selected from Kanke and Bero forest range of Ranchi district in Jharkhand, Athamalik forest range of Angul district in Orissa, and Hijli forest range of Midnapur district in West Bengal. ICFM units were selected from Ranchi district of Jharkhand, and Dhenkanal district of Orissa, and CCFM units were selected from Angul and Dhenkanal districts of Orissa (Table 2.1). The National Tree Growers Cooperative Federation Limited promoted CCFM units. Because Jharkhand did not have any CCFM unit and West Bengal did not have any ICFM and CCFM units, no such sample was taken from these states. The decision to include these forest protection units was guided by approachability and convenience. Thus, a purposive sampling procedure was adopted.

**Table 2.1 :** Profile of Sample FPCs

| Name | Type[a] | Forest Area | No. of House-hold | Organi-sational unit | Population character | Structure of Governance[b] |
|---|---|---|---|---|---|---|
| Khaksi Toli | ICFM | 44 ha | 35 | Hamlet | Homogeneous | GB and MC |
| Jam Toli | ICFM | 85 ha | 200 | Village | Homogeneous | GB and MC |
| Hutar | ICFM | 150 ha | 75 | Village | Homogeneous | GB and MC |
| Dundun | ICFM | 65 ha | 71 | Hamlet | Homogeneous | GB and MC |
| Gobindberani | ICFM | 41 ha | 86 | Village | Homogeneous | GB and MC |
| Shradhyapur | ICFM | 53 ha | 120 | Village | Homogeneous | GB and MC |
| Kankadahat | CCFM | 111 ha | 450 | Village | Heterogeneous | GB and MC |
| Paapsara | CCFM | 330 ha | 373 | Village | Homogeneous | GB and MC |
| Pada | CCFM | 500 ha | 360 | Village | Homogeneous | GB and MC |
| Sundhikatni | CCFM | 33 ha | 120 | Village | Homogeneous | GB and MC |
| Sadma | JFM | 105 ha | 151 | Village | Heterogeneous | GB and MC |
| Semra | JFM | 67 ha | 175 | Village | Homogeneous | GB and MC |
| Berham | JFM | 77 ha | 181 | Village | Heterogeneous | GB and MC |
| Solanda | JFM | 95 ha | 195 | Village | Heterogeneous | GB and MC |
| Chandana | JFM | 103 ha | 372 | 3 Villages | Heterogeneous | GB and MC |
| Harinakhuri – Telebhanga | JFM | 91 ha | 278 | 2 Villages | Heterogeneous | GB and MC |
| Jamsol | JFM | 250 ha | 575 | 6 Villages | Heterogeneous | GB and MC |

[a]ICFM = Indigenous community forest management, CCFM = Crafted community forest management, JFM= Joint forest management.
[b]GB = General Body, MC = Managing Committee.

Except three JFM units of West Bengal, all other units had a Forest Protection Committee (FPC) at single village/hamlet level (Table 2.1). In West Bengal, Jamsol FPC was constituted with six villages, Chandana FPC was formed with three villages, and Harinakhuri-Telebhanga FPC was formed with two villages. Along with these three, another three FPCs — Sadma from Jharkhand State, Kankadahat and Solanda from Orissa State, had heterogeneous population. The remaining eleven FPCs — Dundun, Hutar, Jam Toli, Khaksi Toli, Semra — from Jharkhand state; and Berham, Gobindberani, Papaya, Pada, Snradhyapur, Sudhikatni from Orissa state— had homogenous population where 75% or more of the population belonged to a specific caste or tribe (Table 2.1).

The researcher met two different small groups in each FPC for focus group study. Altogether 34 focus group discussions were conducted in 17 FPCs. Separate discussions were held with FPC officials and records of each FPC were referred to.

*Focus group discussion and secondary sources of data*

For understanding and constructing the reality in the context of community forestry, information was gathered through focus group discussion (Flick, 2002, pp. 112-124), and from the available records of each FPC. At the outset, the researcher met FPC officials, sought permission and then attended one meeting of each FPC. This was followed by two focus group discussions. Focus group discussions were held in evening hours when FPC members were available. The researcher, knowing Hindi and Bengali languages, conducted these discussions and verified records in Jharkhand and West Bengal respectively, and did the same in Orissa with the help of a vernacular interpreter.

The researcher began the focus group discussion by explaining its purpose. Six to eight members comprising a group were asked some open-ended questions. Open-ended questions included questions about evolution of FPC, institutional rules, access rights, benefit sharing, constitution and performance of managing committee, conflict resolution, and leadership. The group was asked to discuss the questions and the replies were transcribed in field diary. The researcher met two different groups in each FPC thereby the replies were triangulated or crosschecked. Besides these discussions, the researcher also discussed such open-ended questions with the president, secretary and treasurer of each FPC and the records of FPC available with them were also verified. This information was compiled and analysed.

## Factors Influencing Social Identity in Indian CBFM

*(a) Evolution*

Community based forest protection units had come into existence owing to two main felt needs for collective action. First need was to regenerate degraded forest patch for meeting the consumption needs, and second to develop and gain access to forest resources with a view to the attainment of social and economic empowerment. ICFM units were initiated by the villagers under the leadership of village leaders or youth groups without any external intervention. These were always organized at single village level (in few cases even at hamlet level as in Khaksi Toli, see Table 2.1) and every household of the village became a member of the protection movement. Social and cultural homogeneity was one of the special features of such units. The villagers framed the institutional rules in conformity with their tradition, cultural milieu, and environmental condition. The access to forest resources was normally confined to the members. CCFM was also evolved at single village level with the joint initiative of crafting agencies like NGOs and villagers. These units were mostly homogenous at least economically if not socially. Crafting agencies played a catalytic role in the formation of CCFM units and framing of their constitutional[1] rules. These rules included rules for membership, governing structures, election pattern, and benefit sharing. CCFM members had the freedom in framing rules that favoured collective choice like representation of different groups in FPC, special benefit to most affected group(s), and operational rules like monitoring schedule, and fixing the date for fuel wood collection. Like ICFM, access rights were confined to the members only. In JFM, FD took the initiatives for regenerating the degraded forest patch with the active collaboration of forest communities. JFM units mostly had larger entity than ICFM and CCFM. These units often included several villages with socially and economically heterogeneous communities. Unlike ICFM and CCFM, in JFM except the operational rules, the state FD framed all the rules and regulations. Collaborating communities were given partial access rights over non-timber and timber produce (Table 2.2).

1. Elinor Ostrom (1990) classified organisational rules into three categories-constitutional, collective choice, and operational rules in order of hierarchy. She opined that change/modification of rules becomes more difficult in the upper hierarchy (constitutional>collective choice>operational rules).

**Table 2.2 :** Basic Features of ICFM, CCFM, and JFM

| *Issues* | *ICFM* | *CCFM* | *JFM Jharkhand* | *JFM Orissa* | *JFM West Bengal* |
|---|---|---|---|---|---|
| Forest category | Village forest, Degraded protected forest | Village forest, Leased land | Degraded protected forest | Degraded forest | Degraded forest |
| Evolution | Villagers | Villagers with the help of NGO | FD and Villagers | FD and Villagers | FD and Villagers |
| Participants | All households of village/hamlet | Entire village | All willing adults | Willing people of adjoining area | Economically backward people |
| Management unit | Single village/hamlet | Single village | Village/group of villages | About 200 ha of forest land | Village/group of villages |
| Constitutional rules are framed by | Villagers | NGOs | FD | FD | FD |
| Collective choice rules are framed by | Villagers | Villagers | FD and villagers | FD and villagers | FD and villagers |
| Operation rules are framed by | Villagers | Villagers | Villagers | Villagers | Villagers |
| Institutional structure | Two tier - GB and MC | Two tier - GB and MC | Two tier - GB and MC | Two tier - GB and MC | Two tier - GB and MC |
| Institution is registered as society | No | Yes | Formally recognised by FD | Formally recognised by FD | Formally recognised by FD |

*(Contd. Table 2.2)*

*(Contd. Table 2.2)*

| *Issues* | *ICFM* | *CCFM* | *JFM Jharkhand* | *JFM Orissa* | *JFM West Bengal* |
|---|---|---|---|---|---|
| People's representation in MC | 7 -10 unanimously selected members, village head/ elders | 11 members (1 SC, 1 ST, 1 women, Chairperson, 7 other elected members) | One *mukhiya, sarpanch*[a], representative of villagers (men and women) | 6-8 members (at least 3 women), *Naib*[b], *sarpanch*, ward members. | 6 elected representatives, *panchayat* representative |
| Voting rights | One vote per household | One vote per household | One vote per household | One vote per household | One vote per household |
| Tenure of the committee | 1-2 year | 3 years | 2 years | 2 years | 2 years |
| Gender representation | Men and women both | Men and women both | Men and women both | Men and women both | Men and women both |
| External FD representa tions | Nil | NGO as observer | Vanpal[c] | Forester/ Forest guard | Beat officer/ Deputy Range Manager |
| Others | Nil | Nil | NGO, Teacher | NGO | Nil |

*Source* : Focus group discussion and CCFM and JFM rules

*a* Sarpanch is elected by constituency of 5000 rural voters for dealing the legal affairs at village panchayat.

*b* Naib is same as Mukhiya

*c* Vanpal is same as Beat Officer.

*(b) Institutional governance*

*Structure*

ICFM, CCFM, and JFM had a similar two-tier governing structure— General Body (GB) and Managing Committee (MC). GB comprises all the members of the forest protection unit. This was a powerful body in ICFM and CCFM. Decisions of GB were final. GB had the right to amend the existing rules and regulation. However, in JFM, GB had no right to change the rules, it could only alter some decisions pertaining to mundane issues. In practice, JFM's GB meetings were convened to apprise the general members about the state of affairs of JFM units. Except election of MC members and ratification of accounts, no other major decisions were taken in such meetings (Table 2.2).

MC is a representative body elected by the GB for functional purpose. The MC usually has the representation from the hamlets/castes/clans sub-groups within forest protection unit. The MC of ICFM was constituted solely by the community members. The president and the secretary were also normally elected directly by GB and MC showed greater accountability to GB. The MCs of CCFM units were constituted in a similar manner except that MC members had the power to elect the president and the secretary. These MCs had greater autonomy than MCs of ICFM. The MCs of JFM were constituted with the representatives of different villages/hamlets/castes/clans, the local *panchayat* member, and the representative of FD. FD representative mostly acted as *de facto* secretary to MC. Like CCFM, MC members of JFM elected the FPC president. MCs of JFM units in practice exercised more power than GB in every matter and at times could even bypass the GB (Table 2.2).

ICFM and CCFM were governed by the principles of democratic decentralisation of power and cooperation. The functioning of these institutions reflected the collective wisdom of their members in managing forests. JFM was also as per its norms, expected to be governed in a similar fashion. However, in many cases (particularly in Jharkhand and Orissa) due to some vested interest, MC members of JFM wilfully deferred the reconstitution of MC for an indefinite period. This prevented the JFM to uphold the democratic values as per the expectation of its resolution.

*Gender issues*

CCFM and JFM had mandatory provision for women representation in the MC (see Table 2.2). ICFM did not have such mandatory provision but it gave importance to the difficulties of women particularly in tribal dominated units. Rules for fuel wood collection and grazing were made so as to suit women. ICFM tried to ease the lot of head loader women by allowing the fuel wood collection quarterly. It also allowed rotational grazing in order to relieve the burden of children who take the cattle for grazing intermittently. Such provisions generated higher cooperation of women and children in forest conservation. In contrast, CCFM and JFM were found to impose total closure with annual fuel wood holiday(s) for collecting fuel wood. During other months of the year, women were forced to collect fuel wood from other nearby forests. This increased the distance of head loading and added to the misery of women. It is evident from the above facts that empathising with the misery of women was more important while making rules than making provision for their representation. Presence of few women in MC hardly influenced the decision-making process in a male dominated Indian society. As women members from Orissa CCFM and West Bengal JFM pointed out that male members shouted and fought among themselves in the meeting, they (women members) became mute spectators of the whole decision-making process.

*Role of external agency*

Studied ICFM units were organised and managed by the villagers. Conversely, crafting agencies like NGOs played an active role in CCFM for (a) mobilizing and consolidating the protection activities, (b) framing constitutional rules, and (c) getting the forest institutions registered under society registration act or cooperative act. Otherwise, NGOs mostly confined themselves to the role of a catalyst and advisor. In the initial stages, MCs of CCFM showed more accountability to catalytic agencies than their GB. However, with the growth of the institutions, crafting agencies' role became minimal and subsequently MC became more accountable to GB. In contrast, FDs role in JFM was not just limited to a catalyst and advisor. Besides framing the JFM rules, FD continued to play an active role in every decision-making process as a major stakeholder. It influenced the process of reconstitution of MC in every case, election of president, and sale of forest produce. Without FD's presence, MC was not authorised to take any major decision. Thus MC of JFM became more accountable to FD than its GB (Table 2.2).

*Access to resources*

In ICFM and CCFM, communities enjoyed the full access over both non-timber forest produce (NTFP) and harvested timber. In JFM, FD and communities jointly shared these access rights (Table 2.3). Sharing terms of JFM varied from state to state. Among the three states under the present study, Orissa gave full access to communities over NTFP. On the other hand, JFM of Jharkhand and West Bengal offered only 1/3 and 1/4 share of various NTFP respectively to the communities. Communities received 50%, 33%, and 25% share of timber harvest in JFM of Orissa, Jharkhand, and West Bengal respectively. Higher access in ICFM and CCFM generated higher motivation and solidarity for forest conservation (Table 2.3).

*Sanction*

Sanctions in community based organisation have two important dimensions: (a) restriction on free riding, and (b) rectification of rule-breaking by imbibing a sense of repentance (Gupta, 1985). Graduated sanction works more effectively than standardised sanction (Ostrom, 1990). Graduated sanction emphasises innovative sanctioning procedure to change the attitude of offenders. Such sanctions are determined on the basis of (a) gravity of violation, (b) experiences of past sanctions and their consequences, and

**Table 2.3 :** Access Rights, Sanction, and Conflict Resolution Process of ICFM, CCFM, and JFM

| *Issues* | *ICFM* | *CCFM* | *JFM Jharkhand* | *JFM Orissa* | *JFM West Bengal* |
|---|---|---|---|---|---|
| Access to resources | Villagers alone | Villagers alone | Villagers and FD | Villagers and FD | Villagers and FD |
| Share of members - NTFP, fuel wood | Full collection right on NTFP. Fuel wood collection is allowed on prescribed days only in collective manner. | Full collection right on NTFP. Fuel wood collection is allowed on prescribed days only in collective manner. | Forest produce will be provided to members at market price, 1/3 of income will be deposited in Village Development Fund (VDF) | Leaf, fodder, thatch grass, broom grass, brushwood, fallen lops/tops/twigs free of cost. Leased out NTFP collected against prescribed wages. | 25% of Cashew, Sal seed, Tendu leaf, honey, wax on approved tariff, rest free. |
| Share of members - timber | 100% ownership. Villagers deposit stipulated amount to Village fund for personal use. | 100% ownership. Villagers deposit stipulated amount to Village fund for personal use. | 1/3 share of proceeds would be deposited in VDF | 50% of the total produce | 25% of net income except in North Bengal and Darjeeling Hills. |
| Share of village fund | 75% of net earning is equally distributed | 75% of net earning is equally distributed | 75% of net earning is equally distributed | 75% of net earning is equally distributed | 75% of net earning is equally distributed |
| **Sanctioning power of FPC** | | | | | |
| a. Punishment | Generally MC decides the punishment | Generally MC decides the punishment | FPC is empowered to take local action | FPC can lessen or cancel share of household if found guilty | Can impose stipulated fine with the consent of FD |

(Contd. Table 2.3)

*(Contd. Table 2.3)*

| *Issues* | *ICFM* | *CCFM* | *JFM Jharkhand* | *JFM Orissa* | *JFM West Bengal* |
|---|---|---|---|---|---|
| b. Cancel membership | For very serious case, GB may even ostracize the guilty | For very serious case, GB may even ostracize the guilty | YES | NO | Undecided |
| **Sanctioning power of FD** | | | | | |
| a. Cancel membership | NIL | NIL | YES | YES | YES |
| b. Dissolving the FPC | NIL | NIL | YES | YES | YES |
| Sanction procedure | Decisions are taken as per the gravity of violation | Decisions are taken as per the gravity of violation | Standardise punishment | Standardise punishment | Standardise punishment |
| Conflict resolution at intra-village | Done mostly by consensus at GB | Done mostly by majority opinion at GB | Done by the arbitration of MC and or FD (in serious conflict) | Done by the arbitration of MC and or FD (in serious conflict) | Done by the arbitration of MC and or FD (in serious conflict) |
| Conflict resolution at intra-village | Done mostly by mutual agreement between villages, some time with the help of *panchayat* | Done mostly by mutual agreement between villages, some time with the help of *panchayat* | Done by the arbitration *Panchayat* and FD | Done by the arbitration *Panchayat* and FD | Done by the arbitration *Panchayat* and FD |

*Source* : Focus group discussion and CCFM and JFM rules

(c) cultural conduciveness. For instance, in Shradhyapur FPC of Orissa some members cut few Sal (*Shorea robusta*) trees illegally. MC of Shradhyapur FPC after discussing the matter prohibited those offenders and their family members from collecting dry leaves (used for cooking) and Kendu leaves (used for wrapping local cigar—Bidi) for one year from its forest. The offenders were forced to go to other adjacent forests for collecting dry leaves and were ridiculed. Further, non-collection of Kendu leaves caused economic loss to their family. Contrarily, bureaucratic sanctions follow simplified and standardised policies. Such punishment was found to be limited to monetary fine in the studied FPCs of CCFM and JFM units. This often fails to change the attitude of the offender. ICFM units were found to practise graduated sanction and consequently had experienced a decline in the intensity of rule violations. CCFM followed a system of graduated as well as standardised sanction policy. Conversely, JFM management preferred to impose sanction as per standard rules. Such sanctions controlled the rule violation in the short-term but not in the long-term. Furthermore, while JFM sanctions were imposed mostly in the form of monetary fine, ICFM and CCFM sanctions varied from monetary fine to social boycott. In ICFM and CCFM, sanctions were imposed after discussing either in MC meeting for general offences or in GB meeting for serious offences. In JFM, the president and the forest guard generally took such decisions. For mass offence, FD reserved the right to dissolve the unit and form a new JFM unit. However, such cases have not been reported so far (Table 2.3).

*Conflict resolution*

Resolving conflicts is an acid-test for organisational efficiency. In forest management, conflicts usually occur among members (intra-village) or between adjacent villages (inter-villages). For intra-village conflicts, ICFM and CCFM mostly sought solution through dialogues between the conflicting parties. If the conflicts were not resolved through dialogue, matters were normally referred to the GB. While the GB of ICFM tried to take decisions through consensus, the GB of CCFM preferred to take decisions mostly through majority opinion. JFM committees, however, preferred to resolve the conflict through bureaucratic arbitration either by MC members or FD representative (Table 2.3). In the event of inter-village conflict, ICFM and CCFM tried to resolve the matter through dialogues, with or without the help of local leaders. Many a times, while resolving the inter-village conflicts, ICFM and CCFM successfully motivated the adjacent villages to initiate forest protection. One such example was found in Khaksi Toli, which motivated two adjacent villages— Jam Toli and Ber Toli— to undertake forest protection activities. Such examples abound in Orissa. However, JFM banked totally on bureaucratic processes for managing such conflicts. Besides MC and FD, *Panchayat Raj Institutions* also played an active role in settling inter-village conflict in JFM. Although *Panchayat Raj Institution* has the legitimate rights to settle village conflict, people tended to avoid such resolution because of its political bias. In many cases, involvement of *Panchayat Raj Institution* added more complexity to resolve the conflict.

*Activities*

(a) Protection of forestlands was the primary activity of FPC. This activity inculcated a sense of ownership, and collective responsibility. In ICFM and CCFM, people in group patrolled the forest on rotational basis. Similar practice was also prevalent in many JFM. However, some JFM appointed watchmen for this purpose, and community members contributed towards meeting their salary expenses. Higher access rights acted as a moral booster for sincere patrolling in ICFM and CCFM. Low access rights led to low motivation in JFM. Some JFM units of Jharkhand and West Bengal allowed the patrolling team to collect the fine directly from the offender. These fines were used for the entertainment of the patrolling team to boost their spirit.

(b) Meeting constituent's forest-related consumption needs is another crucial challenge for forest management. Forest communities, living on subsistence economy, depend on various forest resources for their survival. Each forest protection unit evolved its norms for use of different forest produce to meet different needs of its constituents which are given below :

- Fuel wood holidays: Days were fixed for fuel wood collection and distribution in the form of dried twigs, branches and trees. Such holidays in ICFM were offered quarterly and in CCFM and JFM annually.
- Fixed time for collection of fodder: Due to abundance of vegetation in eastern states of India, none of the forest type restricted fodder collection. However, in a drought year, instances of restricting the number of fodder collectors per household were reported.
- NTFP: ICFM and CCFM allowed only predetermined number of persons per household for collecting the NTFP. In JFM, such restrictions were often not followed.
- Access to poles for house construction: Villagers use poles (wooden log having around 20 to 25 cm diameter) for making thatch- or local tile-roof. Every FPC provided poles to its members with nominal charges for house construction every three to five years.
- Allowance for non-members: No FPC offered any benefit to non-members except the collection of dry leaves and twigs for fuel. Frequent intrusion of non-members disrupted the protection in JFM. These problems were better handled in ICFM and CCFM. Some times, ICFM and CCFM successfully motivated the intruders to initiate the forest protection in their (intruders) village/hamlet.

*Benefit sharing*

Benefit sharing had wide variation between ICFM, CCFM and JFM. The benefits were economic, material and social. They were accrued at individual or collective level. At the individual level, economic benefit was accrued in the form of wage employment generated during resource development; material benefit came in the form of fuel wood, NTFP and timber; and social benefit was accrued in inculcating in-group feeling and voicing one's opinion in the decision-making. At the collective level, economic, material, and social benefits were accrued in the form of community development fund, forest wealth, and increased solidarity respectively.

Evidently members of ICFM received the highest benefit followed by CCFM and JFM. However, crafting agencies and FD mobilized funds for forest regeneration that eventually flowed into the hand of members of CCFM and JFM respectively. Such funds were not available for ICFMs (Table 2.4).

**Table 2.4 :** Ranking of Benefit Flow in Three Forms of Forest

| Benefits | | ICFM | CCFM | JFM |
|---|---|---|---|---|
| Individual | Economic | Nil (No wage employment) | Moderate through wage employment | Moderate to High through wage employment |
| | Material | High | High | Low |
| | Social | High | Moderate | Low |
| Collective | Economic | High | High | Low to moderate |
| | Material | High | High | Moderate/ Partial |
| | Social | High | Moderate | Low |

*Source* : Participatory appraisals

*Other governing rules*

Members of GB and MC in ICFM and CCFM had the power to convene the respective meetings as per their suitability. These meetings were held at regular intervals. In the initial years, NGO representatives attended these meetings regularly in CCFM. Besides regular scheduled meetings, if 50% or more members of GB or MC desired, extra ordinary GB or MC meetings could be convened.

**Table 2.5 :** Rules for Meeting, Election, and Amendment of Rules in ICFM, CCFM, and JFM

| *Issues* | *ICFM* | *CCFM* | *JFM Jharkhand* | *JFM Orissa* | *JFM West Bengal* |
|---|---|---|---|---|---|
| Convening the general body meeting | Decided at village level | Decided at village level | With the consent of FD | With the consent of FD | With the consent of FD |
| Holding the meeting | MC- weekly; GB- quarterly | MC - monthly; GB - Annual (special meeting can be held if 50% members seek it) | 1. Presence of FD is required for taking any new policy decision 2. MC - quarterly; GB – Annual | 1. Presence of FD is required for taking any new policy decision 2. MC - quarterly; GB – Annual | 1. Presence of FD is required for taking any new policy decision 2. MC - quarterly; GB - Annual |
| General Body meeting | Held in regular interval | Held in regular interval | Irregular | Irregular | Irregular |
| Election | As per the decision of general body | Once in three years | Once in two year can be prolonged or reduced as per the wish of FD | Once in two year can be prolonged or reduced as per the wish of FD | Once in two year can be prolonged or reduced as per the wish of FD |
| Election of President of FPC | By the GB - mostly natural leaders are unanimously chosen | By the MC members | By the MC members and FD representative | By the MC members and FD representative | By the MC members and FD representative |
| Framing of rules | GB 's prerogative | GB 's prerogative | FD | FD | FD |
| Revision of rules | Always done in the GB | Always done in GB | Except operational rules, FD can only revise the rules | Except operational rules, FD can only revise the rules | Except operational rules, FD can only revise the rules |

*Source* : Focus group discussion and CCFM and JFM rules

JFM meetings, however, were convened only with the consent of FD representative. Although instances of holding meetings without FD representatives were not rare, no major decision could be taken in such meetings (Table 2.5).

Election of new MC or president or both normally took place at regular intervals in ICFM and CCFM. Time and mode of election were decided by the constituents alone at the time of framing the rules. Despite regular election, change of office bearers was not a very common phenomenon in ICFM. CCFM on the other hand, witnessed frequent change of office bearers at the turn of every election. JFM elections were not held regularly except in West Bengal. Elections in JFM took place only in the presence of FD representatives. Non-availability of FD representatives often postponed elections for years in Jharkhand and Orissa (Table 2.5).

In both ICFM and CCFM, GB had the exclusive rights to amend the rules. However, where CCFM was registered under State Cooperative Act, GB had to abide by the rules of the cooperatives. In such cases, GB of CCFM could amend the rules not specified in the cooperative rules. In JFM, FD reserved the exclusive rights to amend any rules as per its convenience and priority.

### *(c) Power and function of managing committee*

#### *General management*

MC is entrusted with the role of guardian of the institutional arrangement. MC is expected to be transparent and accountable in all matters by sharing all information with GB, ensuring distributive justice, resolving the conflicts impartially, maintaining the accounts properly, holding election on time, ensuring appropriate monitoring and sanction, and taking decision in participatory manner. MC was appreciated most when it protected local rights, secured the territorial authority over forest, and allowed time-tested local knowledge of conservation to work while discharging its duties. ICFM and CCFM units were found to be more successful in meeting these varied expectations. ICFM compared to CCFM made their MC forum more open. Normally MC's meetings of ICFM were conducted in a common place and general members were

**Table 2.6 :** Functioning of Managing Committee of Three Forms of Forest

| *Issues* | *ICFM* | *CCFM* | *JFM Jharkhand* | *JFM Orissa* | *JFM West Bengal* |
|---|---|---|---|---|---|
| Meetings | Weekly and it's regular feature | Monthly and it's regular feature | Quarterly but not a regular feature | Quarterly but not a regular feature | Quarterly but not a regular feature |
| Information sharing with other members | Any villager can be silent observer of MC meeting, decisions are made known regularly | Through notification and general body meeting | Not a regular affair, suspicion prevails | Not a regular affair, suspicion prevails | Not a regular affair, suspicion prevails |
| Maintenance of account | Highly satisfactory and shared with GB regularly | Satisfactory And shared with GB regularly | Satisfactory but not shared with GB regularly | Satisfactory but not shared with GB regularly | Satisfactory but not shared with GB regularly |
| Distribution of benefits | Equally | Equally | Equally as per FD guidelines but suspicion prevails | Equally as per FD guidelines but suspicion prevails | Equally as per FD guidelines but suspicion prevails |
| President's image | Participatory and nurturing | Participatory but in some cases autocratic | Participatory but in some cases manipulative | Participatory but in some cases manipulative | Mostly manipulative |

*Source* : Focus group discussion and CCFM and JFM rules

encouraged to be silent spectators of the proceedings. In contrast, CCFM and JFM units held their meeting at segregated places and preferred to maintain certain degree of confidentiality (Table 2.6).

*Financial management*

MC also looked after the collective fund and distribution of financial benefits to all members as per the resolution of GB. MCs of ICFM maintained more transparency in financial matters. Financial matters of ICFM were always presented before the GB more frequently than CCFM and JFM. CCFM accounts were also shared with general members annually. However, in JFM financial matters were not shared with the GB regularly. CCFM and JFM funds were kept in banks, which was not followed always by ICFM committees (Table 2.6).

*(d) Leadership*

ICFM affairs were guided by participatory values. Leadership in these institutions took decisions by taking all members into confidence. ICFM leadership preferred to spend longer time for collective negotiation in order to develop consensus on each issue. CCFM leadership although acted mostly in participatory manner, presence of authoritarian leadership was also noticed. JFM leadership on the other hand, was perceived more as manipulative. Participatory spirit of ICFM leadership helped in imbibing more solidarity within the organisation than CCFM and JFM. In JFM, leader's/MC's habit of bypassing the GB and taking decisions by themselves only left negative impression and de-motivated its members (Table 2.6).

**Enhancing the Participation: Essential Paraphernalia**

*Freedom of choice*

Study has revealed that for effective participation people must be given freedom of choice in every decision-making process. Diffusion of democratic rights and values is essential prerequisite of participation (Molinas, 1998; Narayan, 1996). JFM largely curtailed the process of democratic diffusion by taking all major decision at FD level and thereby limiting the scope of individual members in exercising their freedom of choice. Likewise in CCFM, crafting agencies also imposed certain basic rules/clauses at the initial stage that curtailed freedom of people. However, they gradually educated people to take appropriate decision on those imposed clauses in order to reduce the feeling of external imposition. Participation was more spontaneous in ICFM than CCFM and JFM as people themselves took every decision and such involvement increased the sense of ownership and belongingness (Table 2.7).

*Preserving the local rights*

Every community, tribe, or state desires to preserve its local rights, and secure its territory. History of Indian forest revealed that deforestation was increased after colonial power took away the forest ownership right from people's hand (Guha, 1983). Recent studies showed that wherever people could establish their local rights over resources, resources were better managed (Raju, 1998; Sarin, 1996). ICFM and CCFM gave higher scope for people to ensuring their social, economic, and cultural rights over resources and elicit more participation than JFM (Table 7).

*Making use of local knowledge*

Management of natural resources are best learned through experience. Knowledge of local ecosystem helps in sustainable management of resources. Knowledge about species preservation, care of plantation, grazing rotation, and rotation of timbers are found to be recorded as sacred rules among forest dwellers. ICFM and CCFM provided ample opportunities to the local inhabitant to design their forest institutions and management system incorporating those knowledge and values compare to JFM. While JFM forests accommodated mostly commercial timber species, ICFM and CCFM forest found to have many non-commercial species, which not only met diversified local necessities but also saved forest strand from disease pest. Maintaining Indian Neem (*Azadirachta indica*), or Sindwar (*Vitex negundo*) in forest reported as serving the above purposes from many places. In JFM, FD most

**Table 2.7 :** People's Perception of Institutional Governance, Leadership, In-Group Feeling and Participation in Different FPCs

| *Name* | *People's opinion* | | | *Social identity* | *Organistional Citizenship* | *Member's participation* |
|---|---|---|---|---|---|---|
| | *Rules* | *MC's function* | *Leadership* | | | |
| Berham | Satisfactory | Satisfactory | Autocratic | Moderate | Low | Low |
| Chandana | Unsatisfactory | Unsatisfactory | Manipulative | Low | Low | Moderate |
| Dundun | Satisfactory | Highly satisfactory | Participatory | High | High | High |
| Gobinderani | Highly satisfactory | Highly satisfactory | Participatory | High | High | High |
| Harinakhuri – Telebhanga | Unsatisfactory | Unsatisfactory | Autocratic | Low | Low | Moderate |
| Hutar | Satisfactory | Satisfactory | Participatory | High | Moderate | Moderate |
| Jam Toli | Highly satisfactory | Highly satisfactory | Participatory | High | High | High |
| Jamsol | Unsatisfactory | Unsatisfactory | Manipulative | Low | Low | Low |
| Kankadahat | Satisfactory | Satisfactory | Participatory | Moderate | Moderate | Moderate |
| Khaksi Toli | Highly satisfactory | Highly satisfactory | Charismatic | High | High | High |
| Paapsara | Highly Satisfactory | Less satisfactory | Autocratic | Moderate | Low | Moderate |
| Pada | Highly Satisfactory | Satisfactory | Participatory | High | High | High |
| Sadma | Less satisfactory | Unsatisfactory | Manipulative | Moderate | Low | Low |
| Semra | Satisfactory | Satisfactory | Participatory | High | High | High |
| Shradhyapur | Highly satisfactory | Highly satisfactory | Participatory | High | High | High |
| Solanda | Satisfactory | Satisfactory | Participatory | Moderate | Moderate | Moderate |
| Sundhikatni | Highly satisfactory | Highly satisfactory | Participatory | High | High | High |

*Source* : Participatory appraisal

often used exogenous technology guided by its commercial interest as compare to ICFM and CCFM where indigenously evolved technologies were preferred. Exogenous technology mostly restricted the scope of people's involvement in forest management.

*Federation*

Creation of cluster and federation of like-minded institutions help in resolving wider conflict resolution, increase collective bargaining capacity, and improve the liaisioning with external agencies. In the current study CCFM under aegis of Tree Growers Cooperative Federation was successful in achieving legal right over their protected forest right from government of Orissa. This also helped them - (a) in settling the inter-village conflicts more amicably and also entered into negotiation with villages under JFM, (b) in building network with similar kind of federations in other states of India. ICFM had its own limitations in this aspect. Most of the ICFM emerged and being sustained as single identity without having any workable exchange with one another. In Jharkhand state, three ICFMs under the current study- Khaksi Toli, Jamtoli, Hutar however, had developed inter-unit tie up with the help of tribal headship locally known as Parha Raja and managed to secure verbal assurance of non-interference from forest department in their forest territory. Local tribal council also ensured full cooperation in the event of settling conflict with intruders/free riders from adjacent villages. Nevertheless, these examples were few and could happen only when body like tribal council existed. JFM had great opportunity to build such network. However, FDs of three states - Jharkhand, Orissa, and West Bengal showed little interest in exploiting such opportunities. As a result, JFM like most ICFM found to manage situations on single unit basis having little to no interaction with other JFM units. Such missed opportunity also a cause of failure in eliciting mass participation in JFM.

**Conclusion**

People's participation in forest management depends primarily on how a particular institutional evolution and other character help each individual member in embracing social identity, group based identity, and organisational citizenship. Institutional process which ensures individual freedom of choice, local self governance, pre-eminence of local rights and knowledge system, participatory leadership, and federation opportunity found conducive in building social identity and organisational citizenship thereby elicited more participation.

Despite the lack of federation, ICFM structures were successful in eliciting more participation as these were evolved and managed by locally and people found to own both the success and failures in the same spirit. CCFM were also successful in terms eliciting participation and found to enjoy the support of a federating structures but lacked the spirit of ICFM due to relatively less freedom in rule making process and lesser interaction between MC and general body. This retarded the spontaneous participation. Bureaucratic style of functioning of JFM bodies worked against the spirit of participatory management and demand for more decentralised and people centred management was quite evident.

Furthermore, institutional management for forest institutions needs to be more liberal in accommodating the views of weaker sections, minority groups, and women. Building consensus in each decision-making process sometime required longer negotiation. However, such approaches gave more stability to institutional structures as well as enhanced people's adherence to the institutional resolution.

The present study has revealed that ICFM and CCFM were more successful in promoting social identity and eliciting participation than JFM but ICFM and CCFM control only a small fragment of Indian forest resources. Even today, around eighty five percent of official forest resources are under FD's control. More so, while establishing the legitimacy of local people's stake on forest, it would be unjustified to deny the stake of nation state. Therefore, JFM umbrella is an essential pre-requisite for making forest protection a mass movement across the country. For making JFM a more viable alternative to ICFM, and CCFM, JFM need to enhance the level of assurances to win people's confidence by conforming to the ICFM system.

# 3

# INSTITUTIONAL GOVERNANCE INFLUENCING PEOPLE'S PARTICIPATION IN CBFM

The central objective of community-based forest management is to elicit people's participation in the affairs of forest management (Pimbert and Pretty, 1998; Roy, 1992; Sarin, 1996). Participation is a dynamic process through which stakeholders influence and share control over development initiatives and the decisions and resources that affect them (Banki, 1981; World Bank, 1996). This is based on a widely accepted view held by natural resource management activists that members of resource-dependent societies are efficient managers of natural resources. Efficient management requires rule-ordered behaviour of individuals and village communities or groups (North, 1990) geared towards sustainability of natural resources (Balland and Platteau, 1996). Institutional governance provides perspectives for such rule-ordered behaviour.

Institutional governance with wide acceptability among resource appropriators promotes prolific people's involvement in resource conservation, inculcates mutual sharing of responsibility and accountability, lessens conflicts, and reduces free riding (Gadgil, 1998; Jodha, 1986; Ostrom, 1990, 1998; Raju, Vaghela, and Raju, 1993; Roy, 1993; Sarin, 1996; Vira, 1999; Zuhair, 1998). Contrarily, low degree of acceptability provokes free riding, diffuses responsibility and accountability, and hinders collective action (Hardin, 1968; MacKean, 1987).

Local appropriators always do not enjoy full freedom to have the institutional governance of their choice (Chambers, Saxena, Shah, 1989; Pimbert and Pretty, 1998; Saxena, 1987; Shah, 1987). They often have to conform to the demands of external agencies and the state. In India, community-based forest management has emerged in three forms — (a) indigenous community forest management (ICFM), (b) crafted community forest management (CCFM), and (c) joint forest management (JFM). These three types differ from one another on (a) freedom of local appropriators to make rules and norms; (b) conduciveness of institutional rules to local situations; and (c) the extent of intervention of state and other external agencies in institutional governance. The three forms of forest institutions also vary in castes, number of villages and livelihood groups covered in them. In this context, the chapter aims (a) to determine the extent of people's participation in different community-based forest management, and (b) to gauge the extent to which various aspects of the composition and governance of forest institutions influence people's participation.

## Institutional Governance vis a vis People's Participation

People's participation and community-based forest management are inextricably linked (Chambers, 1983; Poffenberger and Singh, 1996). People refer to a group of identifiable individuals living in and around the forest who have a *de-facto* or *de-jure* stake in the forest resources. These individuals may hail from one or more villages/hamlets (Poffenberger and McGean, 1996; Raju, Vaghela, and Raju, 1993). In community-based forest management, these individuals are brought under a common forum for protecting the forest under some common rules and regulations (Malhotra, 1995; Roy and Chatterjee, 1994; Sarin, 1996). Like other common property resource management, community-based forest management emphasises on institutionalisation of forest protection movement with the involvement of stakeholders.

Participation has two dimensions: (a) direct, and (b) indirect. Direct participation includes the involvement of stakeholders in activities like attending meetings concerning forest protection, taking active part in meetings, contributing labour towards forest management, monitoring, patrolling, etc. Indirect participation refers to individuals' obedience to forest protection rules, motivating others as well as their own family members for forest protection, providing moral support to the community for ensuring equity, justice, and transparency in forest management (Ostrom, 1990; Palit, 1993; Pimbert, 1994; Raju, Vaghela, and Raju, 1993; Sarin, 1996; Silwal, 1986; Singh, Ballabh and Palakudiyil, 1996).

From a project perspective, participation can mean informing people about a project either through (a) consulting them, or (b) by delegating managerial power over the project to them (Nuitjen, 1992). While the former type stresses sharing of responsibilities and accountabilities jointly by project planners and members of the community, the latter talks about total community ownership. The individual's decision to cooperate with the community vis-à-vis project planners depends on the level of personal acceptance and conviction about the forestry project, favourable evaluation of institutional rules, and accrued benefits (Ostrom, 1990; Roy, 1992; Sarin, 1996).

## Factors Influencing People's Participation

### *Three forms of forest*

Different community-based forest management institutions — ICFM, CCFM, and JFM -vary from each other in terms of composition of stakeholders in the forest protection body, homogeneity of interest, compatibility of governing rules with local norms, functioning of managing committee, conflict resolution, external influence, freedom in exercising local wisdom, and institutional arrangement that favours involvement of primary stakeholders through devolution of power. Such variations may influence people's willingness to participate in forest management (Gupta, 1985; Raju, Vaghela, and Raju, 1993; Sarin, 1996). ICFM, and CCFM show greater compatibility with local culture and address primary stakeholders' aspirations in a more democratic manner than JFM

(Khare, 1998). However, crafting agencies like NGOs' worldviews often influence the decisions of CCFM. In JFM, the influence of forest department, and local administrative bodies cannot be ruled out. Such influence may prevent fulfilment of local aspirations and discourage people's involvement.

*Composition of forest protection units*

Participation can be influenced by caste composition, livelihood groups, number of villages included in forest protection unit, and community homogeneity (Gupta, 1985; Poffenberger and McGean, 1996; Oakerson, 1986; Ostrom, 1990). Tribal communities may show more interest in forest protection because of their historical association with forests and ethno-religious values (Guha, 1983; Jewitt, 1996). People whose livelihoods are more dependent on forests look for greater stake in them. Oakerson (1986) pointed out that management of natural resources becomes more convenient when the boundary of the unit is small. ICFM and CCFM units are generally confined to single village level. JFM units often include more than one village. Forest protection units having homogenous communities face less complication in solving intra-group conflicts (Gupta, 1985) and evolving a forest protection mechanism through consensus.

**$H_{1a}$:** People's participation would differ in the three forms of forest management.

**$H_{1b}$:** Participation would differ against different castes, livelihood groups, village composition of forest protection unit, and community homogeneity.

*Institutional rules*

Setting-up an institutional governance is a key element for sustainable community-based forest management (Gadgil and Rao, 1994; Lele and Rao, 1996; Pimbert and Pretty, 1998 Agarwal and Saigal, 1996). When multiple individual users become dependent on a particular common property resource like a forest, they are jointly affected by almost everything they do. This lays down ground rules for collective action that each individual must take into account the choices of others while assessing his or her personal choices (Bromley, 1986; Korten, 1986; Ostrom, 1986). In other words, if each user acts independently in relation to a scarce resource pool, the total benefits they obtain usually will be less than those which could have been achieved through some coordinated strategies. Ostrom (1986) points out that this uncoordinated act at a minimum will cause serious imbalances in benefit appropriation at user level and at worst, it will result in destruction of common property resources. Forest conservation can be achieved through organisational efforts (Dove, 1993; Jeffery and Sunder, 1999) by changing the situation from one in which individual users act independently to one in which they adopt coordinated strategies for obtaining higher joint benefits (Deb and Malhotra, 1993; Gupta, 1985; Raju, 1998; Sarin 1996).

To ensure coordinated strategies, local forest institutions set various rules and regulations. Individuals are likely to cooperate with group activity if governing rules ensure equity in access right and benefit sharing process; safeguard participation of all sections in decision making process; ensure appropriate monitoring and graduated (as per the gravity of violation) sanction; do not contradict traditional or existing systems of community governance; and provide scope for modifications/amendments in the existing rules as a response to changed circumstances and demands for sustenance.

JFM enforces uniform governing rules except day-to-day operational rules, irrespective of regional variations. Bureaucratic intervention and standard style of functioning specially in election of managing committee, monitoring, and sanction may reduce people's participation (Chambers, 1983; Hobley, 1996; Jeffery and Sundar, 1999; Saxena, 1987; Shah 1987). The interference of forest bureaucrats and local power groups often prevents weaker sections from voicing their opinions. ICFM and CCFM apparently have an edge in these matters because the governing rules evolve from the communities, and consequently institutional governance becomes more compatible with the people's cultural and social setup. However, certain influences of crafting agencies in framing the institutional rules cannot be avoided in CCFM.

**$H_{2a}$** : Evaluation of institutional governing rules would differ in the three forms of forest management.

**$H_{2b}$** : Favourable evaluation of institutional governing rules would increase people's participation.

*Functioning of managing committees*

Forest management institutions are likely to breakdown when people lose faith and confidence in managing committees and withdraw their participation (Pathak, 1994; Wade, 1982). Creating a transparent and accountable organisational setup can prevent this breakdown. Managing committees can do this through frequent consultations with general body, collective decision-making, down to earth informal leadership, and appreçiating ordinary members views (Sarin, 1996). The involvement of state, block and panchayat administration makes the managing committee of JFM more bureaucratic (Poffenberger, 1990; Sen and Das, 1987; Vira, 1999). In ICFM and CCFM, the involvement of community members in decision-making and its implementation make the managing committee more transparent and accountable (Roy, 1995; Sarin, 1996; Singh, Ballabh, and Palakudiyil, 1996). Managing committee's interaction with general body members is more frequent and elaborative in ICFM and CCFM. Such interaction occurs weekly in ICFM, and monthly or bimonthly in CCFM (Poffenberger, 1990; Sen and Das, 1987; Sarin, 1996) in the form of forest protection committee (FPC) meetings. However, this interaction in JFM is usually brief, formal, and irregular due to the nonavailability of forest officials and political nominees (Raju, 1998). People's participation is likely to increase in accordance with the functioning of managing committee.

**$H_{3a}$** : Evaluation of managing committee's functioning would differ in the three forms of forest management.

**$H_{3b}$** : Favourable evaluation of functioning of managing committee would increase people's participation.

*Conflict resolution*

Conflict resolution has been one of the most pervasive and sensitive aspects of institutional governance (Kothari, Anuradha, and Pathak, 1998; Raju, 1998). Community-based forest management systems are expected to provide mechanisms for the equitable use of resources with a minimum of internal conflict. Rules mutually agreed upon reduce monitoring costs for enforcement of rules and also conflicts over resource use (Berkes, 1986). Conflicts in community organisations arise when members refuse to forego some individual benefits in favour of achieving the common goal. In forest management, conflicts can be classified into four categories: within the members of local institutions, with neighbouring non-members, with external commercial or industrial interest groups, and with the state or forest department. Every local institution evolves effective conflict resolution mechanisms for sustainable resource use. Intra-community conflicts are more common in heterogeneous FPC owing to the presence of different castes and livelihood groups. Intracommunity conflicts can also occur for perceived inequity in the distribution of cost and benefits of forest protection, suspicions over mishandling of funds, obstinacy of some members over accepting common rules, enforcement of sanctions, and partiality of leaders favouring her/his own people (Poffenberger and McGean, 1996; Sarin, 1996).

Conflicts with neighbouring villages arise over unmarked boundaries, denial of permission to collect non-timber forest produce, non-reciprocations of neighbouring villages cooperation, and free-riding attitude of neighbouring villages. Conflicts between forest department and villagers are caused when the forest department tries to sell timber arbitrarily, or it does not honour its own commitments, supports industrial bodies' interest, and refuses to understand communities' problems and priorities.

JFM follows a set pattern in resolving conflict. Bureaucratic interference either by forest or local panchayat officials becomes inevitable (Kothari, Anuradha, and Pathak, 1998; Raju, 1998). Unlike JFM intra- and inter-community FPCs, conflicts in ICFM and CCFM are resolved either through mutual agreement, or neutral mediators or concerned NGOs (in the case of CCFM only), or sometimes through majorities' opinion. Intra-community conflicts are effectively resolved through frequent and regular general body or village meetings in areas having strong traditions of community organisations. Individual satisfaction about conflict resolution boosts participation.

**$H_{4a}$** : The causes and modes of resolving conflicts would differ in the three forms of forest management.

**$H_{4b}$** : The extent of satisfaction with and gain from conflict resolution would differ in the three forms of forest management.

**$H_{4c}$** : The extent of satisfaction with and gain from conflict resolution would increase the people's participation.

## Methodology

### *Sample*

Forest management in the three eastern states of India — Jharkhand, Orissa, and West Bengal— was studied. Seven JFM units— two each from Jharkhand and Orissa, and three from West Bengal; six ICFM units— four from Jharkhand and two from Orissa; and four CCFM units from Orissa were selected for the study. JFM units were selected from Kanke and Bero range of Ranchi district in Jharkhand, Athamalik range of Angul district in Orissa, and Hijli range of Midnapur district in West Bengal. ICFM units were selected from Ranchi district of Jharkhand, and Dhenkanal district of Orissa, and CCFM units were selected from Angul and Dhenkanal districts of Orissa. The Tree Growers Cooperative Federation promoted CCFM units. Because Jharkhand did not have any CCFM unit and West Bengal did not have any ICFM and CCFM units, no such sample was taken from these states. The decision to include these forest protection units was guided by approachability and convenience. Thus, we adopted a purposive sampling procedure. Except three JFM units of West Bengal, all other units had a FPC in each village. In West Bengal, Jamsol FPC was constituted with six villages, Chandana FPC was formed with three villages, and

**Table 3.1 : Profile of Respondents**

| FPC | Forest[a] | Community[b] | Respondent | Sex[c] | | Livelihood[d] | | Caste/ Tribe[e] | | |
|---|---|---|---|---|---|---|---|---|---|---|
| | | | | M | F | AG | NAG | SC | ST | G |
| Berham | JFM | HM | 18 | 18 | | 18 | | 3 | 2 | 13 |
| Chandana | JFM | HT | 37 | 32 | 5 | 32 | 5 | 9 | 13 | 15 |
| undun | ICFM | HM | 9 | 9 | | 8 | 1 | 1 | 8 | |
| Gobind-berani | ICFM | HM | 6 | 5 | 1 | 5 | 1 | | 5 | 1 |
| Harina-kuri-Tele-bhanga | JFM | HT | 28 | 28 | | 27 | 1 | 19 | | 9 |
| Hutar | ICFM | HM | 24 | 24 | | 21 | 3 | | 23 | 1 |
| Jamsol | JFM | HT | 58 | 55 | 3 | 36 | 22 | 27 | 17 | 14 |
| Jamtoli | ICFM | HM | 19 | 19 | | 14 | 5 | 4 | 15 | |
| Khaksi Toli | ICFM | HM | 18 | 18 | | 18 | | 1 | 17 | |
| Kanka-dahat | CCFM | HT | 29 | 20 | 9 | 26 | 8 | 7 | 10 | 12 |
| Paapsara | CCFM | HM | 34 | 29 | 5 | 21 | 8 | | 30 | 4 |
| Pada | CCFM | HM | 32 | 29 | 3 | 30 | 2 | 7 | | 25 |
| Shrad-hyapur | ICFM | HM | 10 | 10 | | 8 | 2 | 2 | 7 | 1 |
| Solanda | JFM | HT | 19 | 17 | 2 | 17 | 2 | 1 | 9 | 9 |
| Sundh-ikatni | CCFM | HM | 18 | 15 | 3 | 10 | 8 | | 3 | 15 |
| Sadma | JFM | HT | 19 | 18 | 1 | 14 | 5 | 9 | 10 | |
| Semra | JFM | HM | 19 | 14 | 5 | 14 | 5 | 2 | 16 | 1 |
| Total | | | 397 | 360 | 37 | 319 | 78 | 92 | 185 | 120 |

[a]ICFM= Indigenous community forest management, CCFM= Crafted community forest management, JFM= Joint forest management; [b]HM= Homogenous; HT= Heterogeneous; [c]M = Male; F= Female; [d]AG= Agriculturist, NAG= Non-agriculturist; [e]SC= Schedule castes, ST= Schedule tribes, G= General castes.

Harinakhuri-Telebhanga FPC was formed with two villages. Along with these three, another three FPCs —Sadma from Jharkhand state, Kankadahat and Solanda from Orissa state— had heterogeneous population. The remaining eleven FPCs — Dundun, Hutar, Jamtoli, Khaksitoli, Semra from Jharkhand state; and Berham, Gobindberani Paapsara, Pada, Shradhyapur, Sudhikatni from Orissa state— had homogenous population where 75% or more of the population belonged to a specific caste or tribe.

Ten per cent of the households were selected from each village adopting systematic random sampling procedure. Persons who represented the household in FPCs as members were interviewed. Interviewees were 397, out of which 86 were from ICFM units, 113 were from CCFM units, and 198 respondents were from JFM units (Table 3.1).

*Measures*

A structured interview schedule was prepared in English. The English version of the interviewee schedule initially contained 30 items for assessing participation, 25 items each for evaluation of institutional rules and functioning of the managing committee, and 12 items for conflict resolution. This was scrutinised by four experts in forest management. The items agreed by all were retained. To conduct the interview in three states differing in languages, this schedule was translated into the local languages in Hindi, Oriya, and Bengali with the help of dual-language experts. To ensure the accuracy of translation, another three dual-language experts back-translated these into English. Three interview schedules in three local languages were pre-tested in three states for their understanding and clarity. The author, who knew Hindi and Bengali, interviewed the FPC members from Jharkhand and West Bengal respectively, and also interviewed the FPC members from Orissa with the help of a vernacular interpreter. Including socio-demographic variables on age, castes, livelihood, village(s) covered by FPC, and village population, the interview schedule measured the following variables.

*(a) People's participation*

Singh (1992) used the scaling method for measuring people's participation in forest management. The scale did not cover all aspects of participation. A twelve-item scale containing 4 items from Singh's scale and other 8 items assessed participation. The response descriptions against each item were given on a three-point Likert-type scale— always (2), sometimes (1), and never (0). All items were keyed positively. When the scores of all items on total sample were factor analysed using principal component analysis, and the factors were rotated through varimax procedure, two factors were extracted which explained 58.53% of total variance (see Appendix I). The first factor had significant loadings on eight items related to 'direct participation'. Sample items include" Did you participate in meetings called by FPC?" and " Did you contribute labour toward forest protection activities?" The second factor had loadings on four items that assessed 'indirect participation'. Sample items include "Do you abide by rules and norms of your FPC?" and "Do you report to the managing committee about violation of rules by any of the members?" Alpha reliability on the current sample was .93 for direct participation and .90 for indirect participation. High scores indicated more (direct or indirect) participation.

*(b) Institutional rules*

Eleven items assessed institutional rules. Each item was measured on fairness of rule— fair (2), neither fair nor unfair (1), and unfair (0); acceptability of rule— acceptable (2), neither acceptable nor unacceptable (1), and unacceptable (0); and desirability of rule— desirable (2), neither desirable nor undesirable (1), and undesirable (0). Such bipolar adjectives were used earlier for evaluation of business ethics (Reidenbach and Robin, 1990). When the scores of these items were factor analysed, three factors were extracted that explained 73.30% of total variance (see Appendix I). The first factor containing six items evaluated general administration. The items dealt with the rules for forest monitoring and patrolling system, punishment of offenders, rights of every member of FPC to choose managing committee members, ensuring representation of different livelihood groups in managing committee, selection/election of president to managing committee, and amendment of institutional rules. The second factor containing three items evaluated personal stakeholding. The items dealt with eligibility criteria for membership in general body, women's rights to take part in general body, and norms for benefit sharing among members. The third factor containing two items evaluated the participation of non-members. The items dealt with the sharing of benefits among nonmembers, and inclusion of panchayat/political members in the managing committee. The alpha reliability was .89 for general administration, .89 for personal stakeholding, and .51 for participation of non-members. High scores indicated favourable evaluation of institutional rules on each factor.

*(c) Managing committee's functioning*

Eight items assessed the functioning of managing committee. All items were measured on a three-point scale— always (2), sometimes (1), and never (0). Only one item was negatively keyed. When the scores of these items were factor analysed, two factors emerged which explained 63.17% of total variance (Appendix I). The first factor contained five items about managing committee's transparency. Sample items include "Did the managing committee maintain proper financial account?" and "Did the managing committee consult general body before revising rules?" The second factor containing three items measured managing committee's accountability. Sample items include "Was the managing committee sincere in protecting the forest?" and "Was the managing committee sympathetic to individual member's need at the time of emergency?" Alpha reliability on the current sample was .82 for the managing committee's transparency, and .73 for the managing committee's accountability. High scores indicated greater transparency and accountability.

*Conflict resolution*

Number of conflicts occurred within previous two years was collected from the respective FPCs. Two questions were asked for the causes and processes of conflict resolution within the village and another two questions for between villages. Multiple responses were given by the respondents. Another six items assessed the satisfaction with and gain from conflict resolution. The response descriptions against each item were given on a three-point scale. Four items were positively keyed — highly satisfied (2), satisfied (1), and not satisfied (0), and two were negatively keyed— fully (0), partially (1), not at all (2). When the scores of these items were factor analysed, two factors emerged which explained 87.49% of the total variance (Appendix I). The first factor containing four items measured the satisfaction with conflict resolution. Sample items include "In the last two years, have you been satisfied with the conflict resolution... within village?" and "... between panchayat and your FPC?" The second factor containing two negatively keyed items measured the individual gain owing to conflict resolution. Items include "In the last two years, to what extent... did conflict resolution de-motivate you for forest protection?" and "... did conflict resolution cause any loss to you?" Alpha reliability on the current sample was .87 for satisfaction with conflict resolution, and .85 for individual gain. High scores indicated greater satisfaction and more gain.

*Procedure*

The interview took place in afternoon and evening hours when the respondents were available. The interviewees were bricfed about the purpose of the study, and then their consent was sought for participation. Responses were procured through face-to-face conversation.

## Results

### *Three forms of forest management and participation*

Descriptive statistics on people's participation against three forms of forest management, castes, livelihood groups, village composition of FPC, and community homogeneity are given below (Table 3.2). ICFM, CCFM, and JFM differed significantly on direct participation, $F_{2,394} = 125.39$, $p < .001$, and on indirect participation, $F_{2,394} = 36.94$, $p < .001$. Post-hoc analysis using Tukey's test confirmed that direct participation was significantly higher in ICFM than that of CCFM, and CCFM than that of JFM. On indirect participation, the trend was similar. Only the CCFM and JFM did not differ significantly on the extent of indirect participation. Thus, people's participation was consistently higher in ICFM than that of CCFM and JFM.

**Table 3.2 :** Participation against Forest Institutions and Composition of FPC

| Variables | | Direct Participation | | | Indirect Participation | |
|---|---|---|---|---|---|---|
| | | *N* | *M* | *SD* | *M* | *SD* |
| Forest | ICFM | 86 | 13.88 | 1.94 | 7.36 | 1.14 |
| | CCFM | 113 | 12.30 | 2.49 | 5.94 | 1.65 |
| | JFM | 198 | 7.14 | 4.79 | 5.65 | 1.66 |
| Castes | SC | 92 | 7.45 | 4.67 | 5.79 | 1.53 |
| | ST | 185 | 11.47 | 4.32 | 6.50 | 1.69 |
| | General | 120 | 9.92 | 4.67 | 5.72 | 1.71 |
| Livelihood | AG | 319 | 10.34 | 4.74 | 6.14 | 1.67 |
| | NAG | 78 | 8.95 | 4.81 | 5.95 | 1.83 |
| FPC[a] | SINV | 274 | 12.79 | 2.53 | 6.45 | 1.58 |
| | MULV | 123 | 4.00 | 2.45 | 5.34 | 1.71 |
| Community | HM | 207 | 12.99 | 2.36 | 6.58 | 1.55 |
| | HT | 190 | 6.88 | 4.70 | 5.57 | 1.68 |

[a] SINV= Single Village, MULV= Multiple Village.

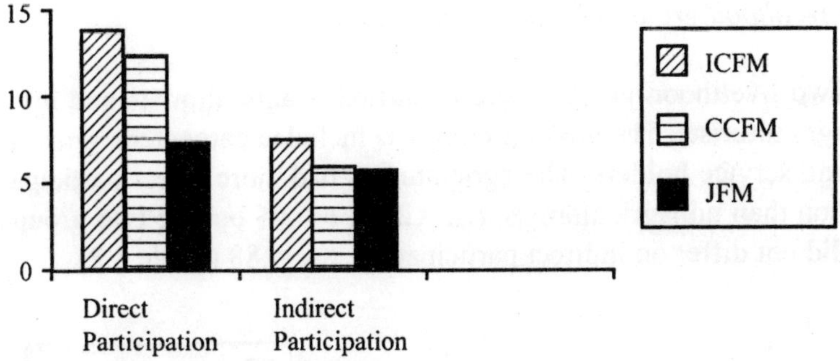


**Fig. 3.1 :** Average Direct and Indirect People's Participation in Three Forms of Forest

*Caste and tribe status, and participation*

Scheduled castes, scheduled tribes, and general castes differed significantly on direct participation, $F_{2,394} = 24.47$, $p < .001$, and indirect participation, $F_{2,394} = 10.21$, $p < .001$. Tukey's test showed that the scheduled tribes had significantly more direct participation than that of general castes, and general castes had more participation than schedule castes. For indirect participation, same trend was observed but general castes and schedule castes did not differ significantly. Hence, scheduled tribes had more participation than that of general castes and scheduled castes (Table 3.2).

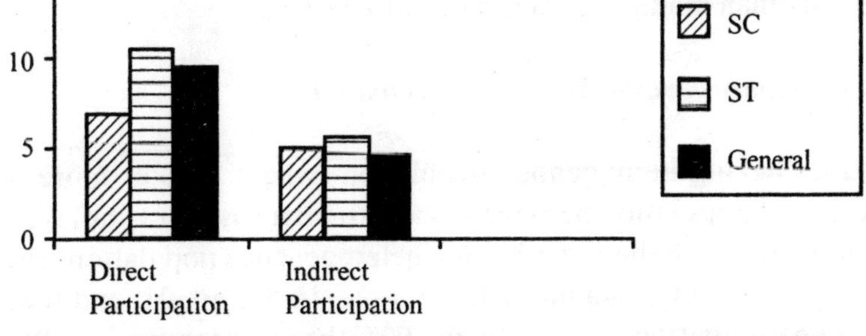


**Fig. 3.2 :** Average Direct and Indirect People's Participation among Different Castes

*Livelihood groups and participation*

Two livelihood groups were identified— agriculturists and non-agriculturists. The non-agriculturists included carpenters, grazers, and service holders. The agriculturists had more direct participation than nonagricultarists, $t_{396} = 2.32$, $p < .05$ but the two groups did not differ on indirect participation, $t_{396} = .88$ (Table 3.2).

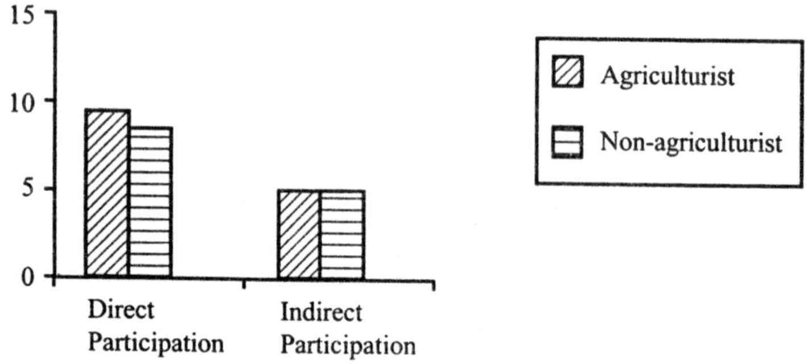


**Fig. 3.3 :** Average Direct and Indirect People's Participation among Different Livelihood Groups

*FPC constitution and participation*

As reported earlier, each ICFM, CCFM unit and four JFM units were constituted in single village, whereas three JFM units were constituted with two or more villages. Single village FPCs elicited more direct, $t_{396} = 32.32$, $p < .01$; and indirect participation, $t_{396} = 6.32$, $p < .01$ than multiple village FPCs (Table 3.2).

*Community composition and participation*

FPCs having homogenous population (where 75% or more of the total population belonged to a particular caste or tribe) were compared with the FPCs having heterogeneous population. Homogenous FPCs had more direct, $t_{396} = 16.56$, $p < .01$, and indirect participation, $t_{396} = 6.20$, $p < .001$, than heterogeneous FPCs (Table 3.2).

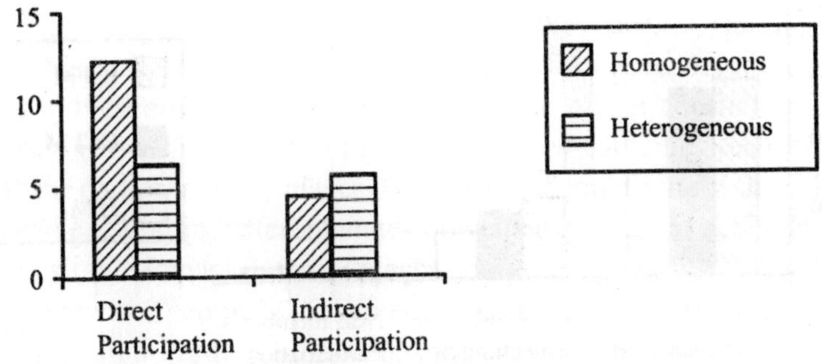


**Fig. 3.4 :** Average Direct and Indirect People's Participation among Homogeneous and Heterogeneous Communities

## *Evaluation of institutional rules*

ICFM, CCFM, and JFM differed significantly on evaluation of rules for (a) general administration, $F_{2,394} = 111.61, p < .001$; (b) personal stakeholding, $F_{2,394} = 62.243, p < .001$; and (c) participation of non-members, $F_{2,394} = 16.124, p < .001$ (Table 3.3). Post-hoc Tukey's test confirmed that rules for general administration, and personal stakeholding were more favourably evaluated in ICFM than that of CCFM and JFM, and CCFM than that of JFM. But, rules for non-members' inclusion in FPC were more favourably evaluated in JFM than that of ICFM and CCFM, and ICFM than that of CCFM.

**Table 3.3 :** Descriptive Statistics on Institutional Rules

| Variables [a] | ICFM | | CCFM | | JFM | |
|---|---|---|---|---|---|---|
| | *M* | *SD* | *M* | *SD* | *M* | *SD* |
| GA | 31.86 | 5.22 | 29.99 | 6.12 | 19.42 | 9.14 |
| PS | 15.81 | 3.19 | 13.17 | 4.84 | 9.82 | 4.47 |
| NMP | 1.87 | 3.26 | .97 | 2.32 | 2.91 | 3.09 |

[a] GA = General administration, PS = Personal stakeholding, NMP = Nonmembers' participation

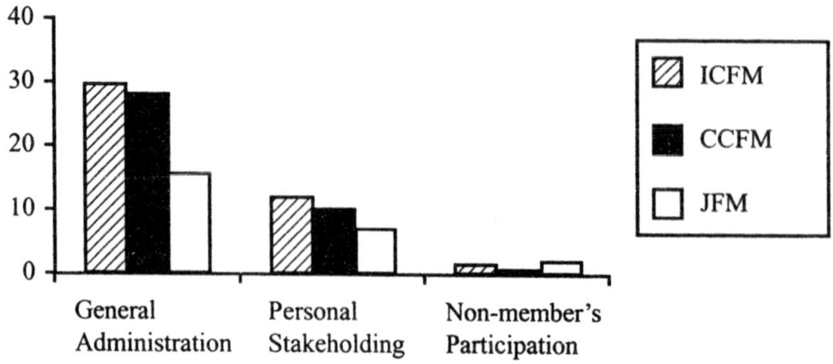


**Fig. 3.5 :** Member's Mean Satisfactaion with Institutional Rules Related to General Administration, Personal Stakeholding and Non-Member's Participation in Three Forms of Forest Management.

Supporting the hypothesis, in regression analysis, favourable evaluation of general administration, personal stakeholding, and non-members' inclusion in FPCs significantly increased direct and indirect participation. The standardized beta coefficients indicated that evaluation of institutional rules was a better predictor of direct participation compared to indirect participation. While evaluation of institutional rules explained 71% of variance of direct participation in ICFM, 67% in CCFM, and 74% in JFM, it explained 22%, 52%, and 42% respectively of indirect participation (Table 3.4).

*Managing committee's transparency and accountability*

ICFM, CCFM, and JFM differed significantly on (a) managing committee's transparency, $F_{2,394} = 74.45$, $p < .001$ and accountability, $F_{2,394} = 59.39$, $p < .001$ (Table 3.5). Post-hoc Tukey's test confirmed that managing committee's transparency and accountability was higher in ICFM than in CCFM, and in CCFM than in JFM.

As expected, in regression analysis, high transparency and accountability of managing committee increased direct and indirect participation in all types of forest management. Increased transparency and accountability of managing committee boost up direct participation compare to indirect participation. Only managing committee's accountability did not predict indirect participation in ICFM.

**Table 3.4 :** Regression Analysis for Variables of Institutional Rules Predicting Participation

| Participation | Variable[a] | ICFM | | | CCFM | | | JFM | | |
|---|---|---|---|---|---|---|---|---|---|---|
| | | *B* | *SE B* | *β* | *B* | *SE B* | *β* | *B* | *SE B* | *β* |
| Direct | GA | .18 | .04 | .47*** | .27 | .02 | .66*** | .30 | .03 | .56*** |
| | PS | .31 | .05 | .51*** | .14 | .03 | .26*** | .30 | .05 | .28*** |
| | NMP | .22 | .04 | .37*** | .16 | .06 | .15** | .29 | .06 | .19*** |
| $R^2$ | | | .71 | | | .67 | | | .74 | |
| *F* | | | 67.74*** | | | 75.23*** | | | 182.88*** | |
| Indirect | GA | .10 | .03 | .29* | .11 | .02 | .39*** | .10 | .01 | .41*** |
| | PS | .10 | .05 | .26* | .15 | .02 | .45*** | .10 | .03 | .22** |
| | NMP | .10 | .04 | .24* | .11 | .05 | .15* | .10 | .03 | .15** |
| $R^2$ | | | .22 | | | .52 | | | .42 | |
| *F* | | | 7.56*** | | | 39.01*** | | | 45.90*** | |

[a] GA = General administration, PS = Personal stakeholding, NMP = Nonmembers' participation.
*$p$<.05, **$p$<.01, ***$p$<.001.

**Table 3.5 :** Descriptive Statistics on Managing Committee's Function

| Variable[a] | ICFM | | CCFM | | JFM | |
|---|---|---|---|---|---|---|
| | *M* | *SD* | *M* | *SD* | *M* | *SD* |
| MCT | 5.30 | 1.07 | 4.87 | 1.25 | 3.47 | 1.44 |
| MCA | 3.84 | 0.46 | 3.52 | 0.86 | 2.68 | 1.09 |

[a] MCT = Managing committee's transparency, MCA = Managing committee's accountability.

*Conflicts and participation*

Occurrence of conflicts in ICFM was comparatively less than CCFM and JFM. On an average, one conflict occurred in ICFM units whereas CCFM and JFM witnessed two and four conflicts respectively in a period of last two years. While all conflicts were found to be resolved in ICFM and CCFM, some conflicts had re-

**Fig. 3.6 :** Member's Mean Satisfactaion with Managing Committee's Transparency and Accountability in Three Forms of Forest Management.

mained unresolved in JFM at the time of survey. Out of total responses, conflicts within the village occurred in ICFM due to improper assignment of duty and responsibility (48.60%), financial irregularity (34.58 %), and theft and sanction (16.82%); in CCFM due to financial irregularity (29.41%), improper assignment of duty and responsibility (20.17%), unequal distribution of employment opportunities (18.49%), benefit sharing (17.65%), and theft and

**Table 3.6 :** Regression Analysis for Managing Committee's Transparency and Accountability Predicting Participation

| Participation | Variable[a] | ICFM | | | CCFM | | | JFM | | |
|---|---|---|---|---|---|---|---|---|---|---|
| | | *B* | *SE B* | β | *B* | *SE B* | β | *B* | *SE B* | β |
| Direct | MCT | .82 | .13 | .46*** | .45 | .14 | .22** | 2.07 | .18 | .62*** |
| | MCA | 2.07 | .31 | .47*** | 1.80 | .21 | .62*** | 1.06 | .23 | .24*** |
| $R^2$ | | | .66 | | | .58 | | | .60 | |
| *F* | | | 80.97*** | | | 74.69*** | | | 145.10*** | |
| Indirect | MCT | .34 | .13 | .33*** | .60 | .11 | .46*** | .34 | .08 | .29*** |
| | MCA | -.11 | .30 | -.04 | .53 | .17 | .27** | .49 | .11 | .32*** |
| $R^2$ | | | .10 | | | .41 | | | .28 | |
| *F* | | | 4.32* | | | 38.26*** | | | 38.09*** | |

[a] MCT = Managing committee's transparency,
MCA = Managing committee's accountability.
*$p$<.05, **$p$<.01, ***$p$<.001.

sanction (14.29%); and in JFM due to theft and sanction (55.83%), financial irregularities (19.17%), benefit sharing (10.42%), improper assignment of duty and responsibility (7.92%), and unequal distribution of employment opportunities (6.66%). Conflicts occurred between villages or FPCs primarily due to unsettled benefit sharing norms, and theft and sanction in all type of forest institutions (Table 3.7).

**Table 3.7 :** Frequency of Causes of Conflicts and Modes of Resolution

| Conflict | Variable[a] | Forest[b] ICFM | | CCFM | | JFM | |
|---|---|---|---|---|---|---|---|
| | | WV (%) | BV (%) | WV (%) | BV (%) | WV (%) | BV (%) |
| | DR | 48.60 | | 20.17 | | 7.92 | |
| | DEO | | | 18.49 | | 6.66 | |
| Causes | FI | 34.58 | | 29.41 | | 19.17 | |
| | BS | | 49.02 | 17.65 | 46.36 | 10.42 | 51.81 |
| | TS | 16.82 | 50.98 | 14.29 | 53.64 | 55.83 | 48.19 |
| Total Response (100%) | | 107 | 102 | 119 | 110 | 240 | 249 |
| | MA | 81.25 | 100 | 51.61 | 62.67 | 11.01 | |
| Resolution | MJO | 18.75 | | 23.87 | | 53.31 | |
| | DG | | | 14.19 | | 17.18 | |
| | PA | | | - | | 8.81 | 18.00 |
| | EA | | | 10.32 | 37.33 | 9.69 | 82.00 |
| Total Response (100%) | | 128 | 86 | 155 | 150 | 227 | 200 |

[a] DR = Duty and responsibility, DEO = Distribution of employment opportunities, FI = Financial irregularities, BS = Benefit sharing, TS = Theft and sanction, MA = Mutual agreement, MJO = Majority opinion, DG = Dominant group's opinion, PA = Arbitration by panchayat, EA= Arbitration by Forest departments / crafting agencies; [b]WV = Within village, BV = Between villages.

In ICFM conflicts were resolved within the village either through mutual agreement (81.25%) or by majority opinion (18.75%). In CCFM such conflicts were resolved by mutual agreement (51.61%), majority opinion (23.87%), dominant group's opinion (14.19%), and arbitration by NGO/crafting agency (10.32%), whereas in JFM these were resolved through majority opinion (53.31%), dominant group's opinion (17.18%), mutual agreement

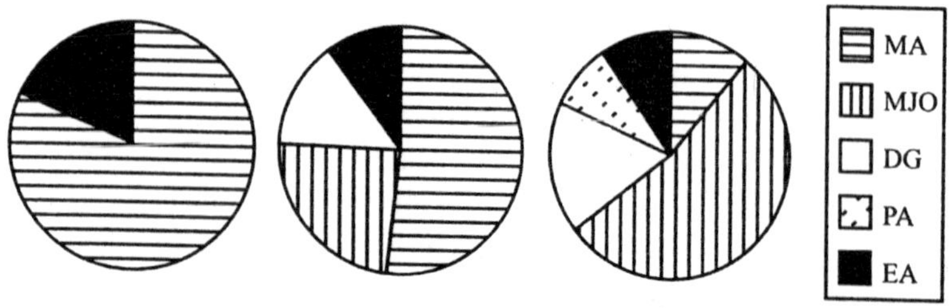


MA= Mutual agreement, MJO= Majority opinion, DG= Dominant group's opinion, PA= Arbitration by panchayat, EA= Arbitration by fforest department/ crafting agency.

**Fig. 3.7 :** Process of Conflict Resolution in Three Forms of Forest Management

(11.01%), arbitration by forest staff (9.69%), and arbitration by local panchayat (8.81%). Conflicts between villages in ICFM were settled through mutual agreement whereas such conflicts in CCFM and JFM were settled through the arbitration by third party — forest department, crafting agency, or panchayat.

ICFM, CCFM, and JFM differed significantly on satisfaction with conflict resolutions in intra-village and between villages/FPCs, $F_{2,394} = 207.29, p < .001$; and on personal gain from conflict resolution, $F_{2,394} = 61.76, p < .001$ (Table 3.8). In post-hoc Tukey's test, satisfaction with conflict resolutions in intra-village, and between villages or FPCs, and gain from conflict resolutions were significantly higher in ICFM than that of CCFM, and in CCFM than that of JFM.

**Table 3.8 :** Descriptive Statistics on Conflict Resolution

| Variables [a] | ICFM | | CCFM | | JFM | |
|---|---|---|---|---|---|---|
| | *M* | *SD* | *M* | *SD* | *M* | *SD* |
| SWINCR | 7.34 | 1.71 | 5.73 | 3.23 | 1.63 | 2.14 |
| GCR | 2.86 | .58 | 2.65 | .58 | 3.48 | .61 |

[a] SWINCR = Satisfaction with intra- and inter-village conflict resolution, GCR = Gain from conflict resolution.

In regression analysis, higher satisfaction with conflict resolution enhanced direct and indirect participation in all types of forest

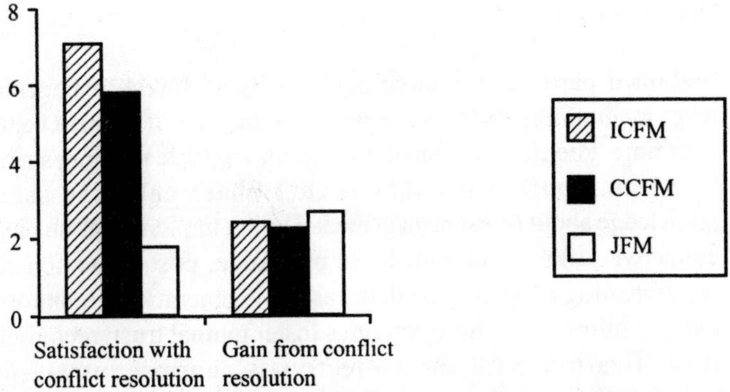


**Fig. 3.8 :** Member's Mean Satisfaction with Intra- and Inter-Village Conflict Resolution and Gain from Conflict REsolution in Three Forms of Forest Management.

management. Gain following the resolution of conflicts increased direct participation in the case of ICFM and CCFM and not in JFM. Such gain could not influence the indirect participation in any type of forest institutions (Table 3.9).

**Table 3.9 :** Regression Analysis for Satisfaction with and Gain from Conflict Resolution Predicting Participation

| Participation | Variable[a] | ICFM | | | CCFM | | | JFM | | |
|---|---|---|---|---|---|---|---|---|---|---|
| | | *B* | *SE B* | *β* | *B* | *SE B* | *β* | *B* | *SE B* | *β* |
| Direct | SWINCR | .63 | .12 | .51*** | .77 | .09 | .61*** | 1.38 | .10 | .70*** |
| | GCR | .54 | .28 | .18* | .63 | .20 | .23** | -.15 | .17 | -.05 |
| $R^2$ | | | .39 | | | .56 | | | .51 | |
| *F* | | | 26.17*** | | | 70.04*** | | | 101.18*** | |
| Indirect | SWINCR | .15 | .05 | .21** | .18 | .09 | .22* | .15 | .05 | .21** |
| | GCR | -.00 | .08 | -.04 | - .01 | .19 | -.04 | -.04 | .08 | -.04 |
| $R^2$ | | | .05 | | | .04 | | | .05 | |
| *F* | | | 5.09** | | | 2.73* | | | 5.09** | |

[a] SWINCR= Satisfaction with intra- and inter-village conflict resolution, GCR = Gain from conflict resolution.

**p*<.05, ***p*<.01, ****p*<.001.

**Discussion**

Sustained participation in community based forest management helps maintaining the resource base and the flow of accrued benefit over time. People's participation in planning (rule making, species selection, conflict resolution, etc.) phase enhances shared knowledge about forest management. During implementation phase, collective tasks are executed like plantation, post-plantation care (or protecting coppice growth in case of regeneration), monitoring and patrolling, etc. These activities foster mutual trust, reciprocity, identification with the collectivists' norms, intra-group communication on forest and allied livelihood problems, and reduce apprehension and anxiety among villagers. With the effective participation in planning and execution phases, willingness to cooperate and stay in FPC becomes stronger. Direct participation entails the voluntary, committed, and sustained support of individual appropriators. Indirect participation incorporates just, fair, and right behaviour of appropriators, and support of family members and fellow villagers towards forest protection.

Tribal communities had higher participation than nontribals because of their historical identification with forest and ethno-religious beliefs (Guha, 1983). Tribal economy was also more dependent on forest and its resources than others. Agriculturists, who perceived short- and long-term benefits from forest, participated more readily. Carpenters and grazers whose livelihood was affected adversely by forest protection, and service-holders and businessmen who had very little dependence on forest registered lower participation in forest management. Villages/FPCs with homogenous population faced less economic and social conflicts (Vedeld, 2000) due to their commonality and mutual confidence that promoted their participation. Single village FPCs had inherent commonality, mutual understanding, and reciprocity compared to multiple village FPCs and accordingly participation was higher in former than in latter.

Forest dependent communities treated forest as assets, savings and insurance both in short- and long-terms (Chambers and Leach, 1987; Foley and Barnard, 1984). Evidence suggested that for eliciting participation, communities and individual choices had to be given appropriate importance (Pimbert and Pretty, 1998; Shah, 1987; Shepherd, 1987). People would participate in a half-hearted manner if external intervention or state legislation undermined local choices (Chopra and Chatterjee, 1990; Pimbert and Pretty, 1998; Shah, 1987). ICFM elicited more people's participation than CCFM and JFM because of the absence of external interference, single village-based management unit with fairly homogenous population. Members of ICFM had full freedom in framing their organisation and its rules as per their priorities, which enhanced their social solidarity and sense of ownership. External interference hampered these and thereby reduced participation in CCFM and JFM. Though CCFM follow ICFM pattern, it had relatively lower participation because of partial acceptance of externally imposed rules and values by crafting agencies. In JFM, too much state interference worked against people's sense of belongingness and decreased participation in forest management.

Evaluation of institutional rules for general administration, personal stakeholding, and inclusion of nonmembers in FPC was influenced by the extent of freedom the communities enjoyed in making such rules. Under full freedom in making rules as in ICFM, the evaluation of such rules was most favourable, when the freedom was restricted as in CCFM, the evaluation of rules was less favourable, and when the freedom was still restricted as in JFM, the evaluation of rules was least favourable. When the constituents of FPCs perceived the institutional rules favourably, their participation increased accordingly. If communities do not have the freedom in forming the institutional rules, appropriators' participation in forest management would be lower and grassroots organization would be fragile.

Managing committee was the governor of institutional rules and the forest resources. To win the FPC members' trust and support, the governor was expected to be transparent and accountable. Depending on the interaction between managing committee and members of FPC in the forms of formal or informal meetings, ICFM's managing committee was most transparent and accountable, followed by CCFM and JFM. The interaction occurred weekly in

ICFM, and monthly or bimonthly in CCFM (Poffenberger, 1990; Sen and Das, 1987; Sarin, 1996), and was usually brief, formal, and irregular due to the nonavailability of forest officials and political nominees (Raju, 1998) in JFM. When members of FPCs perceived the managing committee as transparent and accountable, their participation increased commensurately.

Conflicts cannot be avoided in collective venture. Conflicts were relatively less in ICFM and CCFM than JFM. Conflicts occurred primarily due to theft in JFM that destroyed forest wealth. ICFM and CCFM were successful in not letting the conflicts to cause damage to forest. Conflicts were best resolved when it motivated conflicting parties to fix things by adopting a mutually agreed change to achieve the goal. Conflict resolution through mutual agreement was the strength of ICFM and CCFM. The process not only resolved the problem but also motivated conflicting parties to adopt changed behaviour. Other modes of resolution failed to initiate such positive change and caused reoccurrence of problems in JFM. Although CCFM had much similarity with ICFM, it was not free from certain pitfalls. Weaknesses in some cases were resolving conflicts through the opinion of dominant group or by the intervention of crafting agencies/NGOs. CCFM would have done better if such incidences were reduced.

Satisfaction with and gain from conflict resolution in any collective action had two implications. First, it reduced the scope of violation of agreed norms, and second, it encouraged spontaneous participation. In ICFM and CCFM conflicts were resolved by consensus/mutual agreement rather than majority opinion, whereas conflicts were resolved primarily through majority opinion in JFM. In addition, roles played by crafting agencies in CCFM, and forest department and local political members in JFM could not be avoided. Hence, satisfaction with and gain from conflict resolution were more in ICFM followed by CCFM and JFM. Satisfaction with conflict resolution increased participation. However, gain from conflict resolution could only influence the direct participation in ICFM and CCFM. This happened because any benefit accrued through conflict resolution boosted the immediate moral than long-term conviction. Following statement would clarify the fact:

*"Forest protection is our cultural duty, but when there is conflict, I get demoralised and simply stop cooperating until the dispute is amicably solved"* (Tribal from Semra village of Jharkhand).

*"Look when people work together, conflicts, disputes are but natural. When disputes occur I too get carried away for some time but not for too long because forest is another God to me"* (Inhabitant of Pada village of Orissa).

In contrast, JFM presented a different case. In JFM both types of participation were not affected by feeling of gain. This might be due to the fact that when share of timber yield was distributed among the members, it was mere Rs. 250 ($ 5) to Rs. 300 ($6) per household. This might have dampened people's hope of getting substantial profit from timber sells after years of hard labour. Besides this, people had a suspicion that forest officials did have some conspicuous nexus with timber contractors. When conflicts persisted for long-time, as it happened in some JFM, gain from conflict resolutions failed to solicit direct participation.

Forest institution acted as a collection of self (appropriators) which tried promoting a collective cause. Appropriators, accommodating individual choices, and sacrificing immediate smaller gains in order to have larger collective gains in future, made collective choices for forest management through negotiations and collective decisions. It instilled collective self-confidence, geared coordinated collective action, and promoted collectivists' identity with forest institutions. It also induced (a) greater loyalty to the forest institution, (b) higher obedience to institutional rules, and (c) extra-role behaviour like motivating others for the cause. Any form of external intervention as in CCFM and JFM undermined local choices and priorities, decreased collectivists' identity with the forest institutions, and accordingly dwindled loyalty to forest institutions, acquiescence with institutional rules, citizenship behaviour, and finally group-based activity for forest management. Hence, greater freedom to the constituents would increase collectivists' identity with the forest institution, ensure effective governance of the institution, and elicit more participation in forest management. People's participation would be facilitated if the forest institution was confined to single village, forest-dependent people, and tribals or homogenous communities.

The study has certain limitations that must be acknowledged. While selecting the forest units, we adopted a purposive sampling plan rather than a random sampling plan. The units selected for the study were not statistical representatives of all the forest units in eastern India. Therefore, results should be interpreted in relative terms rather than absolute terms. In addition, leadership styles and values of constituents in forest institutions are important parameters for effective governance. These are not included in this study and are candidates for further research. Notwithstanding the limitations, we developed various scales to measure variables that could be used in similar studies on forest management. To our knowledge, researches on forest management were primarily qualitative in nature. This study used scaling techniques and generated empirical evidence for ensuring people's participation in forest management.

## NOTES

1. Gram (village) panchayat is the lowest strata of governance in India consist of 5000 population belonging to one village or several adjacent villages.
2. In some cases where ICFM forests were raised on forest department's land without prior permission, state forest department adopted them under JFM schemes. They were permitted to be governed by their own rules with minor amendment.

# 4

# LEADERSHIP AND VALUE CONGRUENCE INFLUENCING PEOPLE'S PARTICIPATION IN CBFM

It was argued that local leadership played a pivotal role in the success of cooperatives, water user association, and other natural resource management (Attwood and Baviskar, 1987; Shah 1994a, 1994b; Singh, Ballabh, and Palkudiyil 1996, Vedeld, 1997). Re-involving communities in the act of forest management requires a change in the mindset of the communities through effective leadership (Ballabh and Singh, 1988; Shah, 1991). Evidence suggests that people's participation, commitment, job satisfaction, and performance increase if individual values match with the organisational values (Meglino, Ravlin, and Adkins, 1989; Regan and Grube, 1982; Sange, 1990; Suar, Panda, and Sharan, 1992). Likewise in grassroots forest institutions, members' identification with the institutional values is likely to increase people's participation. This paper examines how (a) the style of leadership and (b) value identification influence people's participation in forest management.

## Leadership in CBFM

Grassroots forest institutions need to recognise that individual and organisational interests should not be conflicting. An effective mechanism for incentives and/or sanctions is required to reconcile the conflicting interests and to facilitate group action. Individual participation in collective action is found to be based on (a) cost of participation in terms of money, time, and energy; (b) expected benefit from collective action; (c) probability of individual action/participation leading to the provision of the collective goods; and (d) leadership viability and trust. Absence of effective leadership causes noncooperation in cooperatives when other factors are congenial (Shah, 1994a). Effective leadership can enhance the probability of success of collective actions by increasing the assurances about the (a) availability of expected benefits to members only; (b) equal distribution of benefits; and (c) exclusion of free riders.

In the case of community based forest management seven critical roles of leaders are identified (Shah, 1991, 1994b). These are (a) generation of ideas; (b) motivating and inspiring the people to participate; (c) acquisition of forestland; (d) holding negotiation with governmental and non-governmental organisations; (e) mobilisation of resources; (f) development of an effective management system; and (g) resolving the conflicts. In CCFM and JFM community leadership are normally influenced by the advice/directives of the crafting agencies and state forest department respectively. However in ICFM, community leaders lead the folk independently in a participative manner. They are mostly village elders or Panch (a group of five people who govern the village affairs), or in some cases youth leaders who continue for years. In contrast, CCFM and JFM follow rotation of leader through election following the completion of a fixed term.

## Leadership and Values Influencing People's Participation

### *Leadership styles*

Leadership style is the way of functioning of a leader. In Indian forest management context, four kinds of leadership style are found — Authoritarian, Participative, Charismatic, and Manipulative (Sarin, 1996; Shah 1994a, 1994b; Singh, Ballabh, and Palkudiyil 1996). Manipulative leaders try to fulfil their own interest by exploiting the simplicity of less literate forest communities. These leaders have the aptitude to appease external agencies like NGO's (as in CCFM) or forest department (as in JFM) in the garb of able organiser. They camouflage their ulterior motives with their well-wisher role. Authoritarian leaders make all decisions for the group/organisation and give detailed step-by-step directions. They keep all information to themselves, maintain a distance from the group members, and praise or rebuke the members according to their personal whims. Participative leaders encourage group members to decide policy issues jointly, choose their teammates democratically, and to settle the problems by themselves. Such leaders share all information with others, decide their actions collectively, and administer reward or sanction based on evidence. Charismatic leaders emotionally charge the people to mobilise themselves and work collectively. They possess magical abilities, exciting speaking aptitude, have transcendent vision/or ideology, show heroism, and propagate radical views (Conger and Kanungo, 1987, p.638). They can deliver the followers out of a crisis or catastrophe. Indian personality traditionally valued charismatic leaders more than rationality (Nandy and Kakar, 1980). Unlike corporate sector, hierarchical relationship between leaders and others is non-existent in forest management institutions. In such cases, members' allegiance to leader depends on leader's credibility and organisational ability. Shah (1991) opined that participative style of leadership mix with some charismatic flavour works better in rural institutions. Too much charisma may lead to over dependency and any falsehood or pretence may disenchant the concerned people. Empirical evidence is inconclusive to suggest which style of leadership more likely to prevail and evoke more people's participation in forest management.

**H 1a** : Leadership style would differ in three forms of forest management.

**H 1b** : Different leadership styles would evoke different extent of participation.

*Leadership traits*

Personal traits or attributes distinguish leaders from non-leaders. Traits are precursor to leadership style and behaviour (Katz and

Kahn, 1978). Shah (1991) analysing the leaders in cooperatives found that the leader has to be a role model, dedicated, frugal, good organiser, and personally able to monitor every activity. The style of leadership in cooperatives may not be fully replicable to forest management institutions because of the lesser volume of financial transaction in latter compared to the former. In forest management, the leaders need to possess idealised behaviour (honesty, integrity, sacrifice, and impartiality) so that the members of the forest community can accept them as role model and can be influenced by them. Traits of the leader like organising ability, eco-conservation, sacrificing nature, impartiality, willingness to make collective decision, tolerance, sincerity, trustworthiness, visionary, sympathetic to the needs of others, mutual respect, and self discipline were reported to be important for forest management (Ballabh and Singh, 1988; Sarin, 1996). Leadership traits are likely to vary among different leadership styles. Leadership traits likely to influence the people's participation.

**H 2**: Leadership traits would influence the people's participation.

*Leader-members closeness*

In a vertical collectivist culture of India, collectivist values of interdependence, social support, cooperation, and interpersonal sensitivity coexist with power distance (Triandis, 1994, 1996). People feel comforted by maintaining strong relationship with higher-ups in the society. They lean for advice, support, and guidance from superiors on ordinary issues, which do not warrant such leaning. They perform organizational activities as a part of positive relationship with the leader (Chattopadhya, 1975; Sinha and Sinha, 1974). Such relationship imbibes people's confidence, and encourages them to participate in organisational activities (Sinha, 1995). More the individual will feel closer to the higher-ups in forest management institutions, she/he is more likely to participate in forest management.

**H 3 :** Higher the individual closeness with leader, higher would be the people's participation.

*Values*

Values are desirable ideals located centrally within one's belief system (Rokeach 1971, 1973). They determine what one ought to or ought not to behave or act. The inward possession of values guides our outer activities. Values develop from early childhood through socialising agencies of family, school and a host of other institutions. Being a member of the community institution, individual's institutional socialisation takes place. Members imbibe the values incorporated in short- and long-term goals of the organization, comply with the rules and regulations of the institution, and interacts with similar others. Each individual attempts to mould his values in the direction of organizational demands and tries to establish a congruency between institutional values and her/his values. Leaders of the grassroots forest management institutions preach and practice the organizational values. Leaders can change the values of constituents in the direction of institutional demands through enforcement of institutional rules, awareness/ conscientization, or through intrinsic (praise, appreciation, etc.), or extrinsic (tangible benefits) rewards. If they do not, members may not participate in institution's activities, and institution may gradually fade away (Roy 1993). As mentioned earlier, three types of forest institutions differ in their management principles and practices and hence the values of them are likely to differ.

**H 4a** : Congruence between the values of organization and its constituents would differ in three forms of forest management.

**H 4b** : Higher the value congruence, more would be the people's participation.

*Forest centrality*

Individual participation in forest protection is dependent on complex decision-making process. More than fifty million world's poorest tribal population depend heavily on natural forest resources for their hand to mouth survival (Ritchie 1992). In spite of this survival struggle, millions of forest dependent individuals are driven by central value to protect forest (Gadgil and Guha, 1992; Lal 1994; Verma, 1990). Recent success stories of forest protection through people's initiatives subscribe to this view. It is not yet confirmed whether personal inclination to forest protection influences individual participation.

**H 5a** : Centrality of forest to lives would differ in three forms of forest management.

**H 5b** : Higher the centrality of forest, more would be the people's participation.

## Methodology

### *Sample*

Sample of chapter III is used for this study also. Besides this, the members, president, secretary, and treasurer of each forest protection unit was also interviewed separately for assessing their value prioritisation on behalf of the organisation.

### *Measures*

A semi structured interview schedule was prepared in English. The English version of the interviewee schedule initially contained 30 items for assessing participation, 4 pen portraits for assessing leadership style, 20 items each for evaluation of leadership traits, and 20 different core values related to forest protection. Besides these, two semi projective items were included for measuring individual closeness to leader and forest centrality. This was scrutinised by four experts in forest management. The items agreed by all were retained. To conduct the interview in three states differing in languages, this schedule was translated into local languages in Hindi, Oriya, and Bengali with the help of dual-language experts. To ensure the accuracy of translation, another three dual-language experts back-translated these into English.

Three interview schedules in three local languages were pre-tested in three states for their understanding and clarity. The author, knowing Hindi and Bengali languages interviewed the people from Jharkhand and West Bengal respectively, and also interviewed the people from Orissa with the help of a vernacular interpreter. Including socio-demographic variables on age, castes, livelihood, village(s) covered by forest protection committee, and village population, the interview schedule measured the following variables.

*(a) People's participation*

Participation index used in chapter III is also used here for this study.

*(b) Leadership style*

Sinha (1995) developed pen portraits for identifying leadership styles. Similarly, four pen-portraits were developed that briefly incorporated the functioning of leaders. These portrays were jotted down on four cards in vernacular languages. Respondents were asked to read and select a character portray which best described their unit's chairperson/president. In manipulative style, the write-up was as follows: "She/he patiently listens to everyone's views and suggestions. She/he although often agrees to act according to the group decision, changes her/his words/decisions later on. She/he favours people of her/his choice and shows favour to those who support her/his action. She/he maintains a good rapport with influential people of *panchayat*, forest officials and political leaders. She/he wants to continue her/his position as long as she/he can." In authoritarian style, the descriptions were as follows: "She/he decides all policies and strategies for forest protection. She/he emphasises obedience to her/his decision and respect to her/him. She/he cares for reputation of her/his forest protection unit. She/he likes those who are loyal to her/him. She/he tries to be a father figure but very strict. She/he puts herself/himself first always." In participative style, the descriptions were as follows: "She/he is people oriented.

She/he along with members of forest protection committee determine the policies and strategies for forest protection. Though she/he is concerned with efficient management, she/he cares a lot for members of forest protection unit. She/he praises appropriate activities of the members and criticizes the inappropriate activities. She/he takes part in all activities like other members. She/he is sympathetic to needs of others at the time of difficulties. She/he encourages in-group feeling." In charismatic style, the write-up was as follows: "She/he tries to motivate members of forest protection unit with future prospects. She/he is a good speaker. She/he is much concerned about forest conservation and often takes personal risk to pursue the goal of forest protection unit. She/he brings out new ideas. She/he is sensitive to the needs and feelings of other members and cultivates mutual liking and respect."

### *(c) Leadership traits*

Thirteen items evaluated leadership traits. Each item was assessed on a ladder having seven steps. Zero depicted the least presence of a trait placed at the bottom, and '6' depicted the highest presence of a trait placed at the top. Each member of FPCs was asked to assess the leader on each trait placing a pebble on the appropriate step of the ladder. FPC members rated their leaders to avoid the overestimation of positive traits by leaders themselves. When the scores on these items were factor analysed, three factors were extracted that explained 54.58% of total variance (Appendix II). The first factor evaluated leader's character and contained the traits of 'eco-conservationist', 'good organiser', 'sacrificing', 'honest', 'collective decision maker', 'trustworthy', and 'self-discipline'. The second factor evaluated the attributes of diplomacy and the items were 'ability to deal with external agencies', 'tolerant to others' views', and 'respect to others'. The third factor containing three items— 'visionary', 'impartial', and 'sympathetic to other's need'— evaluated the charisma. The alpha reliability was .81 for leader's character, .78 for diplomacy, and .51 for charisma. High scores indicated favourable evaluation of leadership attributes on each factor.

### *(d) Leader-member closeness*

This measure was semi-projective in nature. A 100 mm line was drawn on a piece of card. Two dolls of different sizes were used for symbolising the leader and the member. Each respondent was mentioned that the bigger doll was the leader and the smaller one was he himself. The doll representing the leader was kept fixed on one terminal point of the line. The respondent was asked to place the other doll representing her/him on the same line on the basis of her/his closeness to the president of FPC. Distance between two dolls was measured in millimetre. Closeness was assessed by subtracting the measured distance from length of the line (100 mm). Higher values indicated more closeness.

### *(e) Values*

Ten items assessed the values for forest conservation. Values included were: 'sacrificing the present benefit, avoidance of free riding, livelihoods security from forest, communal sharing, equal rights, dutiful, obeying collective decisions, eco-conservation, self governance, strict sanction'. These values were written on ten separate cards in the vernacular language. Each respondent was asked to arrange the cards in order of importance from highest to lowest. Highest importance was coded with a rank of one and the lowest importance a rank of ten. Similarly, the president, secretary, and treasurer of each FPC were asked to rank the same values jointly in order of priority. Such joint ranking indicated the importance of values to the forest institution. Institutional value ranking was correlated with the ranking of each respondent of the same FPC. Rank-order correlation was calculated for each respondent. Higher correlation indicated higher congruence between the institutional and the member's values.

### *(f) Forest centrality*

This item was semi-projective in nature (Sinha, 1990). Centrality of forest to one's life was measured with the help of a circle having a radius of 50 mm. The circle was drawn on a card. Respondents were asked to show the importance of the forest to their lives by putting a dot inside the circle. Distance between the 'dot' and the centre of the circle was measured in mm. Forest centrality was assessed by subtracting the distance from the radius (50 mm). Higher value indicated greater forest centrality to one's life.

## Results

### *Leadership styles and participation*

In ICFM and CCFM, majority of the members opined their leaders as participative. Out of 86 interviewees in ICFM, 73.25% members considered their leaders as participative, out of 113 interviewees in CCFM, 73.45% members perceived their leaders as participative. However, out of 198 interviewees in JFM, 37.37%, 33.83%, and 23.23% members perceived their leaders as manipulative, participative, and authoritarian respectively (Table 4.1). Supporting the hypothesis 1a, leadership styles differed in three forms of forest management.

**Table 4.1 :** People's Participation against Leadership Styles in Three Forms of Forest

| V[a] | ICFM n = 86 | | | CCFM n = 113 | | | JFM n = 198 | | | Total N = 397 | | |
|---|---|---|---|---|---|---|---|---|---|---|---|---|
| | n | *M* | *SD* | n | *M* | *SD* | n | *M* | *SD* | n | *M* | *SD* |
| Direct Participation | | | | | | | | | | | | |
| M | 9 | 11.22 | 3.46 | 4 | 6.00 | 1.41 | 74 | 3.96 | 2.61 | 86 | 4.69 | 3.30 |
| A | 3 | 11.33 | 1.15 | 12 | 9.17 | 2.66 | 46 | 4.13 | 2.13 | 60 | 5.43 | 3.26 |
| P | 63 | 14.33 | 1.25 | 83 | 12.77 | 1.71 | 67 | 11.69 | 3.46 | 214 | 12.87 | 2.56 |
| C | 11 | 14.18 | 1.94 | 14 | 14.00 | 1.62 | 11 | 13.36 | 2.11 | 37 | 13.89 | 1.66 |
| Indirect Participation | | | | | | | | | | | | |
| M | 9 | 6.00 | 1.66 | 4 | 4.25 | 1.26 | 74 | 5.20 | 1.62 | 86 | 5.21 | 1.61 |
| A | 3 | 6.00 | 1.65 | 12 | 4.33 | 1.83 | 46 | 5.20 | 1.72 | 60 | 5.02 | 1.77 |
| P | 63 | 7.60 | 0.77 | 83 | 6.19 | 1.44 | 67 | 6.31 | 1.51 | 214 | 6.65 | 1.44 |
| C | 11 | 7.45 | 1.04 | 14 | 6.29 | 1.90 | 11 | 6.45 | .93 | 37 | 6.73 | 1.47 |

[a]V = Variable, M = Manipulative, A= Authoritarian, P = Participative, C = Charismatic.

$*p < .05$ ; $**p < .01$ ; $**p < .001$.

Because few interviewees reported their leaders to be manipulative, authoritarian, and charismatic in ICFM and CCFM, separate analysis was not carried out for different types of forest. Combined data for different types of forest revealed that the four different styles of leadership elicited different extent of direct, $F_{2,393} = 16.11, p < .001$, and indirect participation, $F_{2,393} = 10.20, p < .01$ (Table 4.1) (Fig. 4.1 and 4.2). Tukey's test further confirmed that charismatic style had evoked higher direct participation than that of participative style, but very few people perceived their leaders as charismatic (9.32%). Manipulative and authoritarian

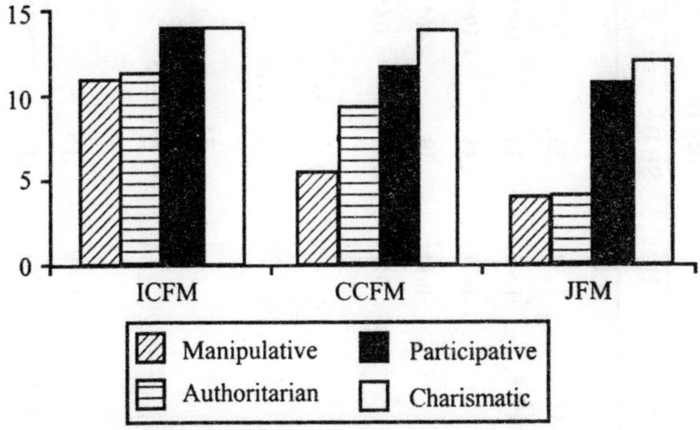


**Fig. 4.1 :** Average Direct People's Participation under Four Types of Leadership Styles in Three Forms of Forest

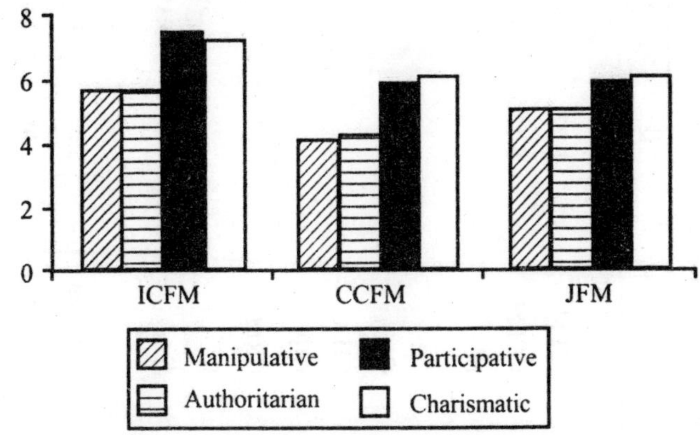


**Fig. 4.2 :** Average Indirect People's Participation under Four Types of Leadership Styles in Three Forms of Forest

**Table 4.2 :** Leadership Styles and Traits Predicting Participation in Three Forms of Forest

| P[a] | Variable[b] | Step I | | | Step II | | | Step III | | |
|---|---|---|---|---|---|---|---|---|---|---|
| | | B | SE B | β | B | SE B | β | B | SE B | β |
| D | Constant | 7.14 | .27 | | 11.05 | .27 | | 7.07 | .72 | |
| | ICFM | 6.73 | .48 | .58*** | 3.52 | .35 | .31*** | 2.54 | .31 | .22*** |
| | CCFM | 5.17 | .44 | .49*** | 1.98 | .33 | .19*** | 1.33 | .30 | .13*** |
| | M | | | | -6.78 | .35 | -.59*** | -5.53 | .32 | -.48*** |
| | A | | | | -6.15 | .39 | -.46*** | -4.60 | .36 | -.35*** |
| | C | | | | .95 | .44 | .06* | .51 | .38 | .03 |
| | CHA | | | | | | | .15 | .02 | .23*** |
| | DIP | | | | | | | .16 | .03 | .14*** |
| | CRM | | | | | | | -.17 | .04 | -.12*** |
| | $R^2$ | | .39 | | | .74 | | .81 | | |
| | *F* | | 125.19*** | | | 216.41*** | | 200.52*** | | |
| I | Constant | 5.65 | .11 | | 6.49 | .15 | | 5.75 | .49 | |
| | ICFM | 1.69 | .20 | .41*** | 1.01 | .21 | .25*** | .74 | .21 | .18*** |
| | CCFM | .30 | .19 | .08 | -.36 | .19 | -.10 | -.54 | .20 | -.14** |

*(Contd. Table 4.2)*

*(Contd. Table 4.2)*

| P[a] | Variable[b] | Step I | | | Step II | | | Step III | | |
|---|---|---|---|---|---|---|---|---|---|---|
| | | B | SE B | β | B | SE B | β | B | SE B | β |
| I | M | | | | -1.36 | .21 | -.33*** | -1.12 | .22 | -27*** |
| | A | | | | -1.46 | .23 | -.31*** | -1.12 | .24 | -.24*** |
| | C | | | | .05 | .26 | .01 | -.04 | .26 | -.01 |
| | CHA | | | | | | | 5.44 | .01 | .24*** |
| | DIP | | | | | | | -8.57 | .02 | -.02 |
| | CRM | | | | | | | -4.93 | .02 | -.10* |
| | $R^2$ | | .15 | | | .28 | | | .31 | |
| | *F* | | 35.82*** | | | 29.76*** | | | 21.93*** | |

*Note* : Hierarchical regression is used for statistical analysis.
[a] P = Participation, D = Direct, I = Indirect; [b] M = Manipulative, A = Authoritarian, C = Charismatic, CHA = Character, DIP = Diplomacy, CRM = Charisma.
*p< .05, **p< .01, ***p< .001.

styles elicited lower direct and indirect participation compared to other two styles and both direct and indirect participation did not differ significantly between manipulative and authoritarian styles.

Effect of leadership styles on participation was assessed by hierarchical regression. In the first step, two dummy variables were entered for three types of forest management. The reference group was JFM. In the second step, another three dummy variables were added for four styles of leadership keeping the participative style as reference group. In the first step, the constant in the regression equation exactly denotes the mean of reference group on participation and the unstandardized betas specify the extent of mean difference from the reference group on dependent variable. Direct participation was higher in ICFM and CCFM than that of JFM, and indirect participation was higher in ICFM than that of JFM. Because the extent of participation differed in three types of forest, the confounding effects of forest types on participation were controlled in the second step of analysis. Second step of regression analysis confirmed that participative style elicited higher direct participation than that of manipulative and authoritarian styles but lower direct participation than charismatic style. On indirect participation, the same trend was observed except participative and charismatic styles did not differ (Table 4.2).

### *Leadership traits and participation*

The effect of three leadership traits on participation was assessed using hierarchical regression analysis. When the confounding effects of forest types and leadership styles on participation were controlled, leader's character ($M$ = 29.44, $SD$ = 7.36) enhanced participation whereas increased charisma ($M$ = 14.85, $SD$ = 3.31) of the leader reduced participation. Diplomacy ($M$ = 13.14, $SD$ = 4.21) of the leader increased only the direct participation (Table 4.2) (Fig. 4.3). Further analysis confirmed that more or less appreciable character was found among the participative ($M$ = 31.62, $SD$ = 5.91) and charismatic ($M$ = 34.03, $SD$ = 4.66) leaders than that of the manipulative ($M$ = 25.67, $SD$ = 7.40) and authoritarian ($M$ = 24.22, $SD$ = 8.16).

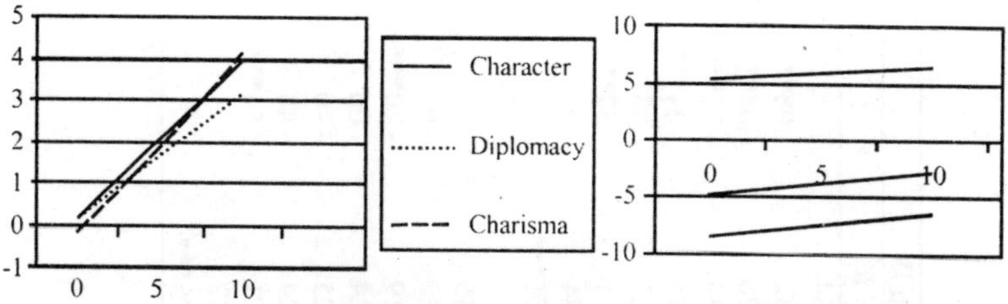


**Fig 4.3 :** Leader's Traits Influencing People's Direct and Indirect Participation

*Leader-member closeness and participation*

Leader-member closeness differed in three forms of forest, $F_{2,394} = 144.01, p < .001$ and under different styles of leadership, $F_{3,393} = 166.39, p<.001$. Post-hoc Tukey's test confirmed that ICFM ($M = 86.41$, $SD = 7.36$) had higher leader-member closeness than CCFM ($M = 75.39$, $SD = 12.37$) and CCFM than that of JFM ($M = 56.25$, $SD = 18.02$). Also, participative ($M = 78.56$, $SD = 11.53$) and charismatic ($M = 82.41$, $SD = 11.45$) styles had higher closeness than manipulative ($M = 48.62$, $SD = 15.48$) and authoritarian style ($M = 50.75$, $SD = 15.00$).

Effect of leader-member closeness on participation was analysed using hierarchical regression. When confounding effects of forest types and leadership styles on participation were controlled, more the leader and the member were close to one another, more was the members' participation (Table 4.3) (Fig. 4.4) and the hypothesis was proved.

*Values and participation*

In ICFM, while values like avoidance of free riding, livelihood security from forest, and sacrificing present benefit received higher priorities, equal rights and obeying collective decisions received lower priorities. In CCFM, higher priorities were given to values like communal sharing, livelihood security from forest and avoidance of free riding and lower priorities were given to eco-conservation and strict sanction. In JFM, values like self-governance, livelihood security from forest, and strict sanctions

**Table 4.3 :** Leader-member's Closeness Predicting Participation in Three Forms of Forest

| Participation | Variable | Step I | | | Step II | | |
|---|---|---|---|---|---|---|---|
| | | *B* | *SE B* | *β* | *B* | *SE B* | *β* |
| Direct | Constant | 11.05 | .27 | | 1.32 | .64 | |
| | ICFM | 3.52 | .35 | .31*** | .88 | .32 | .08** |
| | CCFM | 1.98 | .33 | .19*** | .84 | .26 | .08** |
| | Manipulative | -6.78 | .35 | -.59*** | -3.54 | .34 | -.31*** |
| | Authoritarian | -6.15 | .39 | -.46*** | -3.17 | .35 | -.24*** |
| | Charismatic | .95 | .44 | .06* | .47 | .35 | .03 |
| | Closeness | | | | .14 | .01 | .57*** |
| | $R^2$ | | .74 | | | .84 | |
| | *F* | | 216.41*** | | | 339.55*** | |
| Indirect | Constant | 6.49 | .15 | | 3.20 | .45 | |
| | ICFM | 1.01 | .21 | .25*** | .12 | .22 | .03 |
| | CCFM | -.36 | .19 | -.10 | -.75 | .19 | -.20*** |
| | Manipulative | -1.36 | .21 | -.33*** | -.26 | .24 | -.06 |
| | Authoritarian | -1.46 | .23 | -.31*** | -.45 | .25 | -.10 |
| | Charismatic | .05 | .26 | .01 | -.12 | .24 | -.48 |
| | Closeness | | | | .05 | .01 | .54*** |
| | $R^2$ | | .28 | | | .37 | |
| | *F* | | 29.76*** | | | 38.25*** | |

*Note* : Hierarchical regression is used for statistical analysis
$^*p< .05$, $^{**}p< .01$, $^{***}p< .001$.

**Table 4.4** : Ranking of Values by Members and Leaders in Three Forms of Forest

| V[a] | ICFM[b] | | | | CCFM | | | | JFM | | | |
|---|---|---|---|---|---|---|---|---|---|---|---|---|
| | Member | | Leader | | Member | | Leader | | Member | | Leader | |
| | *M* | R | *M* | R | *M* | R | *M* | R | *M* | R | *M* | R |
| 1 | 3.62 | 3 | 2.91 | 2 | 5.14 | 4 | 6.01 | 6 | 6.13 | 7 | 6.64 | 8 |
| 2 | 2.15 | 1 | 1.63 | 1 | 4.88 | 3 | 4.48 | 3 | 3.78 | 2 | 4.91 | 4 |
| 3 | 3.20 | 2 | 2.92 | 3 | 3.71 | 2 | 2.88 | 2 | 5.29 | 5 | 3.91 | 2 |
| 4 | 5.16 | 5 | 4.98 | 5 | 3.35 | 1 | 1.80 | 1 | 5.17 | 4 | 7.65 | 9 |
| 5 | 7.95 | 9 | 7.29 | 8 | 6.18 | 8 | 6.14 | 8 | 6.90 | 10 | 6.15 | 7 |
| 6 | 7.49 | 8 | 7.76 | 9 | 5.32 | 5 | 5.24 | 4 | 6.01 | 6 | 7.91 | 10 |
| 7 | 8.13 | 10 | 9.16 | 10 | 5.53 | 6 | 6.04 | 7 | 6.30 | 8 | 5.47 | 5 |
| 8 | 7.28 | 7 | 7.13 | 7 | 8.14 | 10 | 9.72 | 10 | 6.66 | 9 | 5.61 | 6 |
| 9 | 5.88 | 6 | 6.52 | 6 | 5.88 | 7 | 5.27 | 5 | 3.68 | 1 | 2.72 | 1 |
| 10 | 4.93 | 4 | 4.71 | 4 | 6.87 | 9 | 7.80 | 9 | 5.08 | 3 | 4.31 | 3 |

[a]V = Variable, 1 = Sacrificing the present benefit, 2 = Avoidance of free riding, 3 = Livelihood security from forest, 4 = Communal Sharing, 5 = Equal rights, 6 = Dutiful, 7 = Obeying collective decisions, 8 = Eco conservation, 9 = Self governance, 10 = Strict sanction. [b]*M* = Mean rank, **R** = Ranking (as per mean rank).

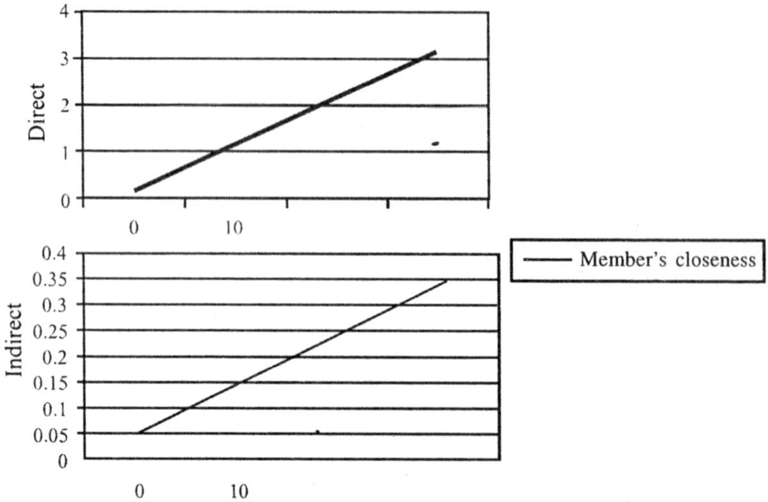


**Fig 4.4 :** Member's Closeness with Leaders Influencing People's Direct and Indirect Participation

were given higher importance and dutifulness, equal rights, and eco-conservation were given lower importance (Table 4.4).

Value congruence differed significantly among ICFM, CCFM, and JFM, $F_{2,394} = 134.36$, $p < .001$. Tukey's test confirmed that

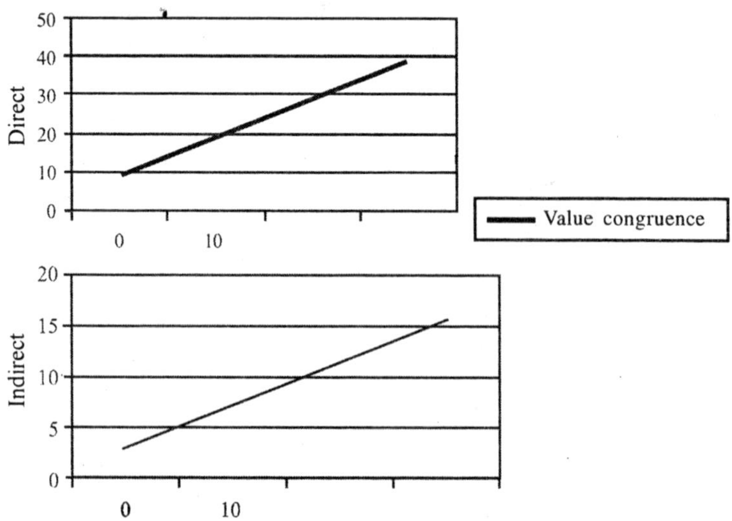


**Fig 4.5 :** Value Congruence Influencing People's Direct and Indirect Participation

**Table 4.5 :** Value Congruence and Forest Centrality Predicting Participation in Three Forms of Forest

| Variable[a] | Step I | | | Step II (VC) | | | Step II (FC) | | |
|---|---|---|---|---|---|---|---|---|---|
| | *B* | *SE B* | *β* | *B* | *SE B* | *β* | *B* | *SE B* | *β* |
| Direct Participation | | | | | | | | | |
| Constant | 7.14 | .27 | | 3.09 | .51 | | .04 | .54 | |
| ICFM | 6.73 | .48 | .58*** | 3.55 | .56 | .31*** | 4.37 | .42 | .38*** |
| CCFM | 5.17 | .44 | .49*** | 3.48 | .44 | .33*** | 2.29 | .41 | .22*** |
| VC | | | | 8.96 | .99 | .42*** | | | |
| FC | | | | | | | .24 | .02 | .54*** |
| $R^2$ | | .39 | | | .50 | | | .60 | |
| *F* | | 125.19*** | | | 128.36*** | | | 197.29*** | |
| Indirect Participation | | | | | | | | | |
| Constant | 5.65 | .11 | | 4.41 | .22 | | 3.98 | .26 | |
| ICFM | 1.69 | .20 | .41*** | .72 | .25 | .18** | 1.14 | .21 | .28*** |
| CCFM | .30 | .19 | .08 | -.22 | .19 | -.06 | -.38 | .20 | -.10 |
| VC | | | | 2.74 | .43 | .36*** | | | |
| FC | | | | | | | .06 | .01 | .36*** |
| $R^2$ | | .15 | | | .23 | | | .25 | |
| *F* | | 35.82*** | | | 39.64*** | | | 42.81*** | |

*Note* : Hierarchical regression is used for statistical analysis.

[a] VC = Value Congruence, FC = Forest Centrality.

*$p < .05$, **$p < .01$, ***$p < .001$.

ICFM ($M = .81$, $SD = .17$) had higher value congruence than CCFM ($M = .64$, $SD = .18$), and CCFM than JFM ($M = .45$, $SD = .17$). The congruence between organisational and member's value was estimated by rank order correlation. Effect of value congruence on participation was assessed by hierarchical regression analysis. When confounding effects of forest types on participation were controlled, higher congruence between organisational and member's values led to higher participation (Table 4.5) (Fig. 4.5). The results proved the hypothesis.

*Forest centrality and participation*

In consonance with the hypotheses, the forest centrality differed significantly among ICFM, CCFM, and JFM, $F_{2,394} = 72.65$, $p < .001$. Post-hoc Tukey's test unfolded that forest was more central to the members of CCFM ($M = 40.89$, $SD = 5.57$) and ICFM ($M = 38.88$, $SD = 6.66$) than that of JFM ($M = 29.14$, $SD = 11.30$). When the confounding effects on participation were controlled, more the centrality of forest to the lives of the members more was their participation in forest management (Table 4.5) (Fig 4.6).

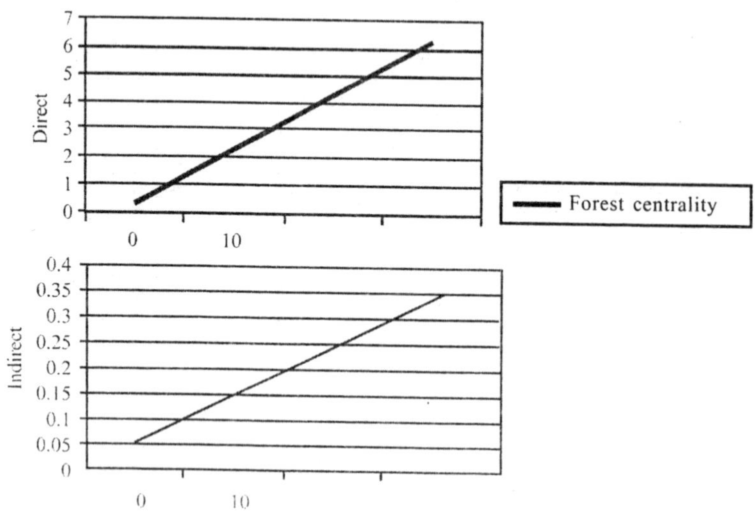


**Fig 4.6 :** Forest Centrality Influencing People's Direct and Indirect Participation

**Discussion**

Notwithstanding the difference among three different forms of forest and the differences in the study area, leadership styles, traits, leader-member closeness, congruence between individual and organisational values, and centrality of forest in one's life did influence the people's participation in forest management.

Governance of forest management institutions depends on intangible attributes of emotional attachment and loyalty to the institution, in-group feelings, and interpersonal sensitivity. Unlike corporate sectors, these institutions do not enjoy any direct economic transaction between governing authority and other members. In such institutions, individual's decision to cooperate with governing authority depends on how leaders exert influence on constituents. With the spread of literacy and awareness among forest communities, demand for transparency and democracy is on the rise. Involvement of members in goal-setting, problem solving, and decision-making ensures transparency and accountability, enhances mutual trust, and instils a sense of ownership (Raju, 1998). Leaders in ICFM and CCFM were predominantly participative because such institutions provided more freedom to the constituents in organisational goal-setting, rule- and decision-making, and conflict resolution. Leaders in JFM were perceived manipulative and authoritarian because of the dominance of forest department in all rule- and decision- making, irregular meeting between managing committee and general members because of the absence of forest officials, and lack of leaders' concern for members.

Members' direct and indirect participation was enhanced under participative leader because such leaders promoted collective decision-making, in-group feelings, and administered reward or sanction objectively. Though few members perceived their leaders to be charismatic, this style evoked only higher direct participation than participative style. Compared to participative leaders, manipulative and authoritarian leaders inhibited participation because of their non-transparent working styles, favouritism, and self-centred decision-making. Hence, irrespective of forest management institutions, charismatic or participative style can enhance peoples' participation (Shah, 1994a).

Regardless of the types of forest and styles of leadership, leader's character enhanced participation while leader's ethics reduced participation. Hence, leader's character associated with charismatic or participative style was the predominant predictor of people's participation. This agreed with the earlier conclusion that too much of charisma fostered dependency syndrome rather than nurtured the rational participation (Nandy and Kakar, 1980) among forest communities.

Irrespective of forest types and leadership styles, more the members were close to their leaders, more was the members' participation in forest management. Because ICFM and participative or charismatic style promoted collective decision, democratic participation, mutual trust, and ensured individual rights, those induced higher leader-member closeness. Indeed, lesser power distance in grassroots organisation ensured higher individual support and cooperation in forest management (Triandis, 1994, 1995, 1996).

Value prioritisation demonstrated an act of balancing between intra- and inter-generational needs. Values like 'livelihood security from forest', 'sacrificing the present benefit', 'avoidance of free riding', and 'strict sanction' were given more importance. For poverty-stricken forest dependent communities, sacrificing any present benefit can be considered as the most difficult task. Members of ICFM and CCFM showed more sensitivity to this task of balancing than their counterparts in JFM. In JFM, people's deprived desire of 'self-governance' was vividly expressed in their most important value. Practice of regular interaction, collective decision-making, and self-governance helped in imbibing common values within the organisation. As these practices were more prevalent in CCFM and ICFM, they succeeded in developing higher value congruence than JFM. When the values of the members matched with the values espoused by forest institution, it found expression in desirable activities for forest conservation and induced greater involvement of members in forest management.

For forest communities, protection of forest is a religious duty (Guha, 1983) and source of meeting livelihood demand in short- and long-run. ICFM and CCFM offered greater benefits to their members and assured more rights over forest compared to JFM. JFM offered lesser short- and long-term benefits to its members that dispirited them to uphold the religious value of forest as a God to them. Irrespective of forest types, as individual valued forest more central to their personal lives, more they assisted in forest protection.

Forest institution acted as a collection of individuals, which tried promoting a collective cause. Regardless of forest types, participative and charismatic styles along with the leader's character and lower power distance between leaders and members induced greater participation whereas too much of charisma dwindled participation. When the values of forest institution and its members were identical, and members considered the forest central to their lives, they participated more in the forest conservation. If the leadership styles and character otherwise do not conformed to the above styles and character, this can be changed by providing training, coaching, and counselling to the leaders of grassroots forest institutions. The value identification and centrality to forest can be enhanced through conducting regular meetings, nurturing interpersonal relationship and exhibiting participative and charismatic leadership styles. By doing so, power distance can also be reduced. Finally, participation of members can be assured if the leaders carry the responsibility to change the mindset of the constituents of forest institutions and help them to re-identify with their eco-friendly cultural heritage.

The study has certain limitations that must be acknowledged. While selecting the forest units, we adopted a purposive rather than a random sampling plan. The units selected for the study were not statistical representatives of all the forest units in eastern India. Therefore, the result should be interpreted in relative terms rather than absolute terms. In addition, people's perception about governing rules, managing committee's functioning, and conflict resolution mechanisms are important parameters for effective governance. These are not included in this study and are candidates for further research. Notwithstanding the limitations, we developed various scales and semi projective methods to measure variables that can be used in similar studies on forest management. To our knowledge, researches on forest management were primarily qualitative in nature. This study used contextual measuring techniques and generated empirical evidence for people's participation in forest management.

# 5

# SOCIAL, CAPITAL AND PEOPLE'S PARTICIPATION

In this chapter we will focus on another pivotal dimension of common pool resource management or simply management of commons, the role of 'Social Capital'. Term social capital in recent time has drawn much attention of academicians and practitioners. In order to examine the contributions of social capital in commons, we may be permitted to use some cases of commons other than CBFM. This is precisely to show that what applies to CBFM can be applicable to other types of commons and vice versa.

Constructive resource management rules and norms are embedded in many cultures and societies, from co-operative water management system of western and northern India; *gouchar* (cattle grazing land) land management of Saurashtra; shifting cultivation system of north eastern India; forest management of tribal groups. But rarely importance of social capital in building and management of such institutions has been recognised. Developmental policy and practice have tended to be preoccupied with changing the behaviour of individuals rather than of groups or communities. As a result, agriculture has had an increasingly destructive effect on environment (Huxley, 1960; Kothari et al., 1998; Palmer, 1976; Ostrom, 1990). In some context, loss of institutions has provoked natural resource degradation. In India, the loss of management systems for commons has been a critical factor in the increased overexploitation, poor upkeep, and physical degradation of natural resources during the past half century. Jodha (1990) reported that only 10% of the studied villages retained traditional practice of regulated grazing in village pastureland causing serious fodder scarcity. Elsewhere, when collective irrigation management system was replaced by private ownership or operation system, resulted substantial degradation of both surface and ground water resources (Kothari et al., 1998; Pretty, 1995; Singh and Ballabh, 1997). One study of 25 completed World Bank agriculture projects found that continued success was clearly associated with institutional building (Cernea, 1987). Out of these, twelve projects achieved long-term sustainability, and in all these projects local institutions were strong. In the others, the rates of return declined markedly contrary to the expectations at the time of project completion. Outcomes were unsustainable where there had been no attention to institutional development and local participation.

Like all public goods, it is difficult to say who is at fault when natural capital (nature's goods and services- Costanza et al., 1997) declines. Without rules, individual tend to overuse and under-invest in it; they are tempted to take benefit without contributing anything - in effect free ride (Hardin, 1968). When such public goods and services are considered free and valued at zero, the market indicates that they can be made valuable by converting into something else. So the profit from converting forest into timber is counted on nation's balance sheet, but all lost services (wild foods, fodder grasses, climate regulation, biodiversity, medicinal herbs) tend not be subtracted. Social institutions based on trust, reciprocity, and agreed norms and rules for behaviour, can mediate such kind of unfettered private action. New thinking and practices are required, particularly to develop forms of social organisation that are structurally suited for natural resource management and protection at the local level. This means more than just reviving the old institutions and traditions. It calls for formation of new forms of organisations, associations and platforms for common action. With this backdrop, the chapter examines the link between social capital of and natural resource development and how social capital can be used for enhancing people's participation.

## Social Capital

Much interest has been shown in social capital in recent times both in academic and development activist circles (Coleman, 1988; Fukuyama, 1995; Granovetter, 1985; North, 1990; Pretty and Ward, 2000; Putnam, 1993; Ostrom, 1998; Rudd, 2000; Woolcock, 1998). The term captures the idea that social bonds and social norms are important basis for sustainable livelihoods. According to Woolcock and Narayan (2000), social capital refers to the norms and networks that enable people to act collectively. It is also described as the structure of relations between actors and among actors that encourages productive activities (Coleman 1988, 1990). These aspects of social structures and organisations act as resources for individuals to use and to realise their personal interests. Local institutions are effective because they permit us to carry on our daily lives with a minimum of repetition and costly negotiation (Bromley, 1993). Co-operation is fundamental for the success of humanly developed management institutions for public goods including natural resources (Ostrom, 1990).

**Social Capital, Natural Resource Management and People's Participation - The Link**

Economic problems involve making choices under conditions of uncertainties and scarcity. Public goods share two characteristics important for collective choice: (i) they are under produced; and (ii) collective actors would be better off if more are produced (Coleman, 1987). A crucial cause of underproduction are incentives rewarding the maximisation of short-term self interest while leaving all participants worse off in aggregate than feasible alternatives (i.e. individual tend to free ride).

If optimal levels of public goods are to be produced and trade gains be fully exploited, shared understandings and patterns of collective action need to be developed beyond immediate kin. Various research findings suggest that humans are more predisposed to social exchange through reciprocity than is expected under narrowly defined rational choice levels (Barkow et al., 1992; Hoffman et al., 1998; Ostrom et al., 1994). Cognitive science holds that a variety of heuristics (Heiner, 1983; Simon, 1996) and reciprocity (Ostrom, 1998) are hard- weird by evolutionary selection. This results in a propensity to co-operate with others not perceived as foes, even if functional mechanisms of reciprocity vary between societies. Collective action is facilitated through the inhibition of short-term self-interested behaviour via a self-reinforcing cycle of trust and reciprocity. At the individual level, norms of trust and reciprocity lead to the formation of reputation thereby reduce transaction cost of interaction (Ostrom, 1998). In the aggregate level, increased returns are achieved via (i) increased levels of generalised trust (Fukuyama, 1995; Putnam, 1993) and (ii) by institutionalising mechanisms of trust, reputation and reciprocity. These two then reduce transaction cost (North, 1990).

Social capital is the productive asset that enables individuals to better fulfil their aspirations through access to goods and services via their social network and through collective action (Castle, 1998). Social capital facilitates co-operations by lowering costs of working together. People have the confidence to invest in collective activities knowing that others will also do so. They are also less likely to engage in unfettered private actions that have negative impacts such as resource degradations. Social capital is deemed to increase production of both quasi-public and public goods by increasing levels of knowledge about production, transformation processes and trading partners, and by exploiting the gains through specialisation. Transaction costs associated with trading are reduced via increase levels of trust between trading partners and the development of institutions that provide incentives for lasting co-operation (Coleman, 1988; North, 1990; Ostrom, 1999; Woolcock, 1998). Social capital, unlike other forms of capital, is not depleted with the use but actually increases in value with its uses (Ostrom, 1999).

In social capital, norms and rule-ordered relationship are viewed as resources that individual can use to reduce risk, access services, obtain information, and co-ordinate collective action (Grootaert, 1998). Collier (1998) identified that overall capacity for co-ordination raises output in four potential ways: (i) social sanctions against opportunism by free-riding individuals reduce transaction costs; (ii) common natural resources can be effectively managed on a sustainable basis; (iii) public goods provision can increase;

and (iv) society can take advantage of economies scale in non-market activities. Social capital can act as an input to the production function for individuals and organisations by constraining opportunism and thereby increasing the probability of collective action to deal with social externalities.

In the light of the above discussion, we will now examine how core factors of social capital- (i) trust; (ii) reciprocity and exchanges; (iii) institutional arrangement; (iv) social network; (v) leadership; and (vi) community characteristics, can help in development and management of natural resources by enhancing people's participation in common property management.

## Social Capital through Self-initiated Process

In 1990, people of Chichkali village in Raipur district organized themselves to utilize the water flowing through the nearby area. The area was frequently hit by drought, and a need was felt for irrigation facilities. Shree Sharma, headmaster of the local primary school, impressed upon the villagers that they could change the situation provided they unite. Villagers getting organized informally constructed a canal, installed few motors, and irrigated nearly 80 hectares of land in the first year. They approached the local (government) authorities in 1993 and were able to get a similar scheme sanctioned. Leadership, informal village institution, priority to local needs and adoption of time-tested technology facilitated development.

We can once again look at Khakshi Toli example. As mentioned in Chapter I that in late fifties, villagers under the leadership of Mr. Simon Oraon (Minj) started protecting the forest on forty hectares of land. But soon Simon felt that the villagers had very few alternative livelihood opportunities and mere forest protection may not offer any viable alternatives. Agriculture, being completely rainfed and subsistence in nature, barely could meet the growing consumption demand. Simon took up watershed-based water harvesting work. A small dam was constructed to store water at higher elevation, which was then connected with three tanks in a series at the downstream. Dam water was used both for ground water recharge and surface irrigation. Agriculture production was increased and multiple cropping became possible. Villagers also took up fisheries in all the tanks. Later on villagers pursued the district administration and with their help a village co-operative was formed. This co-operative received various assistances under tribal sub-plan programme. Today, Khaksi Toli stands out as one of the most progressive villages with a model watershed and forest protection body.

During these year village community also underwent several changes. In the initial year, cooperation among villagers for such activities was a strange affair. Under the able leadership, villagers were motivated to work collectively. Villager helped each other to make contour bunding and terracing so to create new farming land. Each household contributed in the form free labour and bullock for the construction of new farmland. Later on they started pooling up money in common pool. Profits from forest resources and fish farming were added to the common pool. During late eighties, villagers dug several wells for irrigations. But unlike other villages, villagers selected spots for well by which maximum land could be irrigated without disturbing ground water level. As a result, the average water level of wells never goes down below fifteen (15) feet from the surface even on the upland during summer months. During nineties a tractor with all farm accessories were procured for collective use. Well-coordinated work, high mutual cooperation along with both intra-group network and external network with government and NGOs enabled villagers not only to achieve the enviable natural resource pool but also to maintain it with incremental manner over half a century.

Khuls are gravity channels constructed along the mountainsides. These convey surface water from the spring, river stream or glacier points to all agriculture lands. According to census of minor irrigation department, there are 17,000 Khuls in the state of Himachal Pradesh. The local communities manage around 62% of such Khuls. Remaining 32% Khuls were also managed by local communities till recently. At present many of these were taken over by the government. Committees appointed by the government now manage these Khuls. According to directorate of land records, Khuls cater irrigations to around 80,000 hectares of farming land.

Khuls are generally constructed and maintained by the local people themselves. But since independence, some communities started taking assistance from the government for such work. Later on government constructed concrete structures in many Khuls. In the traditionally managed Khuls, farmers who draw the water from Khul form a committee for Khuls construction and maintenance. They contribute mostly in the form of free labour (*Shramdan*), working as water master in rotation to look after irrigation rota and contributing tree trunk for strengthening earthen channel. In state government intervened Khuls, concrete structures are made with the help of government aid. Construction works are normally carried out by the contractors or hired labours. Stakeholders contribute very less to the construction works. Management committee of both traditional and state intervened Khuls are made from among the stakeholders. Social hierarchy dominates in traditional Khuls with regard to the election of committee chief. One study revealed that mutual trust, mutual help and intra-group network and cohesion were much higher among the members of traditional Khuls (Sinha, 2002). In the state intervened Khuls, communities became over dependent on government consequently their sense of belongingness was found to be diminishing. As a result, monitoring of Khul maintenance, and irrigation rota has become irregular. Such activities are still regularly monitored in the case of traditional Khuls. Traditional Khul communities seem to be satisfied with their intra-group network and do not look beyond. This attitude however, prevented them to develop access to external aids for the betterment of Khul structures.

**Economic Development through Social Network**

Village Ralegaon Siddhi, a semi arid village in Maharashtra, has demonstrated amply the power of community-based partnership and networking. The nucleus of the project was water harvesting through community initiatives. Based on the success of the water-harvesting project other development-oriented outputs such as women's liberation and empowerment, school enrolment of girl children and prohibition were realized. The community development partners included the block administration, NGOs, some schools, parent-teacher association, media and local foresters. From a highly degraded village eco-system and a poor economic condition, Ralegaon Siddhi has emerged as one of the richest villages acquiring the status of a unique model village in the country. A survey conducted by the Centre for Science and Environment found that a quarter of all the households had annual income of over Rs. 4.5. lakhs each (Durgaprasad and Rajendran, 2001).

Five hundred semi-arid villages situated in the Aravalli hills of Rajasthan's Alwar district under the leadership of a local NGO, have begun to revive the local traditions of water harvesting. The restoration of the depleted ground water resources has led to sustainable agricultural development, which has allowed the local farmers to withstand consecutive drought-years. It resulted in arresting the out migration as in Ralegaon Siddhi. Studies show that the village domestic product has increased in proportion to the investments made in water conservation. With dozens of villages undertaking water harvesting in the same watershed, nearly five rivers in the area have changed from being monsoon drains to perennial rivers. In one of the river basins, over 25 villages have come together to form the country's first community-based River Water Parliament to jointly manage the regenerated river. For all these endeavours, Alwar villagers had a solid community network and extensions with the local collectorate, the research institutions and environmental activists. The water parliament concept evolved by the inspirational leader Sri Rajendra Singh has begun to make cascading efforts in other dry parts of the country. Similarly the inspirational leader of Ralegaon Siddhi, Sri Anna Hazara is endeavouring to extend the benefits of the project to other parts of the country through NGOs and Self-help Groups (SHGs). Thus, networking and partnership with formal institutions can enhance eco-efficiency and empower the women, poor and the marginalized both economically and socially.

**Building Social Capital through External Assistance**

In Orissa, India, National Tree Growers' Cooperative Federation Limited (NTGCF) identified villages, which earlier had rich forest cover. Subsistence economy, absence of rights over forest resources, and lack of understanding of ecological disaster provoked people to destroy forest rampantly. Through participatory appraisal, NTGCF found that the basic zeal for forest protection was not completely eroded from the minds of people. NTGCF also found that people showed little interest in protecting pure strand of Sal or Teak, which has no tangible benefit other than timber. NTGCF continued its effort for bringing awareness through village meetings, showing documentary films on forest protection, and encouraging progressive individuals to take up the leadership. Instead of imposing a blue print forest model, NTGCF facilitated the villagers to decide upon the nature and type of forest they wanted and to develop their own plan to harness the diverse stock of local knowledge. Villagers opted for development and conservation of mixed forest consisting of trees and plants that met their multifarious needs. But they could not start it by their own, as they did not have any legal rights over forest property. NTGCF persuaded the matter with Government of Orissa and succeeded in getting these activities registered under state cooperative act. NTGCF also helped these village institutions to grow, and frame rules and norms for forest protection. By 1990, 30 such societies were promoted. In 2001, this movement has spread to more than 120 villages in Angul and Dhenkanal districts of Orissa. NTGCF empowered the communities socially and economically giving primacy to local needs, knowledge and skills, and freedom to people to develop their own rules, norms and institutions for forest conservation.

Sambandh, a grassroots NGO is working in Mayurbhanja district of Orissa. The NGO after a series of field visits and discussions in 39 villages of Karanjia and Jashipur blocks realized that though the area received moderate rainfall, people were suffering from crop failure. The problem was discussed in detail with the villagers. Then village resource management exercise was conducted in operational villages through active involvement of villagers and staff members. Sambandh educated the villagers on new technologies of agriculture and other development activities. It facilitated the youth groups and women groups to develop institutional arrangements for execution, operation, and maintenance of irrigation infrastructures and also promoted SHGs, user groups, and forest protection committees. It arranged for demonstration on modern farm equipments and seeds. Villagers were trained on cash crop cultivation, soil conservation, watershed development, community forestry, and leadership development. With the active participation of villagers, it constructed a check dam (with loose boulders) in Dhalabani *Gram Panchayat.* Species having medicinal value were planted. In 2000-01, people cultivated tomato in 50 acres of land. It created the demand for tomato in the local area and people named this as 'Dhalabani tomato'. Land-based income generation activities were initiated through micro-credit to SHGs (Sambandh, 2001). The creation of awareness through discussion and education, capacity building through demonstration and facilitation, the technology appropriate to the villagers and institutional arrangement of villagers were responsible for sustainable income of villagers.

**Preserving Social Capital through External Assistance**

Ratnakiri is the north eastern province of Cambodia with dense forest, fertile soil and low population density. The livelihood of people depends on swidden agriculture and collection of fruits, vegetables, medicinal plants, fibres, and building materials from the forest. Swidden agriculture is a form of rotation cropping that regenerates natural forest in a period of 10-15 years. Old forests are not cleared and moderate terracing checks the soil erosion. Although it did not require any external input except human labour, its productivity was lower than modern cultivation. For generations, people cultivated the land over which they had customary rights. Situation changed since 1993 when Ban Lung people, the business community from the provincial centre, emboldened by economic liberalization began to stake claims on these lands. They put signpost for proposed modern farm in all around the traditional land. Local communities took unified action against these encroachments. But absence of legal rights over land was their biggest obstacle. Understanding their helplessness, few local and international NGOs came forward and mobilized a mass movement.

Impressed by this, King Nordom Sihanouk in 2001 took an initiative to persuade the Cambodian government to pass an act to legalize the rights of indigenous people over mountainous land, forest and river, and to stop transfer of land to outsiders who were not acquainted with traditional land and water management.

This law stopped the conversion 20,000 hectares of upland forest into oil palm farm and many such projects initiated by Ban Lung communities. According to an estimate, land transfer would have displaced 4,500 locals, disturbed the whole landscape by doubling soil erosion and increasing silt in the river. Furthermore, the law also stalled the introduction of external input-based agriculture that could cause permanent loss of regenerating forest. Hence, indigenous social capital can also be preserved by external support from NGO and government. Such external assistance helps in preserving sustainable natural resource management system on one hand and prevent communities to suffer from impoverishment.

## Conclusion and Implications

It is amply clear from the above case studies that social capital of rural communities *inter alia* can play crucial role in managing natural resources judiciously for economic development. Internal or external leadership can play pivotal role in unleashing the power of social capital. In Chichkali village, Khaksi Toli and traditional Khuls local level leadership facilitated in harnessing the benefit of mutual trust, reciprocity and institutional arrangement for economic use of natural resources without impairing the microenvironment. But such local initiatives may not prop up everywhere naturally. It requires certain external assistance. Furthermore, it is evident that people should not confine themselves only to intra-group network. It fosters a narrow outlook. Community that look beyound has better chance of development. Therefore, it is important while nurturing the intra-group network each community should develop liaison with external agencies for accessing to various benefit flow. Spread of social network enhances the magnitude of social capital. Ralegaon Siddhi and community based river water parliament are two successful evidences of amplified social capital.

External assistance can play pivotal role both in reviving and preserving social capital. In Orissa NTGCF and Sambandh facilitated the villagers to rediscover their social capital and thereby ushered them into new era of development. NTGCF tried reviving forgotten or submissive local resource management system by building on the social capital. Villages that suffer from trauma of resource degradation need such intervention to regain their old vitality. Similarly vested interest some time threatens to jeopardise a well functioning social system as happened in Ratnakiri case. Such attack need to nipped at the bud. But only local protest may not be adequate to block such encroachment. NGO and government need to come forward to protect and preserve such system.

Social capital has dynamic qualities. It incites people to participate in sustainable resource use. Appropriate use of it empowers communities towards self-reliance. Both government and NGO can play pivotal role in unleashing the power of social capital by operationalising it through appropriate intervention. In many communities, elements of social capital are in sublime condition. It needs a spark. External agencies (GO and NGO) are required to provide this spark. Once ignited; communities can manage their resources in sustainable manner to rewrite their economy by reducing poverty (Fig. 5.1).

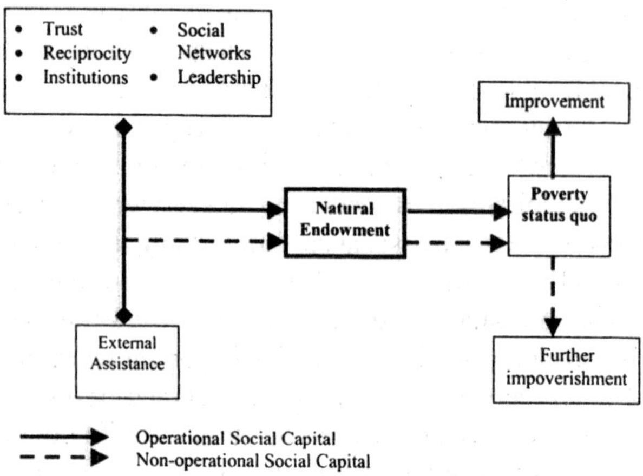


**Fig. 5.1 :** Relationship among Social Capital, Natural Endowment (Resources) and Poverty Alleviation

# PART-II

## Policy and Practices of Community Based Forest Management

# 6

# JFM — AN INTROSPECTION

The New National Forest Policy, 1988, marked a paradigm shift in the history of forest management in India. The new policy acknowledges the subsistence requirements of local people on forest, and places priority on environmental stability, ecology and satisfying the needs of local people.

The Government of India, through a circular to all State Forest Department, legitimised the idea and local communities being invited to help in the conservation and management of state forest. In order for them to do so, the government proposed that they be given a share in the improved productivity of forestlands. This strategy, which is known as Joint Forest Management (JFM), is potentially of great significance since it gives the rural people access to state forestland. The Government resolution on JFM also recognizes the likely contribution which NGOs can make as intermediaries between the state and the people.

The central idea behind this approach of collaborative management is the realization that without the active involvement of the forest dependent fringe communities, the programme to regenerate the degraded forestlands, would meet with limited success. The village communities have been offered the incentives, in form of a share in revenue and formal involvement in the responsibility of forest protection.

Twenty three per cent of India's geographical area equivalent to 76.5 m ha has been declared as forests, which is now mostly under government control. According to the forest survey of India (FSI, 1998), 48 per cent area notified as forests had in 1997 a crown density of more than 40 per cent, 34 per cent between 10 and 40 per cent, and the rest 18 per cent has less than 10 per cent or no tree cover at all. Of the area under forests, 37 per cent is tropical moist deciduous forest (where *Shorea robusta*, better known by its local name *Sal*, is the main species), 28 per cent is tropical dry forest (where teak is the valued species), 8 per cent is tropical wet evergreen forest, and the rest 26% is subtropical, temperate, alpine and other forests.

The FSI estimated current productivity for the entire forests at 0.7 cum (cubic metres) of wood per hectare per year. This includes both recorded and unrecorded removals from forests. These levels are three times lower than the potential forest productivity. JFM is expected to bring considerable improvement in the economic and environmental well being of India's land and people by enhancing forest productivity.

Forests are not spread evenly in India, but are concentrated more in the poorer regions of India. These lands have low agricultural productivity and poor soils, and mostly inhabited by India's indigenous communities, called adivasis or tribal. India's forests have generally speaking not been uninhabited wildernesses. Even in the remote forests, people have either been living traditionally or were brought by the forest department during the colonial period and been settled there to ensure the availability of labour. Today, there are about 100 million forest dwellers in the country living in and around forestlands and another 275 million for whom forests have continued to be an important source of livelihoods and means of survival (Lynch, 1992).

Therefore, changes in forest policy and management over time in India can best be understood in terms of the competing claims and relative influence of the various interest groups and stakeholders. Within an overall structure of state ownership and control, two groups seem to have had a major impact over the last hundred years: foresters and industrialists. For almost a century and until 1988, forest management strategies were decided almost exclusively by the foresters and were markedly biased in favour of commercial and industrial exploitation, with little attention paid to either sustainability or social justice.

## Forest Policy before 1988

In the beginning of the nineteenth century more than two-thirds of the land mass in India was lying uncultivated (Singh, 1986). During that time, adjacent lands to village habitations were enough to satisfy the subsistence needs of the people. Forests remote from habitations were generally under-exploited. Often these virgin forests were concentrated in infertile highlands, with heavy tribal concentration, who were forced in the medieval period to seek refuge in forests, being driven from fertile lands by the more aggressive warrior communities.

The British from the late nineteenth century onwards started making a difference to land and forest usage in India. Guided by commercial interests, the British viewed forests as crown lands, limiting private property rights only to continuously cultivated lands. Uncultivated land remote from habitation was declared by the government as forest and managed under the new forest regulations for timber production. This orientation did not change even after independence, as the forest policy, 1952 declared that village communities should in no event be permitted to use forests at the cost of 'national interest', which was identified with defence, communications and vital industries. The next policy declaration contained in the report of the National Commission on Agriculture (NCA) in 1976 too put its stamp of approval on this commercial approach in the following terms (GoI, 1976:32): 'Production of industrial wood would have to be the *raison d'etre* for the existence of forests. There should be a change over from the conservation-oriented forestry to more dynamic programme of production forestry. The future production programme should concentrate on clear felling of valuable mixed forests, mixed quality forest and inaccessible hard wood forest and planting these areas with suitable fast growing species yielding higher returns per unit area.' In tune with the above recommendation the state stepped up the programme of industrial forestry. For example, in the sixth five year plan (1980-85) of Madhya Pradesh, the central Indian state with highest area under forests, gave special emphasis on production forestry but did not take any special programme to meet tribal demands for fruit, medicinal herbs etc. or upliftment of tribal economy.

Between 1952 and 1980 over three million hectares of plantations were established in India. The major proportion of which were to fulfil industrial needs (CSE, 1985). Out of the total Rs. 670 million spent on afforestation during 1966-74, approximately Rs.560 million was on production forestry alone. The use of bamboo for paper manufacture accelerated from a low of 58,000 tonnes at the end of the Second World War to over 5 million tones by 1987 (Hobley, Cambell and Bhatia, 1996). Plantations have usually been of single species, equally entailing loss of diversity and access, and often on a large scale, and in practice hardly pursuing an objective of benefiting the local people beyond wages (even wages employment becomes insignificant after the first year of plantation). Such trend had onerous effect on poor forest dwellers. An ex-forest secretary of Madhya Pradesh writes, 'This (the policy of giving priority to industries and subsidizing industrial raw material) is clearly discriminatory. The rights of a huge section of society cannot be wiped out in order to benefit a few industrialists. For instance, the Orient Paper Mills was promised a lakh ton of bamboo per year from four districts of the state. This eliminated all bamboo from Rewa, Panna, Satna and Shahdol. When such a situation arises, the Forest Department tells the villagers to fend for themselves because there is nothing in the forests for them (NCHSE, 1987; p. iv)'.

Converting a complex forest into a genetically simplified plantation may help produce industrial raw material, but ignores the basic needs of forest dwellers - mostly tribal - and is therefore, threatens its own sustainability. Conventional forestry based on clear felling disrupts the annual circulation of nutrients, and increases soil erosion (Spurr et. al, 1980 , p.240). Monoculture plantation forestry is also prone to pest attack. Thus, Eucalyptus plantations in Kerala raised after clear felling of dense green and deciduous forest has been devastated by fungal diseases, and the consequent low productivity defeated the very purpose for which they had been raised (Nair, 1985). Similar was the experience of teak plantations in north Bastar, Madhya Pradesh (Anderson and Huber, 1988, p. 63). On the other hand, mixed forests draw and give nutrients to the soil at different stages of their growth, and hence are ecologically far more beneficial than single species plantations. One of the main outputs from forests should be water, which is possible only when forests are considered more in the context of local rather than national needs.

Tropical forests support complex ecological chains while playing an essential and salutary role in regulating the earth's climate and atmosphere. They can return as much as 75 percent of the moisture they receive to the atmosphere. Thus, they have a profound effect on rainfall. Yet these vast natural forests, surrounded by poor populations, were rapidly diminished as they were being converted into plantations to meet market demands.

The entire thrust of forestry during the first four decades after independence was towards the production of a uniform industrial cropping system, created after clear-felling and ruthless cutting back of all growth, except of the species chosen for dominance. Three set of factors have been at work in shaping such policies, first development until the mid-seventies was associated in the minds of planners with creating surplus from rural areas and its utilization for value addition through industry. Hence output from forestlands was heavily subsidized to be used as raw material for industries. The impact of such policies on environment, on the existing natural forests or forest dwellers was not considered to be serious, as the resource was thought to be an inexhaustible. Secondly, tribal and forest dwellers, with little voice or means to communicate were remote from decision-making, and politically their interests were not articulated. Thirdly, foresters were trained to raise trees for timber. Other intermediate and non-wood products were not valued, indicated by their usual description as 'minor products' leading to adoption of technologies, which discouraged their production. The combination of these forces led to perpetuation of a timber and revenue oriented policy that damage both environment and the people, but was argued to be meeting the goals of the nation state.

**Social Forestry**

The NCA however conceded that people's basic subsistence needs should be met from non-forestlands in order to check the process of deforestation and save forests. This was then sought to be achieved through social forestry, a programme of fuel wood and fodder plantations on village and private lands. It is significant that social forestry was not tried on forestlands, except in small measures. Thus social forestry was seen as a programme, which would release industrial forestry from social pressures. The core objective for forestlands remained production of commercial timber. But in order to pacify the people, it was necessary to make them produce what they consumed free of charge using community and private lands for plummeting the pressure on forestlands.

The programme of social forestry had two main components, planting trees on private lands, called farm forestry, and afforestation of village lands. In terms of sheer production of trees the programme of farm forestry had been immensely successful, especially in northwest India, Gujarat, and Karnataka (Arnold and Stewart, 1991). However, later on two serious problems surfaced with this programme. Firstly, its geographical spread has remained confined to a few surplus regions only, and secondly, even in these regions the initial enthusiasm for farm forestry could not be sustained after 1990. The craze for planting Eucalyptus, which was the main farm forestry species, declined as fast as it was risen during the 1980's.

The sustainability of the social forestry component on village lands could not be ensured because, despite the rhetoric, the programme remained essentially a departmental one where local people were not involved; village councils merely transferred common lands to the FD and played no role in decision-making or choice of species. There was no continuity in the management and control of thousands of scattered pieces of planted village lands creating enormous problems of protection. Projects were designed around the ultimate felling of the planted trees, degradation often set in after the trees were harvested. The area available as village lands was also far less than anticipated at the project stage. Projects failed to define, establish and publicise the rights to the trees and the procedures for marketing and allocating benefits. The shares which would go to the individuals, village, *panchayats* and the forest department were not clearly laid down. Insecurity about benefits led to indifference on behalf of the people. Poor soil conditions and tenure insecurity led to a low survival rate of plants, specially in deforested regions and hillsides prone to soil erosion, where trees were needed most (Barnes, Douglas and Olivares, 1988).

Besides these, market oriented trees were planted which did little to improve consumption within the village. Fodder trees were generally ignored. Close spacing to accommodate more trees affected grass production. As projects did little to meet the demand of the poor for fuel wood and fodder, pressure on forestland continued unabated. Finally, as state funds got locked to meet the matching contributions required for external assistance for social forestry projects, forestlands got starved of funds, with several adverse effects. The neglect of forestlands hurt forest dwellers and tribal. It reduced timber supplies to the markets, resulting in price escalation, which further increased smuggling from forestland.

## The 1988 Forest Policy

The rectification of faulty forest policies came in 1988 with a new forest policy which is radically different from the previous two policies. According to this, forests are not to be commercially exploited for industries. But they are to conserve soil and the environment and meet the subsistence requirements of the local people. The policy gives higher priority to environmental stability than to earning revenue. Derivation of direct economic benefit from forests has been subordinated to the objective of ensuring environmental stability and maintenance of ecological balance. It discourages monocultures and prefers mixed forests. The focus has shifted from 'commerce', and 'investment' to ecology and satisfying minimum needs of the people, providing fuel wood and fodder, and strengthening the tribal forest linkages. It declared that the domestic requirement of fuel wood, fodder, minor forest produce, and construction timber of tribal should be the first charge on forest produce. It advises industry to establish direct relationship with farmers who can grow the raw material if supported by industry with inputs including credit, technical advice and transport services. As these linkages may take time, in the interim, it suggested that import of wood and products should be liberalized, but the practice of supply of forest produce to industry at concessional prices should cease.

## Political Underpinning behind New Policy

The striking policy reversal in 1988 suggests that there were no strong political constraints in effecting a radical shift in forest policies. This may surprise political economists and therefore, requires an explanation. In a democratic country with 70 per cent rural population, rural interests cannot be ignored for long. A subsistence oriented forest policy does not hit the rural elite at all; it in fact reduces the control of the centralized bureaucracy, besides curtailing the outflow of forest products to industries. Hence such a policy should not attract political impediments, which are inherent in distributive programmes such as lands reforms.

From the early 70s intellectuals and activists have also picked up the long-standing grievances of forest-dependent communities. Consequently, in the last two decades the working of the forest department has come under close and critical scrutiny. It has been demonstrated that state policies by promoting commercial forestry has contributed significantly to the decimation of biological diversity and to an increase in soil erosion and floods (CSE, 1985; Gadgil and Guha, 1992).

The battles on behalf of forest dwellers have not only been fought in the press on an intellectual plane, but have actually been carried out in the countryside. There have been both armed struggles and political movements to regain control over what they perceived to be their lands. Several heavily forested districts in Andhra Pradesh, Maharashtra, Madhya Pradesh, and Jharkhand are witnessing armed rebellion, called the Naxalite Movement directed against the State. One of the main demands of the Naxalites is better community control over forest resources. In Bihar (now in Jharkhand), in 1978, local people protested in what is called the 'Tree War' against the replacement of natural forests by teak plantations (CSE, 1985).

There have also been peaceful and non-political forest movements in the country. In many places during the 1970s people on their own initiative started protecting forests, of which CHIPKO is a well-known example. It started in 1973 when a local village group was denied access to forests for making agricultural implements, whereas the same coupe was allotted to a sports goods company. This favouritism provoked the villagers who prevented the company from felling trees by hugging them (Gadgil and Guha 1992, p.223). It spread throughout the hills of North India, forcing government to impose a ban in 1979 on all commercial felling in the hills above 1000 metres, which continues till date.

When different interest groups have claims on a resource, policy and politics do not always favour the same group. In the years preceding 1988, while many decisions were taken (Chambers et al., 1989) to make forest policy acceptable to the environmentalists, the state government of Karnataka decided to lease out 30,000 ha of common lands in 1986 to a paper company on a lease rent of 12 per cent of the produce. When agitation and petitions to government did not yield any result, a public interest writ petition was filed by several NGOs before the Supreme Court. The Government of India in this litigation decided to oppose the decision of the state government and sided with the NGOs. As a result, the state government was forced to cancel the lease in 1991 (Hiremath et al.,1994). This was celebrated as a big victory against the lobby of forest-based industry.

In addition to the industry getting discredited in the popular press, two other factors must have weighed upon the minds of policy planners in suggesting a diminished role for forest industries on forestlands in the new forest policy. First, the popularity of Eucalyptus among farmers increased and availability of pulpwood at a cheap price for the paper industry. In some states, such as Gujarat, large farmers even took up Teak plantations, a timber crop which takes 30 to 60 years to mature. Secondly, liberalized imports of timber and pulpwood was permitted which eased the supply for the industry. With new sources of supply, commercial forestry was no longer considered crucial for the industry.

## The June 1990 Guidelines and Joint Forest Management

Although the 1988 policy redefined the objectives of forest management, it did not envisage any direct role for the people in the day-to-day management of forests. It implicitly believed that government alone should control forests, albeit with changed objectives. The case for public management of forests is hinged on a number of factors. Firstly, forest management is associated with a wide range of externalities, as these provide external benefits to the rest of the ecosystem. Secondly, FD has often argued that management of forests requires a level of professional training and scientific competence that lies outside the capacities of peasants and forest users (Shyam Sundar and Parameswarappa, 1987). Thirdly, the time horizons for forest management would favour public ownership and public investment. And lastly, it will allow for major economies of scale and a longer-term planning framework. The strong case for exclusive government management gets diluted because government is not in a position today to enforce its property rights. Forests are subject to intense pressure from human beings, livestock and urban markets. Overexploitation by the people, increased in the last three decades due to several factors. First, increasing marginalization of small landowners has forced them to seek new avenues of income, like head loading. A study (Agarwal, 1987:181) estimated that at least 3 to 4 million people were involved in head loading, making it India's biggest source of employment in the energy sector. Second, as village commons deteriorated, villagers turned to government forests for succour. And third, government policies raising commercial plantations further alienated the people from the resource. More than the official revenues, it nurtured a new culture of rent seeking by those in power. The indiscriminate tree felling by the contractor-official-politician nexus has had a corrupting influence on the forest dwellers, who also wish to make hay while the sun shines.

Unlike other developing countries, extension for agriculture and shifting cultivation, the two familiar causes for deforestation, have not been the main cause of deforestation on forestlands in India at least in the last forty years. The alienation of forestlands from the people who need it for satisfying their needs, and consequently forests turning into open access lands has been one of the main cause for degradation as well as for increasing misery of the people. Till the mid-eighties the response of the government to this crisis of deforestation was to bring more land under the reserved category (which increased from 26 m. ha in 1951 to 46 m. ha in 1988), and plant non-browsable and market-oriented single product timber trees in order to reduce pressure from local population and increase state revenues. This strategy became counter-productive and hastened the degradation process it was designed to prevent.

Given the ease of access to forests, indiscipline and socio-political culture of the country, it has been impossible for the Forest Department to enforce its property rights without people's protest. These weaknesses in the enforcement of access to government property have led to forest areas being exploited as an open access resource by those who have no stake in its health. Realising these realities, Government of India introduced participation of the people in managing forests by issuing a Joint Forest Management (JFM) resolution in June 1990 making it possible for the Forest Departments to involve people in the management of forests. The resolution breaks a new path as it for the first time specifies the rights of the protecting communities over forestlands. Those protecting are to be given usufructs like grasses, lops and tops of branches, non-timber forest produce, and a portion of the proceeds from the sale of trees when they mature. This varies from 20 to 60 per cent of the timber sold. The order exhorts the state forest departments to take full advantage of the expertise of committed voluntary agencies for building up meaningful people's participation in protection and development of degraded forestlands.

Thus in the previous policies people and the environment were seen, all too often as antagonistic. The forest - people interaction was conceptualised as a zero-sum game, in which both parties could not win. According to the JFM philosophy, the conflict model is neither necessary nor useful. To the contrary, ways can be sought in which the interests of people and of long-term sustainability are harmonized in a mutually supporting manner.

## Progress of JFM in the States

Participative policies have taken different forms in different states today. Some forests have been leased to local communities, whereas in some cases, village forest communities share the responsibility for protection with forest department. In some others, villagers on their own had been protecting forests without any guarding from the forest department. By 1997, eighteen state governments have issued enabling resolutions (GRs) permitting partnerships with local people. These states have 80 percent of the country's forestland and 92 percent of the country's tribal population. The JFM programme has now become the central point of future forest development projects funded by the Government of India and the donor agencies. According to government data, it is estimated that 35,000 village communities are protecting about 3.5 million ha of forests, which comprise 5.5% of the total forest cove in India. With more imaginative policies and innovative silviculture, this area could be increased to 15 million ha in about a decade, thus covering about 23% of the total forest cover.

Although the quality of participation is not uniformly good in all the JFM villages, yet the results of involving people in forest management have been quite encouraging in some places at least. For instance, in an ODA assisted project in Karnataka the villagers' earlier fear of FD had declined (Saxena and Sarin, 1998). Indirectly, this has resulted in the VFC (Village Forest Committee) members' improved access to forests for meeting their bonafide requirements of firewood, grazing and fodder. In some VFCs, irresponsible cutting by the local people in forests has been reduced due to improved relations. The consumption of fuel wood had also come down in some places because of the use of fuel saving devices, supplied by the FD. There is substantial goodwill among NGOs towards the project, who are playing an important role in organizing the people, and in helping them through non-forestry activities. Peoples' participation was far higher in those VFCs where NGOs are active. In the eastern states of Andhra Pradesh, Orissa, West Bengal, and Bihar there are a large number of groups protecting forests either on their own or initiated by the forest department, as Table 6.1 would indicate.

**Table 6.1 :** Actual Forest Cover and Area Under JFM in Certain States (sq.km)

| State / UT | Forest cover | Area under JFM | JFM area as per cent of forest cover |
|---|---|---|---|
| Andhra Pradesh | 43,290 | 10,540 | 24.35 |
| Bihar | 26,524 | 7,192 | 27.12 |
| Gujarat | 12,578 | 692 | 5.50 |
| Haryana | 604 | 630 | 104.30 |
| Himachal Pradesh | 12,521 | 60 | 0.48 |
| Jammu and Kashmir | 20,440 | 141 | 0.69 |
| Karnataka | 32,403 | 814 | 2.51 |
| Kerala | 10,334 | 20 | 0.19 |
| Madhya Pradesh | 131.195 | 3,500 | 2.67 |
| Orissa | 46,941 | 4,360 | 9.29 |
| Rajasthan | 13,353 | 1,857 | 13.91 |
| West Bengal | 8,349 | 4,493 | 53.81 |
| Total (including other states) | 633,397 | 34,837 | 5.50 |

*Source*: SPWD 1998

## Impact of the New Forest Policy and JFM on Deforestation

There is some evidence to show that the rate of forest degradation in India has declined after 1989, and that timber and fuel wood prices have stabilized since 1987. Recent remote sensing data is shown in Table 6.2.

**Table 6.2 :** Changes in Forest Cover in India Annually as per Remote Sensing Data

| Period | Area gained / lost annually *(in ha)* |
|---|---|
| 1981-87 | (-) 1,47,000 |
| 1987-89 | (-) 47,500 |
| 1989-91 | (+) 28,000 |
| 1991-93 | (+) 2,200 |
| 1993-95 | (-) 25,000 |

*Source :* FSI 1998

One explanation of the improved scenario could be the general ban on green felling which many Indian states have clamped since the late eighties. The relative contribution of forests to state revenues, similar to land revenue, has been falling dramatically since Independence, because of expansion of economic activity outside land. This has enabled the states to forego incomes from logging. Therefore, it may be premature to suggest that the improvement in forest cover or the fall in wood prices is due to the change in forest policies only; other factors, such as ban on felling, import, spread of Prosopis (*Prosopis juliflora*) shrubs, and the success of farm forestry may have better explanatory power. However, with the success of JFM in certain areas, there are examples of local glut of wood (Poffenberger and McGean, 1996), and such instances are likely to multiply as the protected forests mature for harvesting. If the trend of improvement in forest cover continues for a longer period, it could well be due to participatory policies.

JFM projects have been in operation for more than ten years in many states. The interim evaluation studies highlight two kinds of constraints in scaling up the participatory management of forests, (a) factors which are endogenous to the protecting group, and (b) factors which are in the domain of public policy (Ostrom, 1990 and 1994). The internal variables include: total number of decision makers, inter dependence among the participants, the discount rate or risk perceptions of the group, similarities of interest, leadership, information about expected benefits and costs, and shared norms and opportunities. The external variables refer to the policies of the implementing agency, political climate and government. Locally selected systems of norms, rules and property rights that are not recognised by external authorities may collapse if their legitimacy is challenged or if government does not have faith in the capacity of local communities. Blueprint thinking i.e., imposition of uniform solutions to a wide variety of local problems, centralisation of authority, over-dependence on external sources of help, and corruption or other forms of opportunistic behaviour on the part of external agencies are likely to cause threats to sustainable community governance of common property resources. Besides, government may still continue the old timber oriented technical package while paying lip sympathy to participative policies.

*Community mobilisation*

The management of forests before JFM was such that there was a dichotomy between resource users (including both industry and the people) and those responsible for resource regeneration, the user having no responsibility for plantation and maintenance. Granting the management role exclusively to users however, would succeed only if the village groups have the necessary inclination and management capability.

Whether the local population has been conservation oriented and managed commons in the past is debatable. While Gadgil (1989) has studied people oriented management in a few villages of South India that survived colonial period, other scholars (Nadkarni et. al., 1989; Locke 1995; Buchy 1996) studying the same region have doubted whether such practices were widespread. Nadkarni concluded that historically people's institution existed only in a few villages which managed local commons. Elsewhere forests survived because of limited biotic pressure. Buchy rejects a history of community management on the basis of her archive research and questions the extent to which pre-colonial prohibition over certain types of resource use can be said to constitute a system of communal management. Locke also concludes that it seems likely that although reduced rates of degradation in pre-colonial South India in some cases may have been due to culturally determined patterns of behaviour, for the most part they arose from levels of demand too low to cause depletion. Thus the romantic assumption often made by the environmentalists that the local population has been conservation oriented in the past does not seem to be true.

Exclusive village management of natural resources will require socially cohesive villages, on which there are polarised views. One social science view of an Indian village is an atomised mass, composed of individuals who are not in any organised fold except the family and extended kin-group which form the sub-caste'. According to this view, rigid stratification of village society inhabits development of institutions representing a common will. Grossly unequal land tenure and access to markets ensure that only a powerful minority gains in the name of the community (Eckholm, 1979).

Bandyopadhyay (1983), however, disputes that social and economic inequalities have hindered the possibility of community ownership, participation and control in India. Management of village commons has been a historical reality for two reasons. First, whereas private resources in India were governed by individualistic and class dominated norms, there have been communally shared norms when it comes to community resources. Second, the self-sufficient nature of the traditional village economy guided the exploitation of common resources through a system of self-control. He therefore concludes that there are no structural barriers to achieving community participation in forestry projects. Many environmentalists support this view point (Agarwal and Narain, 1990). It is difficult to settle this controversy.

Why does collective action succeed in some cases and not in others? Empirical evidence discussed in this section, although from limited ecological regions of India, suggests several clues. First, most effective local institutions develop in those small communities where people know each other. Collaboration is easier among small and homogeneous groups (Attwood, 1988). Second, the topography of the upland villages makes their common lands visible from most of the dwellings, so that any unauthorised felling cannot escape notice. If a village is located inside the forest or at the bottom of a slope where the forest is located, individual households can easily provide protection services from their households, thus cutting down on protection costs. In contrast, the area of a flat village in Central South India may well be spread over 5-10 km in one direction which makes it easy for 'free riders' to escape undetected. Third, hill and upland villages usually have better land resources. This attracts better management form the people, as its protection is more vital for their survival. On the other hand, once degradation sets in, people may become indifferent to protection. In Kheda district of Gujarat, grazing lands are so degraded that the dependence of an average milk producer on the grazing lands - and hence his or her stake in their preservation - is low (Shah, 1987). There are thus two syndromes: a valuable resource well managed because it is worth managing well; and a degraded resource neglected because it is degraded. Fourth, remoteness from roads and markets further helps in retaining mutual obligations, and discourages poaching by outsiders. Fifth, in remote villages, fear of reprisals from village elders deters too frequent abuse of common resources. In contrast, the old system of authority in the modernised villages has been undermined without being replaced effectively by a new one, resulting in a hiatus of confidence (Wade, 1987). Sixth, upland settlements are more homogeneous in caste, with one caste or tribe usually dominating both in land and number can effectively issue social prohibition, whereas villages in planes tend to be multi-caste, which makes social control difficult. Finally, collaboration is likely to succeed if all families including the rich are highly dependent on forests for their survival needs of fodder and fuel wood. As the productivity of the common declines, the rich shift to privately grown fodder on their own land, while the poor still use the commons for their sheep and goats. The rich then lose interest in the upkeep of commons, while the poor lack the power and organisation to manage the commons themselves. This may be one reason why in Gujarat, the Indian state best known for community endeavour, only 60 out of 18,000 villages have come forward to start community fodder farms whereas other villages have opted for income generating Eucalyptus plantation on grazing lands (Shah, 1987).

The personal interest of village elite in management of the commons appears a crucial element. Even a market-dominated village may develop collective action, if it is in the interest of all, including the powerful people of the village (Wade, 1985 and 1988). A study of fodder farms on common lands in Gujarat (Shah, 1987) found that some *panchayats* leaders took a great deal of personal interest in setting up and running such farms. They seemed to work for non-economic rewards, such as power, reputation, and social status. Once established, the successful farms were run on business lines, with the interaction between a farmer and the fodder farm similar to that between a buyer and a private seller. An average farmer did not show any interest in running the farm. In fact its success was due more to the initiative of the leader than to community spirit. This makes such enterprises precariously dependent upon quality and integrity of leaders, willing to work for extra-economic rewards.

We conclude, then, that community control and management can work in three circumstances. First, in villages which are small, homogeneous, remote from markets, and dependent upon produce from commons, second, where gains from organisation are high, for both the village elite and the commoners and third, where a leader is willing to run the show for non-monetary gains. Analysing the success of sugar co-operatives in Maharashtra, Attwood (1988, pp. 69-87) reached similar conclusions. According to him, co-operatives succeed not because there are no classes in the village society, but because an alliance between the rich and poor farmers for the successful running of the cooperative sugar factories is in the economic interest of both the classes.

Local collective action has been undermined in the last thirty years by a number of political and economic processes (Bardhan, 1993). Village societies have become heterogeneous, and market forces have commercialised the erstwhile subsistence economies integrating them with urban and national economies. Possibilities for migration and mobility tend to work against cooperation. Intra-group heterogeneity in payoffs may thus adversely affect the sustainability of cooperative agreements. Cooperation works best in small groups with similarity of needs and clear boundaries, and shared norms and patterns of reciprocity. Swallow, Brent, and Bromley (1994) suggest that a group agreement is more likely to collapse where there are more than 30-40 members, whereas the average size of villages in India is about 100 to 200 households. Participatory politics erodes the traditional authority structures, and modernisation improves the options of both exit and voice for the common people. Many rural communities in developing countries are now in this difficult transition period, with traditional institutions on the decline, while new self-governing institutions yet to be born.

The overall result has often been to forestall local action. One way out of this hiatus is 'co-management - cooperative management arrangements between state and local organisations in which states assign group rights to specific resources, establish overall guidelines for inter-group interactions, and help to create more positive environments for the operation of local organisations. The latter can then mobilise local participation in resource management and advise the state on the desirability of proposed management practices' (Swallow, Brent, and Bromely, 1994, p.5). The precise distribution of control and management between the state and the local group should depend on a number of situation-specific factors, such as the ease with which groups can be formed and can retain cohesiveness.

To sum up, emergence of community cohesiveness and participation cannot always be taken for granted, even when the people face distress situation. In Orissa, where success stories can be located in every district, the total area under protection by indigenous groups is even less than ten per cent of the total forest area of the state. This could be enhanced substantially if the problems faced by the groups, and especially the ones which groups cannot resolve on their own, such as inter-village disputes, demarcation, relations with external institutions and markets, are taken care of by the government. This has often been the case in many success stories of JFM, in which forest department helps the group in removing encroachments, providing funds and technical help, mediating in inter village and intra-village conflicts, and taking legal action against free riders. In other words, the capability of a village group to manage commons may be enhanced if the group is supported in its efforts by government.

## Problem of JFM

### *Dual agenda of JFM*

JFM as a programme has a dual agenda which is related at an institutional level. Firstly, JFM intends to create productive assets by way of regenerating and/or afforesting forest lands. Secondly, it aims to achieve the first agenda by way of people's participation and giving them the responsibility of protecting and managing their forests. This dual agenda requires strong, robust village institutions which are representative of the interest of the entire community. Thus, JFM also is a patent instrument for the empowerment of local people. It is important to remind ourselves of the dual nature of objectives, JFM is pursuing, else we might end up repeating the follies of the Social Forestry Schemes.

The JFM programme has undergone considerable progress in the various states and a number of participatory projects of forest management have been implemented under this principle. Analysing the progress of these ventures, it is evident that there is still a long way to go in order to achieve the spirit of forest protection through participation, as envisaged in the programme. The experience of working on JFM at local level has had a limited impact on the revision of policy. A number of donor aided participatory projects are being implemented to make quick progress, but as these programs are not engaged by policy they retain momentum as long as the donors support them. What is needed is a whole process of identification of the various anomalies in the implementation of JFM, at the local level, and creation of space for intermediary institutions at the Regional and National level, to feed these experiences to the policy debate. NGOs, Federations of Village Level Institutions etc. have a great contribution to make in this direction. To achieve progress on this front, the FD at local level will have to become more responsive to seek contribution of NGOs.

*Resistance of bureaucracy to share power*

The keenness of the FD to preserve its own power base and not give away its exclusive position of control over the forest to community institutions has resulted in low level of compliance with the spirit of JFM approach. A frequent complaint against the forest department is that they have still not given up the 'police' image, and are not sufficiently sensitised to undertake extension work. To this charge the forest officials' response is that in the initial stages the community is at a low level of formation, and therefore they cannot dilute their basic responsibility of protection. The forest department also has powers to cancel or dissolve the Village Forest Protection Committee (VFCs), which itself constrains the confidence and autonomy of the village committee. While forest departments will require some statement in the resolution to dissolve the management agreement if their community partners fail to uphold their responsibilities under the JFM programme. It is also important that the identity of the user group is respected. In Rajasthan and Haryana, where the user groups are required to be registered as societies, would extend greater independence. Such groups will continue even if their relations with the forest department are severed. In Gujarat, VFCs are registered as cooperative societies, which in addition to being legal entities provide functional autonomy. Once the user group has a separate legal status this can be used for several purposes.

The FD chooses often literate villagers as leaders. These are generally younger people and therefore, their authority lacks legitimacy. Excessive dependence of the village communities on FD has frustrated village autonomy. Another important element is the response of FD staff to VFCs grievance. In the initial stages,

VFCs look forward to getting support from the forest department in booking offenders, negotiating with other villages / departments etc VFCs also need flexibility, and field staff should not throw rule books at them. Many protecting villages have complained that FD unilaterally overrules their decisions without explaining the reasons thereof. In some places protection is preceded by cleaning, weeding etc. for which the forest department pays wages to the labour (Femconsult, 1995). This must change and the forest department must hand over the responsibility of handling funds to the VFCs. This would make financial dealing more transparent and foolproof against misuse of funds. VFCs will also develop a greater sense of accountability in the process. In Gujarat, the committees raided the houses and confiscated illegally poached wood. When they wanted to conduct auction of the seized material, not only did the FD not permit them to utilise the money so received, but it objected to the place of auction too, pointing to the rules that auction must be conducted at the Range Forest depot only.

With the exception of clauses in the national and West Bengal resolutions, most state guidelines do not address the long-term rights of participating communities. Clear tenure security enhances the authority of community management groups to carry out protection activities, especially when under pressure from neighbouring villages and private interest groups. It is necessary that the time frame for such agreements is clear, as well as the basis for extensions. It may be appropriate for the time period of the agreement to correspond to the production cycle (rotation) of the primary products.

*Restricting JFM to degraded forest areas*

The stipulation of restricting JFM to degraded forest areas raises two sorts of issues. Firstly, the low economic returns from JFM in degraded forest, makes it an unattractive option for the communities involved. Reserving good forest areas under state control and handing over degraded forest land to community questions the basic premise of collaborative management viz-linking responsibility with benefits. The flow of benefits from degraded forestlands put to JFM (especially in Rajasthan) is not commensurate to the responsibility of protection handed over to the communities. Thus, the claim that JFM will lead to sustainable management of the forest through community involvement is debatable. Also such a restriction implies that the community should first degrade their forest areas, so as to bring them under JFM.

*Lack of legal arrangements*

The JFM resolution envisages a big role of the communities in achieving the objectives of the new forest policy. This collaborative arrangement talks about sharing of responsibilities and benefits with the local communities. However, many of these communities are structurally constrained from exercising these responsibilities, as they lack appropriate authority to do so. There is a case for the necessity to 'empower' the local group engaged in forest protection, in a legal sense. This would help them to derive autonomy and authority in dealings with offenders and powerful non-members.

There are examples of forest protection committee members facing penal proceeding for taking to charge powerful and elite offenders. Such incidents bring down the motivation of the members of FPC to pursue the objectives of forest protection. Till the FPCs gather experience and legal authority the, FD has to work in close collaboration with FPCs.

*Tenure insecurity*

JFM arrangement derives its legal legitimacy from the resolution issued by the various state governments. As these resolutions do not have a statutory basis, they are subject to reversal. Hence, the tenure rights of FPCs engaged in forest protection and management are uncertain and insecure. JEM also faces a threat in the form of a massive pull of ad-hoc privatisation by way of regularisation of illicit encroachments on forestlands. Till such an option exists vis-à-vis JFM, there will be little faith amongst the community members to forge horizontal ties of solidarity.

*Institutional change in the forest department*

The present institutional set up of the forest department was designed to protect the forests. Participatory forestry requires a different role for the forest department. While FD has development awareness about benefits of participatory forestry in the recent years, its understanding and commitment to share control and responsibility with people is still partial. Institutional reforms in the FD will benefit the objective of community participation in JFM. This issue should be viewed in light of the dual agenda of JFM viz - Afforestation and Regeneration of forest lands as well as improving local governance. This agenda envisages different roles for the FD and NGOs, involved in JFM. While the FD will have to ensure feasibility of the forest plantations and support to the EPC in related matters on one hand, on the other it will have to involve NGOs in the programme to a greater extent to assist the new FPCs in the complex process of people's institutions.

*Rights of non-protecting people*

The legal and organisational framework for joint management remains weak and controversial. First, the old rights and privileges of the people (usually established in the colonial period) have continued in most degraded forest, and often such rights include free access to expensive timber privileges without corresponding responsibility is counter-productive. Second, often more than one village have their rights in the same forest, with the result that it becomes difficult to promote village protection committees. Third, a large that it becomes difficult to promote village protection committees. Third, a large number of new settlers in a village have their rights in the same forest, with the result that it becomes difficult to promote village protection committees. Third, a large number of new settlers in a village (they may be the poorest) have no traditional rights in forests, as their ancestors did not live in the village at the time of forest settlement they get deprived of benefits, and are compelled to obtain these illegally. Fourth, sometimes people living several kilometres away from forest have customary rights in forests.

They, with no possibility of getting involved in forest management, have been customarily using these lands as an open-access resource without any restriction, for grazing and collection of fuel wood and NTFPs. Migratory tribes from other states too send their cattle for grazing, and their rights have been upheld by the Supreme Court (Vira, 1993). Thus, a forest patch does not have a well-defined and recognised user-group, and may admit the rights of the entire population of that region or the entire forest area (Singh, 1996). This type of right-regime', which makes forests open-access lands, is not conducive to successful protection, as rights of contiguous villages protecting forests may come in conflict with those of distant villages, not protecting but still having rights to enjoy usufruct.

Therefore, at least in JFM areas, use rights should be reviewed in order to put them in harmony with the care and share philosophy which is the basis of JFM. Even in unclassified forests, where no previous settlement has been done, the task is not simple due to the practice of use by a large class of stakeholders. Elsewhere, old settlement rights may have to be modified with a view to make these amenable to formation of viable VFCs. This is easier said than done, as changing customary or legal rights would be perceived as an unpopular step and may face political hurdles. Such a policy can be made acceptable if it is accompanied by other pro-people changes in technology, nature of species, secure rights over produce, etc.

### *Inter-village disputes*

Depriving communities far from the resource but having traditional rights is a ticklish question. Some close communities have solved this by charging fees from distant villages on the ground that they do not have to protect the resource. In West Bengal, some VFCs negotiated with neighbouring communities to clarify rights and territorial responsibilities when they bean to initiate protection activities. As the user groups have a strong incentive to avoid conflicts, they have often demonstrated that they can conduct much of the negotiation on their own or with the help of the *panchayats* (elected village councils) leaders. However the Forest Department holds ultimate responsibility for seeing that management groups do not create conflicts over pre-existing usufruct.

Confusion over forest boundaries is a recurring problem for the VFCs. In one case, members from Chandmura village in West Bengal thought that they were also protecting the Arabari forests. Only when the forest was harvested for timber did they realise that they were not part of the programme. The village took the government to court, thus delaying harvest benefits to others. The problem could have been avoided had there been maps and constant dialogue between the participation villages.

The Rajasthan resolution allows revenue village wise FPC formation, which may consist of several hamlets located separately from each other. This makes the smooth functioning of the VFC very difficult (VIKSAT 1995). Whether multi-hamlet forest protection committees have been formed, field experience shows that the component communities keep their independent identity within the large group maintaining clear boundaries of their area and by retaining exclusive control over harvests in their territory. Often such groups surrounding a large tract of forest form an apex committee to coordinate their activities and represent themselves to the FD. Although the larger group may facilitate joint protection and dispute resolution, informal partitioning of the resource has no validity in law and may not be sustained over a long period.

Most VFCs want their forest tract boundaries to be formally demarcated. Rough agreements between villages over these boundaries may be sufficient when the resource is degraded, but once valuable products are regenerated, conflicts will ensue in the absence of formal notification. Often forest maps are not available which delays formalisation of boundaries. This is not a simple exercise, since natural, administrative and customary boundaries do not coincide. In practice, under existing customary use, different boundaries apply to different products, e.g. grazing and fuel wood. Boundary disputes between neighbouring VFCs are likely to increase as harvesting approaches.

*VFCs and Panchayats*

Another legal problem concerns the status of VFCs versus the village *panchayats*. The state government resolutions recommend VFCs as functional groups. However, these committees have no legal and statutory basis, and it may be difficult for them to manage resources on a long-term basis. Their relationships with the statutory village *panchayats* will need to be sharply defined (Poffenberger and Singh, 1993).

The 1989 West Bengal resolution stated that the local *panchayats* land management committee shall select beneficiaries for constituting the VFC. This indicated that the *panchayats*, which is outside the user group, would determine who could and who could not participate. Although in 1990, the West Bengal Government allowed every member in the village to be a member of the management group, the hold of the *panchayats* remained strong. The Orissa order prescribes that the lady deputy Chief of the local *panchayats* will be the head of the VFC, but the *panchayats* are not working well and her stewardship is not seen as legitimate by the indigenous VFCs.

Experience over the last 20 years from Indian social forestry programme indicates that in many cases *panchayats* had difficulties in effectively managing community woodlots due to their inherent political nature and often-diverse constituencies. *Panchayats* are political organisations based on electoral system, whereas conflict can be quite harmful for the effective functioning of VFCs. Protection can work only if there is almost unanimity and consensus amongst the user group.

Unlike *panchayats*, powers to the VFC are not given under any law, which may affect their powers to check free-riding in the longer run. Thus, most successful VFCs charge fees for collection of forest produce, although this practice is technically against the Forest Act. The illegality can be removed if the allotment of forest land to the VFCs is done under section 28 of the Forest Act. At present it is done administratively.

Due to the increasing importance of *panchayats* in decision-making in India, many field activists feel that community forest management must take place at the smallest possible level of those who actually use the resource. This would require statutory changes in the current *panchayats* laws.

There is also some concern that if JFM groups were absorbed by village *panchayat's* vested interests, it might exert control over decision making. Since small user communities may comprise of less powerful groups, they may lose authority to elite if the management becomes a direct adjunct of the *panchayats*. VFCs are recognised only by the Forest Department, all other government departments recognise *panchayats* making them much more powerful than the VFCs. On the whole, there is need to clarify the relationship of local forest management groups to *panchayats,* simply subsuming them as part of the *panchayats* would almost certainly threaten their effectiveness.

### *Marketing of NTFPs*

The JFM programme is no doubt oriented towards the subsistence needs of local communities. But once the produce of forests increases through proper protection, there is every likelihood of production increasing beyond what can be consumed within the village itself, and so also the importance of marketing. Moreover many NTFPs have traditionally been used by the gatherers to generate cash incomes (Shepherd, 1989). However, old restrictions imposed in the past on their processing and *Sal*es are still in place. The poor have no right to process these items and sell them freely in the market.

As the commercial importance of NTFPs increased in the past, the state governments during the 1960s and 1970s nationalised almost all important NTFPs. These NTFPs can be sold only to government agencies or to agencies so nominated by the government. In theory, these rights are acquired ostensibly to protect the interest of the poor against exploitation by private traders and middlemen. In practice, such rights are sublet to private traders and industry. Thus, a hierarchy of objectives developed: industry and other large end-users had the first charge on the product at low and subsidised rates; revenue was maximised subject to the first objective which implied that there was no consistent policy to encourage value addition at lower levels; tribal and the interest of the poor was relegated to the last level, or completely ignored

(Saxena, 1996).

Studies (Chambers et al., 1989) indicate that while collectors of NTFPs are often some of the lowest income groups in India, they often receive only 5 to 20 per cent of the retail value of their goods. Various governments run marketing and cooperative schemes and have established *para* (hamlet) stalls for this purpose, but these have frequently failed to result in major improvements in prices. The state marketing agencies have reached a stage where they are unable to play the roles for which they were intended. The policy frame wherein a state monopoly was considered necessary to counteract severe market imperfections has also become counter-productive and is encouraging market monopolies. If the poor are to enjoy the fruits of their labour (and of the forests which they are supposed to bring up), a drastic overhauling of the policy frame as well as the supportive institutional framework is necessary so that it is consistent with the 1988 policy objectives.

Practical considerations point out that government is incapable of administer complete control effectively and do buying and selling of NTFPs itself. It is better for government to facilitate private trade, and to act as a watchdog rather than try to eliminate it. Monopoly purchase by government requires sustained political support and excellent bureaucratic machinery. It is difficult to ensure these over a long period and hence nationalisation has often increased exploitation of the poor. Experience shows that open markets may give producers the best chance of gaining a competitive price for their products. For marketing NTFPs government should not have a monopoly, nor create such a monopoly for traders and mills. The solution is to denationalise NTFPs gradually so as to encourage healthy competition. Government should set up promotional Marketing Boards, as distinct from commercial corporations (which are inefficient, and hence demand nationalisation), with responsibility for dissemination of information about markets and prices to the gatherers. The Boards would help in bridging the gap between what the consumers pay and what gatherers get. Free purchase by all and sundry would also be in tune with the current liberalisation and open market climate.

Encouraging setting up of processing units within the tribal areas is also to be recommended. In other cases, NGO- run programmes to develop NTFPs, which makes processing more efficient and improves market access, can enhance the income of forest communities. In West Bengal, the presence of an NGO who provided improved *Sal* plate processing and marketing support allowed village producers to improve incomes to Rs. 11.50 for an eight-hour day equivalent versus Rs. 5 to 6 for other communities dependent on middlemen.

To sum up, with a view to promote people's participation, state governments permit collection of NTFPs from JFM areas. However, this hardly acts as an incentive for two reasons. First, even from non-JFM areas people have *de facto* or *de jure* collection rights. Secondly, the marketing environment for realising the full value from NTFPs is constrained by exploitative governmental regulations restricting *Sal*e, processing and transport. At least in JFM areas, markets must be freed from unnecessary government controls so that gatherers are free to optimise returns on their labour.

### *Insensitivity to gender issues*

Protection of a degraded area under JFM often increases women's drudgery as they have to travel a greater distance to collect their daily requirements of fuel wood and fodder (Sarin 1998). Despite the good intentions of forest protection, community forest management has often burdened women with additional hardships, or concentrated it on the shoulders of younger women. They also had to switch over to inferior fuels like leaves, husk, weeds and bushes. The widespread shift to use of forest sweepings to meet domestic fuel needs has a negative effect on regeneration and nutrient recycling essential for maintaining soil productivity.

Obviously, merely shifting the protection role from the Forest Departments to the community does not provide any immediate relief to women. Further, the gender differentiated impact is not restricted to firewood - it applies equally to other forest produce. For example, protecting *Sal* trees with the existing technology of multiple shoot cutting results in the leaves getting out of reach. This affects the making of *Sal* leaf plates, which is a common source of income primarily for poor women in many parts of West Bengal, Orissa and Bihar.

Another problem is of providing adequate share to women in management responsibilities in JFM committees. In this respect, women's rights and entitlements have been almost totally overlooked in the JFM Rules. For instance, Bihar, Karnataka, Madhya Pradesh and Tripura provide for the membership of only one representative per household; Gujarat, Rajasthan and Maharashtra have left the matter open; Punjab has no provision for a general body at all, and in Jammu and Kashmir, it is unclear whether either a man or a woman or both can represent a household. In cases where one person represents a household, it invariably ends up being a man (except in the case of widows with no adult sons).

Membership in committees is not synonymous with a share in rights or of benefits. One needs to ensure both, and not one or the other. Forced inclusion of women through legislation has not led to genuine participation. Participation of women is cosmetic and symbolic, it is however better where NGOs or a gender sensitive forest official were active (OXFAM 1998). Often meetings are scheduled in the evenings to suit men, but at times when women tend to be cooking. When attending meetings, women feel marginalized and their voices are not given importance. It is considered against Indian culture to talk in the presence of men, much less to question their ideas. Often they get busy in arranging tea and snacks for the male members and thus are unable to concentrate on the deliberations of the Committee. As a result, there is a bias in favour of those forest products of interest primarily to men. In village Kilmora in a *Van panchayats* in UP (Britt-Kapoor, 1994) the female member who has the added advantage of living at the house where meetings are held rarely stayed longer than was necessary to sign the register. In another village Katuul (Britt-Kapoor, 1994) a female member said, *'I went to three or four meetings. My suggestions were never implemented. No one ever listened. I marked my signature in the register. I am illiterate, so I couldn't tell what was written in the meetings minutes. I was told that my recommendations would be considered, but first that the register had to be signed. Later they were uninterested'.*

Given the sex-segregated and hierarchical nature of Indian society, separate women's organisations and staff are needed to work among women, to instil confidence in them, so that they can fight for their rights. Therefore, whenever there is recruitment, more women need to be recruited in the forest department. The village level committees should have adequate representation of women. Forestry staff should be sensitised on gender issues through orientation programmes. As women in many societies still feel inhibited in expressing themselves in mixed gatherings, each committee should have a separate women's cell for the raising their consciousness and for improving their skills. The quality of women's participation and the control they exercise over decision making processes is more important than the sheer number of women present in such bodies.

### *JFM and the poorest*

JFM has often failed to give fair attention to the poorest forest dependent communities, such as artisans, head loaders and *podu* (shifting) cultivators. Although FD does not evict *podu* cultivators, it includes old *podu* lands within the scope of JFM, which increases the fears of the tribal that after wage earning programmes are withdrawn, their food security would be jeopardised (OXFAM 1998).

Not all social groups are hit equally by the decision to protect and keep livestock out of the proposed area to be protected in JFM. For low income rural families to participate, it is important that benefits start flowing as early as possible, either in the form of gatherable biomass or new opportunities of employment. This will require policy shifts and afforestation programmes on other categories of land farmlands, village lands and FD lands remote from village habitation. Otherwise, mere protection of a degraded area may transfer biotic pressure to some other area. Therefore production of biomass through quick growing shrubs, bushes and grasses must be undertaken on more remote lands, so that peoples demands are met in a sustained manner from these bushes and shrubs, while people protect forest lands in anticipation of more valuable NTFPs and forest products. The issue of how to meet the economic needs of the people for the first few years, during which they have to reduce their dependence on the protected land must be faced squarely. It is impractical to expect that people will give up grazing or reduce their consumption in national interest without expecting any tangible gains in return. Simultaneous development of all categories of land in the same region will also provide short-term benefits to the most needy.

One practical implication of including programmes on different types of land in the same project would be that these would have to be implemented in the same Range or group of villages, rather than being implemented, as happens currently, in different Ranges, which loses complementarily.

Coordinating JFM with other departments - Afforestation may be the first priority of the FD but communities felt need may be drinking water, irrigation, or wage employment during the slack months. JFM projects should therefore either include these as entry point programmes, or coordinate the JFM related efforts with the activities of other departments, such as Irrigation, Animal Husbandry and Cottage Industries. It may therefore be desirable if such activities are taken up in the same area as the JFM for better results and multidimensional development of these villages. This will improve relations between people and the forest staff.

Need to develop strategies for conflict resolution - Capitalising on this potential of joint management on a large scale will require significant shifts in investments and strategy, and some of the constraints have already been discussed above. Where regenerating forests are already beginning to increase in value, conflicts will increase between contending resource users such as adjoining villagers, migrating herders, or more distant and periodic forest users. As a more lucrative range of non-timber products begins to mature, and the sharing of timber harvests becomes regularised, questions of equity and the distribution of benefits will create new management challenges and conflict resolution skills. Strategies to deal with these problems are yet to be evolved.

## Some Contributions of JFM

### 1. Mathwa village FPC turned as *Panchayats*

Otherwise low profiled Lalubhai from Mathwa, smiled with a sense of satisfaction on his face for 3 years the entire village fought for the JFM in 465 hectares of degraded forestland under his able leadership as VFPC chairperson. *Sarpanch* and other elite didn't support him initially. Nearly 3 years of fight with strong elite in village and forest based business interest groups in nearby towns, the village gained access to forest resource with the support of DFO and SWDF.

In 1998, the entire village harvested fodder from the forest at free of cost. In other sense for many it was for the first time they received fodder from their own forests. Women as strong partners in the entire process influenced the distribution system. The whole operation was planned and executed by Lalubhai and his fellow members in FPC. With this he gained tremendous confidence and good will of people. But it was an eyesore for the powerful in village who exclusively exploited forests for years together.

Meanwhile village *panchayats* elections came in. Asit was the post reserved for women candidate, *Sarpanch* nominated his wife at his position for village president. But this time Galali ben Solanki who is an active member of FPC and also wife of Lalubhai also filed her nomination. Almost all the women in the village supported her. *Sarpanch* fielded other two candidates to split the votes to secure majority. Elections took place in the month of November 1997. There were 1114 voters in Mathwa. In a remote tribal village where going out to town is considered men's role, husbands generally do filing nomination for Sarpanch. But here the scene is different.

Finally as results declared Galali ben Solanki won by a majority of 564 votes with a lead of 249 votes to her rival. She was elected as *Sarpanch*. In a course of about thee years a simple common family in the village with a commitment for JFM, emerged as a powerful force in the community. And now this husband and wife duo is planning to develop the entire village on the lines of watershed and other employment generating activities. Lalubhai and Galali ben says 'It was all possible because of the support and guidance extended by Sadguru. All these years, we were just victims of various forces now we know how to control them and even how to rule them'.

## 2. Strength of women in JFM

Sharda village near Dahod town has about 300 hectares of degraded forestland being protected and allowed for conservation under JFM. Village FPC has been protecting the forest since 1993 years. As a result the forest is now producing good fodder grasses which is allotted to the FPC for the first time. However, the men in FPC were hesitant to take up the responsibility against the wish of *Sarpanch* who every year exploited the resource. He said that he should be given a major chunk as it is the practised every year. This time again men were ready to give away the folder demanded but women took an objection stating that the forest is protected by village FPC then why should he be given share. This way women's group in FPC proved much stronger than men.

In another incident, *Sarpanch* took the side of adjacent village leader who apparently belong to same political party who involved in illicit cutting of wood from Sharda forest. When villagers protested it, and the clash turned violent, he conveniently took a neutral stand stating that it is clash between two families and not the case of forest tress pass. Women all along fought the battle and stopped the illicit cutters.

## 3. The Arabari experiment in JFM

There is a growing body of experience available from India and abroad showing that joint protection and management of forests by the forest departments and local people living in and around forests can effectively protect degraded forest lands thereby allowing them to regenerate. The Arabari experiment in joint protection and management of natural forests has now become well known in India and abroad (Singh, 1991). The experiment was started by the forest department of West Bengal in 1971-72 in the Arabari forest range which is located in East Midnapur forest division, about 30 km away from Midnapur town and 200 km west of Calcutta. In 1972, as part of its project, resuscitation of *Sal* Forest of southern West Bengal, the forest department launched an experiment in natural forest regeneration in Arabari. The then DFO, Dr. A. K. Banerjee, soon after taking over charge, realised that it was difficult to regenerate and protect the Arabari forest without the co-operation of the local people who depended on the forest for fuel wood, fodder, wood grazing of animals, minor forest produce and even cash income from sale of fuel wood. Consequently, he started meeting people in the neighbouring villages and informally discussing with them the need for forest protection and regeneration.

The DFO promised to help solve the problem of livelihood of the local people in the lean period, provided they were ready to co-operate with him in the task of regeneration and protection of the forest. With the consent and assurance of the local people, he demarcated 1,272 ha of degraded forestland for plantation and protection by the people. The plantation work was to be taken up in full swing only in the lean period, and all the local people were asked to form a Forest Protection Committee (FPC) for managing and protecting the plantation. The committee was assured of work under various on-going rural employment schemes and given exclusive rights to all non-wood forest products, free of cost. Their immediate needs for fuel and fodder were also taken care of.

Initially, the villagers were allowed to cultivate paddy, fodder crops, *Sabai* grass, Maize and Groundnuts on some of the degraded forestland. Honeybee hives were established in eucalyptus groves on an experimental basis as a possible source of supplementary income to the villagers. Poles were provided to the villagers for house construction, repairs and making cots for sale at subsidised rates. The participating villagers were given exclusive rights to all minor forest products such as *Sal, Kendu* leaves, dry twigs, seeds of *Mahua, Subabul*, *Sal* and *Aakashmani* trees etc. Fruits like Mango, Guava, Jack fruit, *Kendu* fruit, etc. and valuable medicinal plants were also allowed to be collected and sold in the market by them. The villagers earned substantial amount from the *Sal* of these products

While the committee was organised in 1972, it was not formalised until 1977 when the list of beneficiaries was checked by the forest department and the *Panchayats*. The FD as well as the Indian Statistical Institute, Calcutta conducted a demographic survey since the initial list received from the *panchayats* was biased. All the 618 families residing in and around the project area were included in the list. Only the head of households were enrolled as members of the committee. The committee was headed by the president and consisted off 11 members, one each from the participating villages. It had a secretary to handle routine office and other matters.

When the committee started functioning, 22 persons from the 11 participating villages (one man and one woman each) guarded the forest in the daytime. Some forest guards and *van mazdoors* (forest labourers) also accompanied them on patrol. The *van mazdoors* were landless labourers hired from all the 11 villages. Night guarding was not done, as it was not considered necessary. If a person failed to turn up for his/her duty he was called for an explanation. Each member was assigned to the patrol duty for one week, every two months.

Anyone spotted cutting wood or destroying the forest was fined by the villagers or handed over to the forest department. The fines range from Rs. 2 to Rs. 5. The FPC feels that a heavier fine, say, Rs. 100 to Rs. 500, will be too much for the villagers and even if they manage to pay the fine, they will try and recover the amount from the forest in retaliation. If a member of the committee is at fault, he is presented before the committee. The members tell him about the merits of conserving the forest and the sentiments of the villagers toward the forest. They listen to his problems and assure him work within the village, only if he promises to stop cutting the trees.

The protection provided by the participating villagers allowed the forests of Arabari to regenerate. Consequently, by 1988, 700 ha of fine *Sal* coppice and a plantation crop of over 305 ha had been raised. AT the 1988 price, 700 ha of *Sal* forest were valued at Rs. 12.6 million and the expected benefits exceeded the expected costs by over then times. This encouraged the FD to formalise the partnership through a special Government Resolution issued in July 1989 which was later modified and re-issued in July 1990. Both the original and the modified Resolutions stipulated, *inter alia*, that (i) the members will have to protect the forest /plantation for at least five years to be eligible for sharing of the usufruct; (ii) each usufruct from the final harvesting not before the crop attaining the age of ten years; and (iii) the concerned forest official shall set apart 25% of the net sale proceeds at every final harvesting of the concerned plantation/forest for distribution to the eligible beneficiaries.

### 4. Kadalipal Forest Protection Committee

The Kadalipal FPC is a FD initiated FPC. The Kadalipal FPC is protecting a part of the forest resource for which there are a number of claimants. The Kadalipal village is falling in the range forest of Kamakyanagar division. The Sundherkol reserve forest and Kadalipal reserve forest form one of the two main reserve forest in this range. There are a number of villages that are located between this Sunderkhol range and the Brahmini river. All these village communities have been past users of this reserve. The FD, at the instance of the Government Order has formed a number of FPCs that are about 2-3 years old in the villages in the immediate vicinity of Sunderkhol reserve and has allocated forest area for protection by the FPCs. As a result, numbers of village communities located away from the reserve are deprived of the access to the forest resource. An under current of conflict is prevailing in this area. Prior to the formation of FPCs, FD used to issue permits to people for collection of firewood by charging Rs. 1/- per cartload.

By bribing the forest guard people could collect more from forest, than was permitted. Later on the Kadalipal FPC had imposed a much higher fee of Rs. 20 - Rs.30 per cartload of fuel wood. According to the Khuntabati people even this collection is possible only if one is acquainted with the FPC members of Kadalipal. The poor in the village cannot afford to pay for fuel wood and they have never paid in the past. The Khuntabati further accuse the Kaladalipal FPC of being more interested in building up the village development fund by selling their forest than in forest protection.

Similar views echoed in Kuntabath village also. In Sirimala 35 families of Dama caste also face the deprivation of access to bamboos of Sundherkhol reserve. They make a number of articles from bamboos for their livelihood. Their traditional rights are now threatened.

The people also put forth certain options:

1. Revival of FD permit system,
2. Allocation of forest area on the basis of population so that each village is given a patch for protection,
3. A joint protection committee of user villages 'Kuntabatti' people were willing to contribute by cash or by sending people for patrol,
4. Handover protection to *Panchayats*. *Panchayats* can then arrange to apportion share of produce,
5. Opening of FD operated fuel wood depots,
6. Form an apex committee of all villages to decide upon mode of distribution of produce. The immediate villages may do the protection with contributory (in cash or manpower) support from farther villages.

The interesting phenomenon is that these villages have been protecting their *Khesara* (village) forests for a number of years but now their forest resources have become scarce.

*Profile of Kadalipal*

The hamlet Kadalipal is located 3 kms. Off the main road from and 13 kms away from the Kamakyanagar town. The hamlet belongs to the Annapurna Khamari revenue village of Kantia Kateni *Gram Panchayats*, Kamakyanagar block of Kamakyanagar subdivision. Its forest is under the jurisdiction of Kamakyanagar Range Forest Division (West).

The people of this village were the sebaks (servants) of the erstwhile queen Annapurna. About 30 years ago, the queen's land was given on lease to some of the families and the community began a settled life. At the time of settlement in 1970s land ownership entitlement was done. In the earlier times, the people even gave revenue to the queen in lieu of land lease. Forest was dense at that time and wild elephants often destroyed the crops and people could not pay the revenue. The king Raja Sankar Pratap Singh later hunted down the elephants.

Kadalipal has tribe of Juang, Kandhas and Para and has about 30 families. The total area of the hamlet is 189 ha. The forest area under FPC protection is 160 ha. The village has a primary school. Other facilities are available at Alwajharana village located on the main road. All the families have agricultural land and paddy is the main crop. There is a pond which acts a source of irrigation and people grow winter crops like pulses. Sugarcane is grown in some areas too. Maize and Black gram and grown in autumn. Cattle of indigenous type are kept for dung and draft power and they graze mainly in the forest.

*Forest protection committee*

Some semblance of forest protection was started about 8 years ago. Within 2 years some disputes about forest jurisdiction took place with Baliarpur hamlet. Regular protection was abandoned. In October 1990, the forester organized a meeting and informed about the Government order and urged the people to form a FPC. Since 2 years, regular patrolling has been going on.

*Structure of the committee and decision making*

One member from each of the 30 families constitutes the general body. There is a committee of 7 members who look after the functioning of the committee from within the village. There are also government nominees like forester, *Sarpanch*, revenue inspector as per the government order. Like the FPCs discussed earlier it is the village representatives who actually decide and implement the decisions. The *Sarpanch* concerned was not even aware of the committee or the Government Order. However the cases involving wood smuggling are handed over to the FD through the forester.

The FPC is recognized and finds a mention in the official records of the FD. A map demarcating the FPC area has been prepared and is given to the committee. A Dhandi (foot path) has been made for ground level demarcation.

*Rules and regulations*

Once again the underlying principles of consumptive use norm provides the basis for rules. The members are allowed to use the forest for meeting fuel wood NTFPs and timber requirement only for self-consumption. A species-use and frequency of use norm is followed.

**Table 6.3 :** Use of Various Tree Species by Kadalipal FPC

| *Purpose* | *Species* | *Frequency* |
|---|---|---|
| Fuel wood | Attendi, Khukundi, Nahalbelli | Once in 15 days |
| Small timber | Khakadi, Karada, Bamboo | Once in 2 years |
| Pole | Patuli, Asana, Bahada | Once in 4 years |
| Beam | Halda, Kanso, Seedha, Khakadi | Only at the time of house construction |
| Plough-making | Mainly Sal otherwise any timber species available | Once in a year |
| Long Pole | Sal | Once in 3 years |

The committee mentioned that it does not permit outsiders to use their forests. But this is obviously not the case as was mentioned by neighbouring villagers. The committee uses such opportunities to build their village development fund.

*Conflicts between villages*

Kadalipal FPC experience raises the issue of access to forest between immediate and far away communities. Undercurrent of resentment is reflected in the sentiments of Katiakateni and Kuntabathi. Often such situations can flare up as in the case of conflict between Negiapasi and Beltigiri.

In January 1992, Nagiapasi village was assigned 307 ha. of forest area in the Kapilas reserve for protection in the presence of collector and the members of legislative Assembly. This forest has a reasonable vegetative cover. The neighbouring village Beltigiri was assigned 200 ha. of another patch in the same reserve but much more degraded. A sketch map-8 depicts the above scenario. Because of better forest cover in Nagiapasi's patch, Biltipuri people entered the area for the use of forest. This led to a conflict. The *Sarpanch* who belongs to Biltigiri is the format president of both the FPCs but has taken the stance beneficial to his home village. The collector intervened in the conflict and put forward the following proposal.

1. FD will open a fuel wood depot to meet Beltigiri's requirement
2. Plantation on 20 ha. of fuel wood species on Beltigiri's patch
3. Beltigiri could send their women twice a week for fuel wood collection. No one else would be allowed

The *Sarpanch* in turn has put forward another proposal

1. Revision of area allotted
2. Men should be allowed, as women from certain high caste do not go for fuel wood collection.
3. Permission for chipping of wood into certain sizes for easy bundling while carrying.

No compromise has been reached so far. In the meantime the Beltigiri people have closed access to Banks, dispensary and college for the Nagiapasi people. But conflict indirectly improved the forest protection and forest offences to some extent have been reduced.

# 7

# FOREST MANAGEMENT IN SOUTH EAST ASIA

Having studied India's JFM programme intrinsically, now we will look into a few governmental forest programmes of South East Asia. Purpose of such study will be relevant for two reasons. First, like India many or most of the South East Asian countries' forest policy was originally designed by their colonial ruler to meet their own interests. These policies have increasingly imposed governmental control over the region's forest resources through their centralized forest department or such agencies. Land legislation either ignored or little recognized the customary rights of long-term occupants or indigenous communities. The accelerated deforestation indicates the failure of centralized forest management system. Many scientists argue that population growth and commercialisation of natural resources are responsible for deforestation. However, the most crucial reason for failure of centralised management may be the institutional failure or absence of proper institutional arrangement for forest management.

Second, in recent time many of the previously existing common property management regimes of Asia have collapsed under variety of pressure (Jodha, 1990). Population growth and commercialisation of forest produce may be one of the major reasons for such collapse. But one can hardly deny that alienation of locals from forest management is also largely responsible for it (Poffenberger, 1990). In this chapter, first we shall analyze the process of social forestry development in South and South East Asia in general and then we shall look into the forest management systems of Java and Philippines in particular. This will help us to understand how important people's participation is for sustainable forest management.

**Social Forestry in South and South East Asia**

Concept of social forestry has rapidly gained acceptance since its inception in the second half of the 1970s. Since that time many efforts have been undertaken for operationalising the concept. Often on, many of these efforts took place within the framework of internationally sponsored forestry development programmes and projects on experimental basis. But increasingly social forestry has been included within the forestry development strategies of the national forestry service in tropical countries. Consequently, social forestry has now become firmly incorporated in the repertoire of accepted approaches towards forest management. Concurrently an increasing amount of scientific studies have been carried out to assess the major impact of the social forestry programme. Main thrust of these assessments was to identify and describe the diversity in activities involved in social forestry, and to evaluate the potentials and constraints of different social forestry practices. Since its inception, much has been learned about the principles of social forestry and the relevance of various approaches towards implementation of this concept. Here a review will be given about the reasons for emergence of the concept and about the major lessons learned during the decades of social forestry development in South and South East Asia. The concept of social forestry incorporates both forestry development policies and forest management practices. It will be argued that this conceptual ambiguity can be overcome by making an analytical differentiation between social forestry as a concept in forestry policy and community forestry as a concept for forest management. Such differentiation assists in obtaining a better understanding about the diverse roles and responsibilities of the various actors involved in social forestry development. Moreover, it illustrates a theoretical perspective, in which the interaction between social forestry policies and community forest management practices is considered as a social interface problem. Such a perspective can assist in better appreciating that social forestry development is not just a linear process of transferring improved forestry practices from professional foresters to villagers. It is rather a social negotiation process whose outcome is subject to various factors outside the scope of influence of social forestry projects. Therefore, stimulation of social forestry calls for a new perspective in forestry. This perspective focuses not only on technical practices but also on processes of social interaction.

*The emergence of social forestry*

In the mid 1970s, important changes in thinking took place about the role of forestry in rural development. One of the first signs of this new thinking was the introduction of the term 'social forestry' in India in 1976. In a report of a National Commission on Agriculture it was recommended that rural people should be stimulated to contribute towards the maintenance and regeneration of forest and tree resources:

> *'Free supply of forest produce to the rural population and their rights and privileges have brought destruction to the forest and so it is necessary to reverse the process. One of the principle objectives of social forestry is to make it possible to meet the needs (for forest products for rural people) in full from readily accessible areas and thereby lighten the burden on (industrial) production forestry' (GoI, 1976 in Chambers et all, 1989).*

In the same year FAO started a new programme on forestry for local community development. In 1978, this programme published an overview paper about the role of forestry or local community development in which the term 'community forestry' was introduced. This term involves a community either through activities by individual households or through community as a whole (FAO, 1978). The objectives for community forestry were as follows:

a. the provision of fuel and other goods essential to meet the basic needs at the rural household as well as community level,

b. the provision of food and environmental stability necessary for continued food production,

c. the generation of income and employment in the rural community.

Additional stimulus to the evolution of the new concepts of social and community forestry was provided by an influential World Bank review of forestry development policy (World Bank, 1987), the IRDC study on 'Trees, food and people' (Bene et al., 1977), as well as the deliberations at the 8th World Forestry Congress held in Jakarta in 1978.

The Indian report highlighted the role of social forestry as a contribution to improve forest management. In contrast, the FAO report put more attention on the rural development context of community forestry as well as its contribution towards improved land use. The World Bank report emphasized that the major contribution of forestry to development will come from its impact on indigenous people. The IRDC report elaborated this point by stressing the importance of paying more attention towards the possibility to integrate forest production and crop cultivation.

After several initial discussions about the precise definition and interpretation of the terms social and community forestry (FAO, 1985; Arnold, 1987 and 1991; Wiersum, 1990) in the middle of the 1980's, it became generally agreed that the concepts are basically synonymous. It can best be defined as any forest management activities of situations, which closely involve local people in forestry and tree growing activities, for which rural people assume (part of the) management responsibility, and from which they derive a direct benefit through their own efforts (Gregersen et al., 1989; Wiersum,1990). This definition emphasizes that social forestry is a collective name for variety of forest management strategies. These strategies pay special attention to the equitable distribution of forest products in relation to the needs of various groups within the population (often, but not exclusively, with special emphasis on the fulfilment of forest related needs of the underprivileged groups of the population). The main aim is elicit participation of local organizations and people in the management of forest resources and wood biomass. There is not just one objective for stimulating social forestry, but rather a group of objectives, which are partly overlapping and partly divergent (FAO, 1985):

a. to increase the utilization of human resources for managing degraded and marginal lands to counteract the process of deforestation,
b. to contribute to the general socio-economic development of rural people through employment generation, institution building and by promoting agricultural production,
c. to ensure that rural people can produce, or have better access to certain basic needs in the form of essential forest and tree products and services,
d. to address the needs and aspirations of specific underprivileged groups within the rural population, such as subsistence farmers, landless families or other sectors of the rural poor.

These concepts do not involve one specific forestry development approach, but rather a group of different approaches. The original Indian report indicates farm forestry, extension forestry and rehabilitation of scrub and degraded forests. The FAO report mentions farm forestry, woodlot management, forest product manufacturing and forest utilization by forest dwellers. Gradually it became accepted, however, that rather than characterizing social forestry strategies on the basis of their technical dimensions, they can much better be differentiated on the basis of their social dimensions. Important differences still exist in respect to what organization is primarily responsible for managing the forest/tree resources. Broadly speaking, such management responsibilities may belong to the community at large or communal groups, to private households or to the public sector. These different organizational arrangements are of primary importance for deciding the kind of management strategy to be pursued. Consequently, three general social forestry strategies are distinguished: community or communal forestry, farm forestry and publicly managed forestry for local community management. Another factor of diversification is the actual degree of control, use right or ownership of the forest manager over the forest/tree resources. Once again, a major differentiation can be made between community, private or public control. Many additional characteristics can be used to delineate the strategies even further, e.g. whether they concern basically subsistence or commercial activities (FAO, 1985, Arnold, 1987, Wiersum, 1990). Obviously, each of these different approaches has its merits and constraints. Many of which only became apparent as a result of the gradual experience obtained during their implementation.

### *A decade of social forestry development*

The strategy for forestry development has received much attention since the need to develop social forestry was identified. Many of the international donor agencies quickly accepted this new approach to forestry development. Since the early 1980's, an increasing number of social forestry projects have been implemented. As result of all this action, much practical experience and empirical information have been collected about the specific characteristics potentials and constraints of various social forestry strategies (FAO,1985; Arnold, 1987, 1991; Aquino et al. 1987; Wiersum 1990; Gilmour and Fisher, 1991; Skutsch, 1994). This has enabled us to distinguish social forestry development into three broad phases viz. an experimental phase, a consolidation phase, and a diversification phase (Table 7.1).

**Table 7.1 :** Phases in Social Forestry Development

| *Period* | *Social Forestry Approach* |
|---|---|
| Experimental phase (late 1970's to mid 1980's) | Emphasis on village woodlots and individual tree growing based on scaling-down of conventional forestry practices as a means to address fuel wood and desertification problems |
| Consolidation phase (2nd part of 1980's) | Increased understanding about the role of trees in livelihood strategies of villagers. Less emphasis on firewood, more on multi-product systems and integration of tree growing with agriculture. Increased recognition of significance of indigenous agro-forestry practices. Less emphasis on community forestry approaches. |
| Diversification phase (early 1990's) | Increased emphasis on conservation and management of existing forests, including controlled utilization of non-wood forest products. New understanding about the role of common property and joint forest management. Recognition of the need to conserve the cultural integrity of tribal forest dwellers. Increased attention to integrate forestry activities in local-level land use planning. |

Two of the main factors underlying the emergence of the concept of social forestry in the mid 1970's, were the concerns about the poor man's energy crisis and desertification. To overcome these problems increased rates of reforestation was considered essential (Spears, 1983). Consequently, in developing social forestry initially much attention was focused on the establishment of new tree plantations. Much attention was given to the establishment of village woodlots. This approach was based on the consideration that forests were public property, which should be managed for the general good of local people. Furthermore, it was assumed that such communal management would allow economics of scale in establishing and maintaining a forest cover. These assumptions were thus still rather similar to the assumptions underlying the model of conventional plantation forestry. Only difference was that this model was scaled down so as to fit the level of village institutions rather than state institutions. In addition, this approach was also favoured for reforestation of communal wastelands. Many of these first communal forestry projects met with less than anticipated success. Important factors which contributed to this disappointing result were identified as the lack of social homogeneity at village level, the presence of conflicting local interests and an unequal power base in participation (FAO, 1985, Arnold, 1987, 1991).

Only in some specific cases the communal approach to social forestry was successful. Two early examples were the village forestry programme in Korea and the Azad Kashmir project in Pakistan. However, these two projects differed from the usual village forestry projects in some important aspects. In Korea, the reforested lands were privately owned and the communal management organization was carried out as a cooperative activity. This approach fitted very well with the prevalent government policy to stimulate agricultural production through a national system of rural cooperatives (Gregersen, 1982). In Pakistan, reforestation activities were carried out in such communal lands which had in fact already been informally partitioned into private land (Cernea, 1985). A third example of a relatively success was the community forestry programme in Nepal (Gilmour and Fisher, 1991, Bartlett, 1992). Here, as well as in other countries, it was found that social forestry development could well be based on traditional indigenous forest management systems (Olofson, 1980; Fisher 1989; Persoon and Wiersum, 1991).

Due to the disappointing results of these village forestry projects, gradually more attention was given by development planners to the stimulation of tree growing practices by private people. Several early farm forestry projects, such as the PICOP project in the Philippines (Hyman, 1983) and the Gujarat Social Forestry Project in India (Spears, 1983) were considered very successful. Especially in Gujarat, many more trees had been planted than originally envisaged. However, it was gradually recognized that such farm forestry projects may have several undesired social consequences and that they are not suitable under all land tenure conditions. The stimulation of commercial farm forestry had in several cases benefited relatively well-to-do farmers. Landless people were mostly negatively affected by these projects because of loss of employment opportunities as agricultural labourer and loss of access to previously existed free fuel wood resources. In these cases, the different interpretations of the objectives of social forestry became clearly demonstrated. While some people were impressed by the mass scale plantation (more than what was targeted) (Spears, 1983), other people strongly criticized the results for their undesired social consequences (Shiva ct al., 1982). Later group even questioned moral of social forestry programme and termed it as perversion of a rural development effort and anti poor programme (Blair, 1986). The different viewpoints clearly illustrate the different interpretations as to whether social forestry should be based on the objective of increased utilization of human resources for better managing forest resources, or on the objective of addressing the needs and aspirations of underprivileged groups within the rural society (Seymour, 1991). As a result of these discussions the potentials and constraints of farm forestry became clarified, and the need to give more attention to the integration of tree growing and agricultural activities was recognized (FAO, 1985; Arnold, 1987, 1991; Wiersum, 1990).

At the end of 1980's, it became gradually recognized, that the reforestation approach needed to be augmented by giving more attention to forest management issues. This understanding arose as a result of several observations:

a. In spite of the increased rates of reforestation, the process of deforestation and forest degradation continued unabated. Consequently, it was recognized that in addition to creating new forest resources, equal attention should be given to the maintenance of the still existing forest resources.
b. From an ecological point of view, it became recognized that the scope of natural regeneration of degraded forest areas was much greater than the anticipated target. In several cases it was found that in case of effective protection, the productivity of the natural vegetation was at least equal to that of plantation (Bajaj, 1990). Such protection should be ensured by changing the uncontrolled open-access utilization practices into community-controlled utilization and management practices. Furthermore, also

the newly established plantations needed protection and a proper management regime.

c. As a result of the experiences gained with the first generation of social forestry projects, much had been learned about the variable ways in which these resources have been traditionally managed. The improved knowledge about the different kinds of indigenous forest utilization and management systems indicated the scope for further stimulation and adaptation of community management of natural forests (Fisher, 1989; Arnold, 1991).

Concomitantly interest arose again in the potentials for development of communal forestry due to the recognition that increased attention needed to be given to the proper management of the existing vegetation. The experiences of the first generation communal forestry projects resulted in an understanding that the joint residence in a village and presence of communal lands form an effective basis for communal forest management. Communal forest management is normally best assured by common interests (Cernea, 1989; Arnold 1993;, Mol and Wiersum, 1993). For instance, the experiences with the community forestry programme of Nepal had revealed, that the communal approach at specific user groups consisting of villagers with similar forest related interests is better than administrative village units (Gibbs and Bromley, 1989). A second factor which contributed to the renewed interest to communal forestry, was the emergence of a new scientific interest in the management of common properties (Gibbs and Bromley, 1989; Arnold, 1933; Mol and Wiersum, 1993). This resulted in the recognition that a clear distinction should be made between open access resources utilization and common property resource utilization. The rural poor better understood the complementary role of the common property resources compared to private resources. Finally, the major requirements for effective common property management were identified, i.e. the existence of a local organization with the following characteristics (Gibbs and Bromley, 1989):

a. A structure for group members to make decisions on the required resource management practices, group control over the behaviour of the group members, which ensures that the planned management practices area carried out, ability to control the distribution of collected forest products, ability to exclude outsiders.
b. Local organization may consist of either a specific user group or cooperative with selected membership from within a village, a village organization, of a tribal organization at supra-village level.

These new insights were not only important in reassessing the potential for communal forestry but they have also been instrumental in the development of a new approach to social forestry in the form of so-called Joint Forest Management. This approach has been particularly developed as a means for managing the still existing forest vegetation and regenerating degraded forestlands.

The social forestry approach is based on the assumption that the conservation of still existing (natural) forests is best assured by official legal state control coupled with active involvement of local villagers in managing the forests for local community needs. In this case the official ownership as well as the overall responsibility for formulating the executive management plan rests with a public forest management organization. But a major part of this responsibility is delegated to local community groups once they receive a (long-term) forest occupancy right or forest utilization permit. This cooperative forest management approach was pioneered since the early 1980's in both South East Asia and India (Poffenberger, 1990). These early experiences as well as the growing understanding about the scope for common property forest management has contributed significantly to the recognition of the potential of the social forestry strategy.

In addition to these developments with the realm of social forestry, a rather independent development within the realm of nature conservation also contributed to the growing interest in forest management by local community groups. In the first place, for proper conservation of national parks and nature reserves, it was found that increased attention should be given to the conflicts that often arise from incompatibilities between the livelihood strategies of local people and conservation objectives. Consequently, the attention became focused on improved methods for managing the boundaries (of Buffer zones) where these incompatibilities are most pronounced (Sayer, 1991; Hall and Rodgers, 1992). The integration of rural development activities and forest management for local needs should pay the way towards more successful nature conservation.

In the second place, it became increasingly recognized, that in many cases indigenous people had been able to utilize and manage their forest resources in a relatively sustainable way (Olofson, 1980; Denslow and Padoch, 1988; Persoon and Wiersum, 1991). Especially with respect to the problem of deforestation in tropical rainforests areas, it was increasingly argued that indigenous forest utilization and management practices are intrinsically more sustainable than large-scale commercial timber exploitation. This may be due to these people's dependency on non-timber forest products which they try to sustain for their own survival. Hence further stimulation for fostering such sustainable practices was strongly felt. It also became increasingly recognized, that many tribal people living in forest areas are culturally dependent upon these forests. Thus they can justly claim forestland as their ancestral lands. Consequently, it is gradually being acknowledged that the traditional land rights and forest management systems of tribal people should be officially recognized. The social forestry approach in which forest management responsibility is returned to tribal groups has especially gained credit in Latin America (Redford and Padoch, 1992), but is not much practiced in Asia.

The growing interest in community involvement in managing natural forests has brought a change in the profile of target group of social forestry projects. Originally, when social forestry primarily addressed the energy and desertification concerns, the attention was mainly focused on involving the sedentary farmers living in tree scarce areas outside the major forest complexes. The new approach towards community involvement in natural forest management however, involves the people living in the forests. In many cases this concerns tribal people engaged in shifting cultivation and /or forest gathering activities. Consequently, the objective of the social forestry has gradually become interpreted to include the need for protection of the cultural integrity of tribal forest dwellers.

The understanding about the pluralistic way in which local people interact with forest resources in dependence of socio-economic and cultural conditions has greatly increased. This happened due to the increased attention paid to the diverse patterns of forest resource use by either sedentary agriculturist, shifting cultivators or hunter-gatherers (Padoch and Vayda, 1993) and the different ways in which they can be involved in forest management. This understanding led to the question how to deal with such heterogeneity. It was acknowledged that a combination of social forestry development measures was necessary to address the different target group and diverse local needs. In order to assure that such activities do not overlap or compete with each other, attention should not only be given towards stimulating forest management practices but also towards improving forest land use planning. In the first place, agreements have to be made with respect to which kinds of forest products can be collected by different user groups in different land use zones. Further, the agreement need to be worked out on division of management responsibility for various zones. For instance, if various forest user groups are involved in managing the forest, clear boundaries between these various areas have to be established (Sarin, 1993). Gradually various approaches towards local level land use planning can be incorporated in social forestry projects (Hardcastle, 1989; Van der Bliek, 1991; Ven der Hoek, 1991).

*Key learning*

All these experiences have greatly broadened the empirical knowledge base about the strengths and weaknesses of different approaches of social forestry. Gradually, new important insights emerged in respect to both technical and social aspects of social forestry. A decade of social forestry has significantly increased the understanding about:

a. the diversity of social forestry strategies, each having its own specific characteristic, advantages and limitations with respect to various forest management and social development objectives,
b. the variable ways in which rural people depend upon forest and tree resources for their livelihood strategies, and the fact that they often have organized themselves already either at household or communal level for carrying out forest management activities. In many cases, social forestry projects may be directed at further adaptation of such indigenous forest management practices in order to adjust them to changes in external conditions (new forest legislation, increased commercialisation).
c. the importance of giving attention to all technical aspects of forest management (forest land-use planning, forest rejuvenation, forest protection, controlled forest utilization) rather than to some selected components such as reforestation only. Forest management does not only refer to such technical arrangements, but also the social arrangements involved in the protection and controlled utilization of forests resources. Thus in social forestry attention should be given to both the need for possible introduction of new technical forest/tree resource management practices as well as the need for creating effective local forest management organizations to ensure an equitable distribution of the forest products.
d. the major differences between conventional forestry and social forestry, both with respect to the kind of actors involved, as well as its technical and organizational characteristics are given in Table 7.2.

**Table 7.2 :** Key Characteristics of Conventional and Social Forestry in Tropical Countries

| *Role of actors involved* | *Conventional forestry* | *Social forestry* |
|---|---|---|
| Forest users | Mainly urban people and forest industries | A large variety of rural and urban groups |
| Forest managers | Professional foresters | Both community groups, farmers and professional foresters |
| Function of professional forester | Omnipotent manager | Either advisor or co-manager with local people |
| Technical Characteristics Natural systems | (Semi) natural forests and timber plantations with emphasis on trees, soil and water and wildlife | All kinds of (semi-) natural and cultivated wood biomass and associated forages, crops and /or livestock |
| End products | Mainly timber, some minor forest products, regional environmental services | All possible wood and non-wood forest products for subsistence and commercial use, environmental services at local and regional scale |
| Problem identification | Government based sustainable output of required products and Regional environmental protection | Village-based Maintenance of production capacity of forests and associated agri-cultural lands |
| Organizational characteristics West ownership | State or commercial enterprises | Either state, communal or private |
| Fanning process | Professional blueprints | Process approach at local level |
| Control functions | State forest service backed by legislation | Combined local and state control |
| Arrangement between manager and user | Formal | Both formal and informal |

## Forest Management in Java

*Changing face of forest management policy in Java*

The government of Indonesia recognizes some 6000 forest villages in Java. The island has almost one fourth of its area as official forestland (more than three million hectare). Till recent Tsunami devastation an estimated twenty million people were reported as highly dependent on forest resources for food, fodder, fuel wood and building materials. Many of the Java's poorest residents own little or no land and residing far from alternative employment opportunities (Peluso and Poffenberger, 1989).

*Perum Perhutani*, State Forest Corporation (SFC) for Java classifies most forestland in Java as production forest. Earlier SFC focussed mainly on revenue generation and stringent law enforcement. It considered any activity of forest dwellers in forest area as an act of intrusion. SFC is one of the most legally and financially powerful body in Java. Later on it was given a mandate to take up income and employment generation programmes for forest villages.

Rural people particularly forest dwellers, however, have generally been terrified by the SFC. They perceived SFC as paramilitary force who is quick to use repressive measures to restrict people's access to forest resources. SFC mostly treated forest dwellers as trespassers except when SFC engaged them in reforestation programme as labourers. Such engagement was done mainly in two forms, a. *Cemplongan* - in which villagers are paid daily wages for land preparation and tree plantation, and b. *Tumpang sari* or *Taungya* - in which villagers are allowed to cultivate food crops on forest land during first two years of plantation and establishment in return for the planting and caring of tree seedlings.

Since 1940 dispute over landownership and forest degradation began which later on became serious threat to SFC. Forest management through law enforcement was gradually proven increasingly non-functional in the face growing rural food insecurity and demand for cultivable landownership. While *Cemplongan* and *Tumpang sari*, welcomed by villagers as temporary sources of wage income and access to land, did not provide them any long-term incentive for forest protection. In 1980s, SFC was compelled to rethink its land management policies owing to the continuing loss of forest cover due to theft, fire, and uncontrolled grazing, as well as frequent violent confrontations between SFC and villagers.

Since 1970s, the SFC leadership started supporting various

income generating programmes in order to minimize the conflict between SFC and villagers. However, when such measures failed to pacify the villagers, SFC initiated social forestry programme with the assistance from Ford Foundation. The primary aims of the social forestry programme was to reduce conflict by responding to rural communities' need and reviving traditional (pre colonial) forest management system to some extent.

*The Java social forestry programme*

In 1986, with further support from the Ford Foundation, the SFC launched thirteen social forestry pilot projects on degraded forestlands in west, central, and east Java. Although based on the traditional *Tumpang sari* reforestation system, the social forestry pilot projects incorporated marginal but potentially significant modifications in the agro forestry system as well as its earlier social approaches. Compared to traditional *Tumpang sari*, social forestry is designed to offer the farmer greater volume of benefits, a wider range of benefits, and benefits over a longer period. Because the timber trees (species such as teak or pine) are spaced more widely than in traditional *Tumpang sari*, farmers participating in social forestry have both more space and additional seasons to plant food crops before the canopy closes. Farmers are also allowed to plant non-food crop species, such as fodder grasses and fuel wood trees, as well as fruit trees and other horticultural crops previously forbidden on forestlands. Finally, at social forestry sites, farmer's access to the land can be extended until the timber is harvested, allowing them continued access to non-timber products and the opportunity to cultivate shade-tolerant species beneath the forest canopy.

The social forestry programme has also attempted to stimulate a gradual change in the relationship between SFC personnel and participating farmers different from that of traditional *Tumpang sari* relationship. Forest rangers were given training on how to approach forest villages as community development agents rather than as law enforcement officials. Villagers, rather than relating to the SFC as individual contract labourers, are encouraged to form 'forest farmer groups' (*Kelompok Tani Hutan*, or KTH) to enter into forest management agreements with the SFC on a collective basis. Although, each farmer is allocated an individual plot of approximately 0.25 ha, KTHs plots vary in size, but are usually divided into subgroups of 10 to 20 members. Programme guidelines assert that KTH members are to be involved in planning the social forestry site and are to be given a degree of choice in the non-timber species to be planted. The KTH is to meet regularly with SFC staff and to organize cooperative workdays and savings-and-loan activities.

*Contractual agreements*

The forest management agreement or contract currently in use in Java was drafted at a workshop in 1986 (Barber 1989) and is based on the *Tumpang sari* contract used by the SFC for labourers in reforestation projects. The contract specifies the agro-forestry system to be implemented and the rights and obligations of each party. It is signed by all members of the KTH and a district-level SFC official and is witnessed by a local government official.

The only right of participating farmers recognized by the old contract was the right to food crops grown on the site. In contrast, the social forestry contract recognizes farmer's rights to horticultural products and their rights to receive technical assistance and input loans from the SFC. As per new contract the SFC is obligated to provide technical assistance and input loans in addition to seedlings. The SFC retains the right to determine the agro-forestry system, rights to the land and the tree stems, and the right to terminate the rights of those who violate the terms of the agreement. KTH members are obligated to follow SFC direction, repay loans, and participate in guarding and protecting the forest at the planting location and surrounding areas. The contract includes seedling survival standards to evaluate farmer performance, but these standards are to be waived if the SFC fails to deliver obligatory services.

An important difference between the old contract and the new is the renewal opportunity of the latter. While regular *Tumpang sari* contracts expire after at most 2½ years, the social forestry contract can be extended at 2 years intervals throughout the length of the timber rotation. The renewal of the contract was intended to assure farmers of their continued access to products from horticultural and shade-tolerant species. The process of completing the contract was envisioned to serve as a catalyst for a participatory process between SFC staff and KTH members.

The training of SFC field staff in community organization skills has been conducted by *Yayasan Bina Swadaya* (Foundation for Community Self-help, henceforth *Bina Swadaya*) with financial support from the Ford Foundation. *Bina Swadaya*, a nationally prominent NGO, has also fielded one advisor in each province to provide back up for field staff in KTH development. Although the pilot projects are staffed by a mix of internally and externally recruited field workers, project sites opened during the last 4 years of expansion depend on regular SFC forest rangers and guards who have been given special training in community organization techniques. Early program experience has been documented by the Center for Development Studies of Bogor Agricultural University. With support from the Ford Foundation, undergraduate, masters, and doctoral students have conducted case study based researches at pilot project sites.

Initial positive experience with the pilot projects has motivated the SFC to expand the program to some 150 additional sites in 1987 and 1988, and expansion for the 1989-93 period is slated to cover almost 50,000 ha. An evaluation revealed that the rapidity of the program expansion simultaneously indicates and threatens the programmes initial success. The addition of new sites has outpaced the training of personnel to staff them. It has overburdened an already weak planning and monitoring capability of SFC officials who are attempting to incorporate social forestry's major features into the agency's standard operating procedures.

### *Problems*

In addition to problems directly related to the rapid expansion, other problems have emerged and are awaiting attention from overstretched programme proponents. Poor and landless farmers are supposed to be given preferential access to participation in the KTH. However, preliminary evidence indicates that many factors other than equity, including past performance in *Tumpang sari* and ability to make an irregular payment to forestry officials, come into play in participant selection (Sunderlin 1990). Poor households are unable to take time away from wage labour opportunities to make the initial investment in cultivating a social forestry plot. Further, the opening of a social forestry project represents the closing of an open access resource albeit one of low productivity. This exclusion of poorer elements of the KTH community could easily make them worse off.

Significantly, the rest of the community apparently does not respect the rights conveyed to the farmers over fruits, fuel wood, and fodder products. Non-KTH members continue to treat these products as open access resources, so the participating farmer is seldom the one to enjoy them. The fact that KTH members have not chosen to press the issue with village officials or to set up a rotational guard system (such as that used in West Bengal) to protect their plots may be an indication of the low value of the products lost through such pilferage. One reason that the potential benefits to each farmer are so low is that at many sites all applicants were accepted into the KTH resulting in tiny individual plot size. While programme guideline specify that each farmer should receive 0.25 ha, in some sites plots are as small as 0.10 ha.

Low production per plot, pilferage by other community members, and the yet-to-be proven viability of shade-tolerant crops in the agro-forestry system raise serious questions about the sustainability of the social forestry programme. Ironically, KTH members (rather than the foresters) have begun to unilaterally abrogate contracts, abandoning their plots after the tree canopy closes. It may be that for the programme to succeed, the SFC will have to provide a longer period of agricultural benefits to participating farmers, perhaps through alley-cropping, or entitle them to a share of timber at harvest.

Activists stressed upon the role of the contract in protecting SFC rights. Apparently the most important role of the contract has been to reassure the SFC that expanding and extending farmers access rights- particularly the addition of horticultural species to the agro-forestry system-would not lead to unwelcome claims to ownership of the land or the trees. It was reported that a new clause was to be added to the contract in the near future, forbidding signatories from disputing the status of the land. The existing contract already implicitly affirms the SFC's property right, and program guidelines forbid the inclusion of disputed lands. Nevertheless risk of the contract being misused has intimidated farmers into relinquishing claim to such lands. When confronted with this possibility, two suggestions were by and large emerged at activists circle: 1. an exchange of rights (in the form of pending claims on disputed forest land) for program benefits (by singing a contract relinquishing their claims) would be a good deal for the farmer, and 2. the function of the contract to specify farmers responsibilities. A case was cited in which an SFC official used the terms of the contract to convince a KTH to expel a member who was not fulfilling his obligations. So far lip service has been paid to the role of the contract in specifying farmer's rights and SFC's responsibilities. All acknowledge that due to the extreme imbalance of power between the two parties, these elements of the contract would have little meaning in the case of a dispute. The validity of these contracts has yet to be tested in court.

The role of the contract in regulating KTH membership also appears weak. Unofficial transfer of plots within and between households is apparently common. Wives of the predominantly male KTH members do not appear to be anxious over the fact that only their husbands sign the contract. However, when prodded by a researcher over what would happen in the case of divorce or polygamy, one group of women took a sudden interest in becoming co-signatories. Most forestry workers and male farmers dismiss the need for co-signatories. They insisted that community norms regarding inheritance in the case of death or abandonment would be followed regardless of the contract format. The potential role of the contract in educating the farmers as to their rights and responsibilities appears to be undermined at many sites by poor implementation. Workshop participants reported contracts being signed without a public reading, which is critically important in areas of high illiteracy. The contract itself is usually stored in the SFC sub district office, and copies are not routinely distributed to KTH. Formal extension of the contracts after the initial 2-year period is reported to be haphazard. Unfortunately more systematic data on implementation of the contract do not exist. None of the organizations that cooperate with the programme has focused on the agreement as a particular topic for research and monitoring. Programme managers from Bina Swadaya and the SFC have been slow to respond to the need for a special contract implementation handbook for field staff and an explanation of the contract in layperson's terms for farmers.

Java Social Forestry Programme has succeeded in achieving various secondary goals, including raising participants' income in the short run, increasing the variety of species they are allowed to plant, and establishing a working relationship between a forestry agency and an NGO. However, it appears to have fallen well short of achieving the primary objective of developing a community forestry management system. The potential of the contract to strengthen farmer's rights and catalyse genuine participation in forest planning and management has not been realized. While prior existence of the *Tumpang sari* system provided a basic legitimacy for granting farmers limited rights to forestlands and products, lingering colonial era attitudes on the part of both farmers and foresters have proven difficult to overcome. Probably, social forestry programme is becoming more like a regular *Tumpang sari* rather than the reverse.

**Forest Management in Philippines**

People living on upland public forest area have been a major factor in preserving the remaining forests of the Philippines. Their presence and management practices have helped to deter large-scale logging operations and encroachment by people from the lowlands. Many of these residents of forestlands practice indigenous agro forestry, an essential element of sustainable development in the Philippine uplands (Gasgonia, 1991).

Unfortunately, the Philippine government, since the Spanish

colonial period to the present, has been generally prejudiced against upland dwellers. People living within classified forestlands have long been indiscriminately labelled as destructive *Kaingineros* (i.e., slash and burn farmers). They have also been indiscriminately referred to as squatters on government lands (Act No. 274, 1901, Presidential Decree No. 705, as amended, 1975). It was only in 1982 (Letter of Instruction No. 1260, 1982), the long-term upland dwellers became eligible to participate in the Integrated Social Forestry Program of the then Ministry of Natural Resources. This recognition gave these dwellers official status with a definite government program that allowed them to stay where they were. Since then, many policies have changed, programmes have been strengthened, or forgotten, or cancelled, and new programmes have been initiated. Yet public awareness remained relatively low about the rights of Philippine's upland dwellers, especially indigenous cultural communities living within what are officially classified as public forestlands.

In the meantime, large-scale timber and non-timber concessions continue to deplete forest resources. The logging roads provide access to the forests from the lowlands, resulting in a steady influx of lowland migrants. Settlements of lowland migrants with slash- and burn farms using tilled mono-cropping methods have been continuing on both sides of these logging roads. This phenomenon accounts for accelerated resource depletion and increasing population densities in the remaining forests.

Long-term forest occupants face tremendous pressures to make quick decisions that may spell ecological disasters. Material benefits from cash crops work against traditional swidden farms that require long fallow periods. At the same time, national prejudice against cultural communities perpetuates ignorance of the ecological importance of indigenous methods of agro forestry. If upland dwellers are to be given a fair chance, decades of disenfranchisement and injustice must be eradicated and public sentiment must sway in their favour.

The time has come for both government and non-government organizations (NGOs) to ensure that long-term upland dwellers do not succumb to the prejudice that labelled them as forest destroyers. The issues of property rights and development assistance relative to large-scale concessions and other upland programmes need to be addressed. For its part, the government must take clear and decisive actions towards more community-based and environmentally sustainable programmes.

With the 1987 Constitution as its mandate, the government can establish and/or strengthen the necessary institutions to prioritise programmes for long-term upland dwellers. The rationale for these programmes is best expressed in Department Administrative Order No. 123, series of 1989:

1. The conventional practice of awarding forest product utilization permits/licenses to timber companies has denied legal access to these resources by rural communities.
2. Despite many decades of forest products extraction, poverty is still widespread in the uplands.
3. Forest conservation is an imperative precondition to sustainable development and requires the active participation of rural communities.

The historical as well as official significance of these words proclaims a policy shift towards forest management by upland dwellers. It follows that upland dwellers should now be better able to acquire legal rights to use natural resources within the traditional territories they occupy. This improved status should counteract the assumption of the Regalian Doctrine that all public lands are owned by the state.

Government policies and programmes in favour of upland dwellers already exist. Access benefits have trickled down to some communities, mostly to those with cultural and political unity. In many cases, however, where procedural and technical channels are clogged, immediate evaluation is necessary to institute corrective measures. Furthermore, the task at hand is not to merely ensure that benefits trickle down to target communities, but that they sweep through the entire nation, appropriately and efficiently.

*Government programmes*

The Department of Environment and Natural Resources (DENR)

has jurisdiction over public forestland in the Philippines. The DENR's mission is to promote the well being of the Filipino people through sustainable development of forest resources, optimal utilization of lands and minerals, ensuring social equity and efficiency in resource use, and enhancing effective environmental management. Under this mission, several DENR programmes and policies target people living on public forestland or upland dwellers as beneficiaries. These programmes can be grouped into (1) the Integrated Social Forestry Program (ISFP), and (2) The Action Task Force (TF-AD).

The ISFP, oldest among these DENR programmes, is centred on the concept of stewardship. Upland dwellers within public forestlands can secure a certificate of stewardship form the DENR and acquire exclusive rights to use and occupy land for 25 years, renewable for another 25 years (Letter of Instructions No. 1260, 1982). Stewardship certificates are issued to individuals and associations or indigenous communities.

The National Forestation Programme (NFP), through their more recent programmes, offers various livelihood opportunities to upland dwellers. The most popular program is contract reforestation, which is primarily a short-term employment agreement to undertake government reforestation projects (DENR Administrative Order No. 39, 1988). Contracts are awarded either through the family/community approach or through the corporate approach. The latter includes private corporations, NGOs, local government units, and other private sector entities.

By 1989, after the first year of implementation of contract reforestation, upland dwellers became apprehensive about their long-term prospects because employment is assured for only 3 years and tenure is not a project component. Their growing concern was addressed when the DENR offered a subsequent agreement under the NFP, called the Forest Lease Management Agreement, or FLMA (DENR Administrative Order No. 71, 1990). Holders of the FLMA may harvest, process, sell, or otherwise use the products grown on land covered by the agreement for a period similar to the ISFP.

*Other community-based program*

Community Forestry Management Agreements (CFMAs) offers

same 25-year lease period to upland dwellers as the ISFP does (DENR Administrative Order No. 123, 1989). The CFMA gives limited rights to upland dwellers to undertake timber-harvesting operations. Unlike the LFMA, the CFMA emphasizes community organizing and planning, and NGO involvement.

**Table 7.3 :** The Various Types of DENR Documents Issued

| *Program* | *Individual/Family* | *Community* | *Indigenous Peoples* |
|---|---|---|---|
| ISF | CSC | CCFS | CSC or CCFS |
| NFP | FCR | CCR | FCR or CCR |
| | FLMA | FLMA | FLMA |
| | CFMA | CFMA | |
| | MFPP | MFPP | MFPP or negotiated contract |
| TF-AD | CALC | CALC | |

CALC = Certificate of Ancestral land Claim, CCFS = Certificate of Community Forest Stewardship, CCR= Corporate Contract Reforestation, CFMA= Community Forestry Management Agreement, CSC= Certificate of Stewardship Contract, FCR = Family Contract Reforestation, MFPP = Minor Forest Product Permit, FLMA = Forest Lease Management Agreement, NFP = National Forestation Program, TF-AD = Ancestral Land Delineation Task Force.

The DENR is currently undertaking a nationwide delineation of ancestral domains through regional and provincial task forces as an exclusive service to Philippine indigenous cultural communities. The first task force, created in the Cordillera Administrative Region, serves as a model for other areas (DENR Special Order No. 31, 1990). Basically, the task forces seek to delineate the boundaries of ancestral domains through actual ground survey, and in the process, identify the specific indigenous cultural communities that have rights to these areas as traditional territories. The communities or individual members thereof are eventually issued Certificates of Ancestral Land Claims (CALCs). In terms of development assistance and land tenure, for a comparison of the government programmes see Table 7.4.

**Table 7.4 :** Comparison of DENR Programs

| *Program* | *Tenure (yrs)* | *Development Assistance* |
|---|---|---|
| ISF | 25 | Infrastructure support, credit assistance, planting stock production |
| Contract Reforestation | 3 | Employment for planting weeding, monitoring, evaluation |
| FLMA | 25 | Production sharing of income from the sale of timber harvested |
| CFMA | 25 | Community organizing, on-the-job training in forest management planning and conservation, livelihood opportunities in forest resource rehabilitation |
| Rattan | 10 | Rattan plantation establishment and development |
| TF-AD | - | Not specified |

CFMA = Community Forestry Management Agreement, FLMA = Forest Lease Management Agreement, ISF = Integrated Social Forestry, TF-AD = Ancestral Land Delineation Task Force.

## *Program analysis: Property rights and social benefits*

Each program has strong and weak points that can be used by upland dwellers to strengthen tenurial security and gain access to government services. These programmes give upland dwellers a choice of opportunities to work with government for advancing their interests. In turn, the government hopes this will result in better management of the uplands. Unfortunately, implementation is much impaired because of the confusion about these different programmes.

Large-scale concessions given by the DENR to business enterprises controlled and owned by a few rich individuals generally have priority over social forestry programmes. These concessions are given through TLA (Timber License Agreement), TPSA (Timber Production Sharing Agreement), PLA (Pasture Lease Agreement), AFLA (Agro-forestry Farm Lease Agreement), AGLA (Agro-forestry Grazing Land Lease Agreement), ITP (Industrial Tree Plantation), and IFP (Industrial Forest Plantation), among others. These permits prohibit further leases, agreements, or contracts even for areas covered under the NFP and the Community Forestry Programme. Even the ISFP has to forego its reforestation obligations and its commitment to upland dwellers if any party manage to acquire the above permits.

For instance, the ISFP can cover areas within existing large scale concessions, provided the area has been developed by the upland dwellers before 1982 and awarding the area to them will not conflict with the reforestation obligations of the licensee/ leaseholder. Tracing the origin of this provision is quite interesting. In 1988, Secretary Factoran issued the revised regulations for ISFP (DENR Administrative Order No. 97, 1988). In that order, he included TLA, PLA, AGLA, etc., as prohibited areas for ISFP. On 27 February 1991, he revoked the provision, so that upland dwellers can apply for areas within TLA, PLA, or AGLA, provided they can prove development activities before 1982 (DENR Administrative Order No. 04, 1991). This shift in policy must be interpreted to mean that the licensee is no longer preferred over the prospective ISFP participant.

Only reforestation obligations of the licensee/leaseholder can dislocate the prospective ISFP participant. Unless licensee/ leaseholder is able to indicate the actual reforestation that was undertaken by 1982 under ISFP, no protective cover would be given to licensee/ leaseholder. This operations plan should have been submitted and officially received by the then Bureau of Forest Development latest by December 1981. Rationally if no reforestation has been undertaken by the licensee/leaseholder by this time, the ISFP applicant should have been given the option to undertake this, with costs to the licensee/ leaseholder. Further all trees planted should be co-owned by the DENR and the ISF stewardship holder.

With respect to the recent programmes under the NFP, these licensed/contracted areas are listed as prohibited areas. Unlike the ISF stewardship contracts, the FLMA and the CFMA cannot be availed of by upland dwellers if the area is covered by licenses, agreements, or contracts. Facts and figures about these large-scale concessions provide distressing signals. In 1989, timber licenses, tree farms, forest plantations, or agro-forestry landholdings and grazing lands covered 5.490 million ha. Findings of evaluation of state of the Philippine uplands found it illogical to allow such large landholdings to persist and continue to breed poverty not only in the uplands but also in the entire nation. A similar argument against industrial and grazing agreements was also made.

**Table 7.5 :** Areas under Concession in Philippine (in million ha)

| *Agreement* | *1979* | | *1989* | |
|---|---|---|---|---|
| | *Number* | *Area* | *Number* | *Area* |
| Timber | 284 | 9.156 | 113 | 4.67 |
| Industrial | 45 | 0.039 | 375 | 0.468 |
| Grazing | 3,633 | 0.967 | 903 | 0.352 |
| Total | | 10.162 | | 5.490 |

*Source : Philippines Forestry Management Bureau (1989).*

There is a clear need for natural resource accounting to put implementation priorities in a more rational perspective. Without this, the false dichotomy between the economy and the environment leads policy makers to ignore or destroy the latter in the name of economic development (Gasgonia, 1991). Along this line, the DENR recently initiated studies in natural resource accounting in a deliberate effort to recognize the productive role of natural resources in state economy. Coupled with the strengthening of the Environmental Impact Assessment System in Philippines, the DENR is taking steps to recognize social benefits and social costs. The next step would be to remove the burden of social costs from the upland dwellers and redistribute them among the other communities. This is realistically correct if large-scale concessionaires cannot be made to answer for these costs. As a corollary to this, social benefits should be allocated to the upland dwellers who play crucial roles in sustainable development and not to the elite.

Consistent with these steps, a DENR administrative order need to be issued, revoking all provisions in its regulations that prioritise large-scale landholdings under social forestry programmes. The

Secretary to the DENR can make the areas within public forestlands available to social forestry programmes for national interest abrogating all permits and leases. It is possible because these permits, agreements, or contracts have provisions that allow the issuing authority to cancel, revoke, or revise the same for public interest. This unilateral authority may not even have to be invoked if a thorough performance evaluation determines that cancellations are warranted due to violations of forestry laws. In other words, there are various ways explicitly legal to get the same result. Therefore, it is a basic question of prioritising grassroots concerns over conservative policies that favoured economic and political elites.

Another important and urgent matter that needs attention is the right of indigenous cultural communities to their ancestral domains. The DENR has begun providing technical assistance to indigenous people by conducting ground surveys of their ancestral claims. Delineation is a mere preliminary step, nevertheless indigenous people have been able to assert their rights more eloquently because of its official stature. In practice, however, when these claims overlap with licensed areas, even the DENR surveyors and foresters need to get permission of the licensee to conduct the survey. Otherwise, they risk the ire of the licensee's guards who are often armed.

### *Development assistance*

From a regulatory standpoint regarding development assistance, there is confusion over whether the different DENR programmes, especially social forestry programmes, are mutually exclusive. Namely, the NFP takes priority over the ISFP, which in turn takes priority over licensed /contracted areas. Yet licensed/contracted areas take priority over NFP. There is a circuitous ambiguity here. Once the area has been declared for ISFP, the upland dwellers who are awarded ISFP contracts should not be excluded from the livelihood benefits of the more recent programmes under NFP. The strong but short-term appeal of NFP, as opposed to ISFP, is immediate cash through direct compensation by contract reforestation. This incentive should not work against the upland dwellers who may opt for the short-term NFP reforestation contracts by causing them to forfeit their privilege to avail of ISF stewardship contracts. In the same manner, if upland dwellers decide to apply for ISF contracts, they should not be excluded from the livelihood and financial benefits offered under other DENR programmes.

This exclusivity situation appears to have surfaced due to DENR's commitment to ISF stewardship contract holders that everything they produce within the area belongs to them (including trees, whether fruit or hardwood). Under contract reforestation, which is financially supported by loans from the Asian Development Bank, the DENR holds a major share in the trees planted in the area. Thus it has been argued that if a reforestation contract is given to ISF stewardship contract holders, the DENR loses its share in the trees planted and will have problems in repaying the loans obtained.

Without going into the intricacies of government debt service, the speculated problem of loss of share/ability to repay the debt can be easily answered by an administrative circular that specifies such sharing arrangements whenever ADB loan/fund assistance is availed upon by ISF stewardship contract holders. Under this method, upland dwellers, as well as forestry officials, will not be forced to select one program to the exclusion of others. These arguments also apply to indigenous peoples who have opted for Certificates of Ancestral Land Claims (CALC). Where physical inaccessibility no longer provides protection from encroachment, ancestral domains are kept intact through contractual arrangements with government agencies and private parties. These include employment, royalties, leases, and use of forest product privileges. The indigenous peoples insist on recognition of their ancestral rights more than anything else. Yet they are constrained by lack of legal documents to apply for social forestry programmes and abate immediate displacement. In fact, most of their rights, especially to ancestral domains, have never been directly recognized, in contrast to prior and vested rights of Spanish origins. The fact is that the indigenous peoples should be entitled for better privileges.

There is already some speculation that with the creation of TF-ADs and the issuance of CALSs, indigenous peoples will no longer participate in ISFP or the NFP in general. But when they do decide to avail of the livelihood and technical assistance under these programmes, they should not be turned away. Their participation in these programmes is not only for their own benefit, but also more to the benefit of government and society. It is because indigenous people hold their ancestral domains sacred. This is the essence behind the inclusion of the non-waiver provision is ISFP contracts concerning ancestral land rights.

## *Conclusion*

The DENR has been under new administration since 1987. Former Secretary Factoran has opened up greater opportunities for upland dwellers to gain legal access to forest and land resources. Policy changes and programme implementations have been responsive to the initiatives of NGOs and private voluntary organizations (Seymour and Rutherford 1990). Subsequent administrators should work toward streamlining the different social forestry programmes and coordinating efforts to give better services to upland dwellers. The DENR needs to make a clear and immediate pronouncement of priorities regarding its different programmes, with a definite emphasis on social forestry as conceptualised under the ISFP.

However, policy pronouncements and comprehensive programmes will remain empty promises if the DENR's key field officials do not take the necessary actions. Having a hung bureaucracy with a wide spectrum of concerns, the DENR serves upland dwellers through a decentralized structure. Successful implementation at the field level depends on the Regional Executive Directors (REDs). The REDs should receive clear instructions and motivation to implement social forestry programmes, and institutional support to strengthen their ability to follow up.

The basis for evaluating their performance should also give more weight to the impact of social forestry as a key result area. Evaluation should include not only number targets such as number of certificates issued and areas covered, but also socio-economic and cultural impacts of the programmes. This would allow the REDs to concentrate on coordinating the efforts to ensure greater impact. Furthermore, the REDs who work closely with NGOs and private voluntary organizations (PVOs) should be given better performance ratings. Social forestry programmes in the Philippines enjoy greater success by upland dwellers when NGOs and PVOs are present in the area. An ISFP can be a pragmatic institutional framework for upland dwellers if it is properly implemented and prioritised. It incorporates environmental enhancement and protection with livelihood technologies based on sustainable agro-forestry in the Philippine uplands. Eventually the upland dwellers will gradually assert their rights to these resources in all areas. They must be able to use the official documents to put pressure on government to prioritise social forestry programmes and to acquire better recognition of rights, including ownership, communal titles, and self-determination with respect to ancestral domains.

## End Notes

### Forest Management in Java

1. In addition to the reference cited in the text, this section is based on several formal and informal reports available to the author.
2. Land disputes have been a chronic headache for the SFC and have often concerned areas planted to perennial crops following the disruptions of the 1940s and mid 1960s.
3. KTH membership is predominantly a male domain. Although women provide a substantial share of total labour at the social forestry sites and often attend KTH meetings formal KTH membership is usually limited to the head of household, traditionally defined as the husband. However, most KTHs include few female heads of households, usually widows, as full members.

### Forest Management in Philippines

1. Philippine civil law recognizes possessor's rights over land when exercised in an open continuous, exclusive, and notorious manner for 30 years or more. However, jurisprudence is not settled about 'public forest land' and 'native titles,' or ancestral domains.
2. In this context, agro-forestry is defined as any sustainable land-use system that maintains or increases total yields by combining food (annual) crops

and/or livestock on the same unit of land, either alternately or at the same time, using management practices that suit the social and cultural characteristics of the local people and the economic and ecological conditions of the area.

3. 'Upland dwellers' refer to those who have occupied forestlands before 1982, as provided for in the Integrated Social Forestry Program, and shall include indigenous cultural communities and upland farmers.
4. As of 1989, there were 15.88 million ha of classified and unclassified forestlands, or about 53 percent of the total Philippine land area (Forestry Management Bureau 11989).
5. The ISFP imposed 1982 as a cut-off date for eligibility of upland dwellers to secure stewardship agreements. In accordance with the constitutional mandate for equality before the law, the licensee/ leaseholder must have conclusive documentary proof that an operations plan for 1982 was duly submitted and officially approved before 1 January 1982. Without such proof, no presumption lies in his/her favour.
6. Since the priority given to large-scale concessions was done through administrative regulations, the same can be revoked administratively (see Annex D for a draft Administrative Order).
7. The authority to revoke or cancel contracts because of national interest finds basis in the 1987 Constitution, Art. II Sec. 10, 22, and 23, Art. XII, Sec. 5, Art. XIV, Sec. 17.
8. The 1987 Constitution contains several provisions about the rights of the indigenous cultural communities to their ancestral domains / lands and makes reference to their customary laws as basis for the delineation of their traditional boundaries.
9. A CFSC area is a large area with the perimeters defined such that the resources within are for the exclusive use of the community. Within the CFSC area, there are individual and common areas that can be better developed through NFP technical and financial support. The CFSC is also popular among the indigenous peoples who practice integrated individual and communal forest management.
10. For commercial harvests that would involve transportation of goods from the area to the market or buyer, permits are required from the DENR.
11. The DENR has established regional NGO desk offices, directly under the supervision of the REDs. These NGO desk officers act as information centres and coordinate with NGOs and PVOs regarding implementation and policy reviews of DENR Programmes (DENR Administrative Order No. 120, 1989, memorandum from the Head Executive Assistant Gozun to all REDs/Project Managers, 23 August 1989).
12. Development in other arenas likewise needs to be attended to, especially those in Congress where the following bills are pending: Public Land Management Code, Forestry Code, Mining Code, and Ancestral Domain Commission.

# 8

# SELF-INITIATED AND NGO PROMOTED CBFMs IN INDIA

With increasing awareness for conservation and development of forests, increasing number of village communities are coming forward to participate in the management of village commons, particularly the forests. Village Committees/Village Forest Committees are the usual institutions constituted to enable them to manage forests on sustainable basis. These institutions emerged out of local initiation or crafted by various NGOs. The pattern of management, although same in principle, varies substantially depending on availability of community land, demands of the dependant communities, conditions, composition and age of the forest crop, local political and institutional arrangement, and ecological conditions. Taking these factors into consideration, various models are discussed here.

## Lapanga Forest Protection Committee

Lapanga is a large village located on the State Highway from Sambalpur to Rourkela at a distance of about 40 kms from Sambalpur. The total number of families in the village was about 335 in the year 2000, represented by all castes. The extent of village commons managed for forest production is of the order of 200 hectares. The important species are Sal and usual associates in dry zone like Terminalias, Kuruma, Kendu, Mohua etc. All age classes of trees are represented from over-mature to poles and saplings of coppice origin.

The village committee consists of members from both high and low castes of the village. The village committee is functioning since 1960s. The members are replaced as and when required. Amongst the office bearers of the committee, prominent are the president, secretary and treasurer. The committee usually sits for deliberations two to three times a year but additional sittings take place depending on exigencies. The committee is apolitical.

Management, distributes the forest products to every family on the basis of one share for one kitchen, besides ensuring protection of the community forest. Usually every family pays certain amount in cash every month for payment of wages to two watchmen engaged by the committee for protection of the forests. The committee also takes decisions regarding the amount of fees to be paid by each family in addition to the normal watch and ward fees for appropriating the usufructs. The treasurer maintains the detailed accounts of the funds collected. A part of the funds is utilized for community functions in the village like annual fairs, worship of village deity etc.

Besides meetings, the genuine and essential requirements of the villagers in respect to small timber, the committee time to time undertakes fuel wood and revenue generating tree felling. During past 40 years, the committee, beginning with the establishment of one Middle School, have now established a High School for the children of the village and neighbouring villages. Construction of school building, payment of salaries to the teachers, purchase of library books and science equipments etc. are done by utilizing the funds collected from the forests. This is a vivid example of the potential for development of villages by proper management of common property resources by the village committees without taking the support from the government.

*Strengths and weaknesses of the committee*

The members selected as office bearers are mostly natural leaders, representing various sections of the community. They are usually self-less, dedicated and committed workers. The committee usually remains free from political wrangling in the village. People normally have faith in the committee and never question their integrity. This is probably the biggest strength of the committee.

However committee suffers from certain weaknesses too. First, the committee does not have the legal backing for management of forests. The forests have never been declared as village forests. As per rules, the committee is not supposed to sell or barter the forest produces, but utilize it for own consumption. But they have been selling the surplus produce for developmental purposes because of sympathetic tolerance of the administration. Second, the members lack the technical know-how for the scientific management of the forest resources. Although restricted felling are usually carried out to remove the over matured trees, tending operations for improvement of the tree crop, are rarely undertaken. Harvesting is done manually only once, giving preference to retaining the economically beneficial species like Sal, Asan, Bija etc. The other species are usually felled for utilization. In the process, a mixed deciduous forest has almost turned into a pure crop of Sal with a few associates. Because of over-grazing by cattle and uncontrolled fires, natural regenerations fail to get established. These defects call for urgent amelioration. Third, because of lack of legal backing, protection against theft poses a problem.

*Can it be replicated?*

The village committee of Lapanga, probably is the oldest one in the state of Orissa engaged in management of forests on community land on a sustainable basis. The success achieved and the benefits derived by the villagers of Lapanga on a sustained basis, have motivated neighbouring villages to establish such committees for protection, management and development of natural forests. Hundreds of such village forest committees have already come up in the neighbouring areas comprising Rengali, Jharsuguda, Kulabera, Laikera, Kirimira, Govindpur, Laxmanpur, Kuchinda, Barkot and Rainmal C.D. blocks of Sambalpur District. There is ample scope for replication of such patterns in other areas with certain modifications as discussed in this book.

**Bichhakhani Village Forest Protection**

Bichhakhani is a small village in Barkot C.D. block of Deogarh Subdivision located about 15 kms away from Deogarh towards Calcutta on National Highway six. Youth Club of the village is very active. When the Social forestry programme in Orissa was launched with SIDA assistance, the members of the youth club came forward to participate in protection of natural forests and creation of new forests on barren community land. A path of degraded forests existed in about 30 hectares of land within the jurisdiction of the village. The youth club members decided to tend the degraded forests and protect it. They sought the support and guidance from the social forestry project and assistance was given for plantations activity on barren community land.

A village forest committee was constituted in 1988 taking members from all sections of the community as decided in a general meeting of the villagers in accordance with the provisions of Orissa village forest rules, 1985. With the active participation of the members of the youth club, the village forest committee functioned exceedingly well. Youth club members carried out the works like site preparation, nursery raising, planting and tending operations by voluntary contribution of labour. During 1988 and 1989, 10 hectares and 4 hectares of plantations were taken up respectively in the village. Besides these, rehabilitation of 20 hectares of degraded forestland was also taken up.

Since the members contributed labour voluntarily for execution of work, the funds earmarked for plantations were deposited in a passbook and village forest fund was created for development of forests during 1990. On the third year of committee formation and community plantation, the project personnel proposed a management plan in consultation with the village forest committee. Two members of the village forest committee were given crash training in forest management principles and practices.

According to the management plan prepared, first harvesting of the usufructs in shape of pruning, thinning and cleaning was taken up during November and December 1990. Usufructs were distributed on the principles of one share for one kitchen in the village after maintaining detailed accounts in a production and distribution register. The first test of the knowledge acquired for application came during the aforesaid operations, which they meticulously executed. The local youth club with the support of the leaders in the village contributed to the management of commons and for the development of the village. As of now the system has turned out to be fairly self-sustaining.

## Badamala Village Forest

Badamala is a medium-size village located on state highway from Sambalpur to Rourkela, 3 kms from Jharsuguda towards Sambalpur. There are five hamlets in the village with about 180 families representing all castes. The social forestry project started operating in this village from 1987. A village forest committee was constituted as per the provisions of the Orissa village forest rules, 1985. The most active member in the committee, besides others, was the president, who happened to be the *Sarpanch* for a pretty long period and hailed from the same village. He was the single most driving force, for successful management of man-made forests on village commons.

In 1987, an area of 10 hectares, which was the only piece of total barren community land in the village was selected for creation of a village woodlot. As per the decision of the committee, small timber species like Sesame, Gmelina, Dalbergia, Albezia and Bamboos were planted with fuel wood species like Cassia, Eucalyptus, Acacia, fruit trees namely Mango, Jack fruits, NTFP yielding species like, Neem, Karanj, Tamarind and fodder species like Subabul, Bahunia etc. As per the decisions of the committee, the seedlings were raised in three types of nurseries: one managed by the youth club, the second by the women's group and the third, by individual family. Plantations were done during June 1987 with lot of pomp and ceremony where the entire village community participated.

The village forest committee provided protection by collecting contributions from each family in cash and kind. This account was maintained by the committee and used for the payment of watchman engaged for the purpose. Acute scarcity of forest products probably motivated the villagers to pay their shares for development of forests with expectations to get the usufructs share during harvesting much in excess of the contribution paid.

The project personnel in consultation with the village forest committee prepared a management plan after a thorough inventory of the surviving plants. Two members of the village forest committee were trained in management principles and practices under a crash course organized by the project. The first harvesting was done sometime during December 1989 in the form of pruning, thinning and cleaning in the protected natural forests. The usufructs were distributed in the village as per the decisions of the committee. Some fees, as decided by the committee, were collected from each user of forest and were deposited in the village forest funds.

The village forest committee motivated individual families to take up nursery raising in their own house-hold premises for creation of forests in private wastelands and along boundaries of agricultural fields and homestead lands. It appears from the results achieved so far, that the village is going to become self- sufficient in respect of forest products on sustainable basis. The community plantation is also being managed scientifically.

## Bania Forest Protection Committee

Bania is 25 kms away from Dhenkanal town. It falls under the Sorsiapada Gram *Panchayat* of Gondia Block, in Dhenkanal subdivision. The village is about 60 years old. In 1930, there were 5 families of Dahuri caste, settled here. Then one Munda tribal family moved here from Mayurbanj district. Other castes came afterwards. Village was developed gradually as more and more forestland was cleared and brought under agriculture by the people who immigrated here.

The Forest Protection Committee (FPC) at Bania was formed by a NGO, People's Institute for Participatory Action and Research (PIPAR) in the year 1981-82 as a result of a mobilization against wood smuggling. Bania falls in the Sadangi range, notorious for wood smuggling activity. Kapilas and Ramia are the two major reserve forests of this range. These reserves are close to the Cuttack district, well connected by a state highway and were under constant pressure of smuggling. At one time forest staff used to refuse to stay at the forest quarters for fear of personal safety. Then the patrolling of forests used to be done by forest guards and casual labourers employed by forest department moving in a group of two to three persons. Smuggling went unabated and later it was found that some of the watchmen and ward staff had become agents of the wood smugglers and were misinforming the forest department.

In the year 1981-82, a NSS camp was organized by PIPAR and the wood smuggling operations going on in these reserve forests were discovered. Village communities were aware of the forest reserve being plundered but were unable to stop the more organized and powerful smugglers. PIPAR, with support from the forest department and collector mobilised the communities against the smugglers. *Lathis* (Bamboo sticks) and whistles were provided to the communities for protection and easier communication. And in a mass action about 200 cartloads of smuggled wood was confiscated. Since FD and collector supported the main action, smugglers did not retaliate. Form then onwards there has been a major decline in smuggling activity. Village communities gained confidence and formed FPC. Sadangi Range has now 47 FPCs covering 3780 hectares of reserve forest and in fact leads the district in FPC formation. There is a primary school and a non-formal education centre run by PIPAR in Bania. The nearest high school is at Sorsiapada, 4 kms away from the village.

The total area of the village is 179.2 hectares out of which forest area is 63.8 (35.6%) hectares. Agriculture land constitutes 42.18% of total area i.e. 75.6 hectares. Agriculture is mostly rainfed and local paddy is the main crop. Maize and Mandia or Ragi (coarse cereal) are other crops grown. Under tank irrigation vegetables like Potatoes, Brinjal, and Ladies finger are grown. People have started using fertilizer for irrigated crops. There is no landless family in the village.

People are dependent on the forest for a number of vegetable items used for cooking. Three types of tuber viz. Panialu, Mesihaalu and Kantaalu are available during the monsoon and post monsoon seasons. A person could collect 5-6 kgs of these tubers every day. Two varieties of Mushrooms, namely, Patra and Nada are also collected for consumption. Different types of leafy vegetables like Indian spinach and Bhadavadaha are used for curry making.

Agriculture per se meets only their cereal requirement. In 1930s, the Munda headman had migrated here looking for agricultural land. Cultivation was difficult at that time because of the attack of wildlife specially elephants on crops. During 1950-70 a lot of coupe felling organized by the FD took place. The commercial felling stopped after 1970s and smuggling of wood increased. Deforestation drove the wildlife away and some land was cleared for agriculture. Wild elephants are still a threat for the crops especially, when the crops get ready.

Agriculture is supplemented by rearing of cattle (indigenous) and goats for dung, milk and meat. In emergency, cattle and goat are sold. Normally, children take them to the forest for grazing. Bania has not much to do with the local markets or economy. It comes close to being a self-sufficient village.

*Forest and its uses*

Forest wealth in Bania is rich in diversity and since 1980s it is fast regenerating. In 1930s when the Munda headman first came here, forest was extensive and wild elephants were the kings of forests. People dare not venture out of their homes after dark. Plenty of small game was available for hunting. By 1970s the forest were extensively damaged. The wildlife more or less disappeared. With regeneration of forests, small animals like rabbit, foxes are resurfacing once again. Even wild elephants visit the forest occasionally.

Consumptive use of forests was however, the prevailing norm until commercial felling was introduced by the forest department. It would require ethno-botanical studies to document the biodiversity and the use of forest to do any justice to the Bania forests. The forest provides several types of vegetables and fruits which are important supplementary diet to cereals produced from agriculture. Various types of oilseeds are collected from forest and enough oil is extracted for consumption. Oil extraction is a noteworthy example of the consumptive use norm. Firewood, material for fence, thatch, poles, beams, agricultural implements, paddy dehusking contraption are all collected from forests. Medicinal plant processing provides a wide range of treatment items useful for a number of local ailments. Sale of Kendu leaves and Sal leaf plates provide some cash income. Kendu leaves are collected by women and children and sold to Kendu leaf division. Sal leaf is made into plates at leisure by women and sold to the local trader. Sal seeds are not sold but are used for oil extraction.

*Forest protection committee*

The Mundas have formed their own FPC consisting of 35 families. The FPC excludes other caste groups. By consensus they have chosen seven members including a women members who is literate. She also works for PIPAR and her awareness is quite high. The Munda headman is the leader of the FPC. The government representative is the Sarpanch (Formal President), Revenue Inspector, Forester, and the village agriculture worker.

In practice it is the seven members who meet twice a month i.e. on 15th and 30th day and discuss protection related issues. The general body of 35 members also meets once a month. The general body is the final authority to take decisions and evolve rules. The Government nominees play a negligible role in the affairs of the FPC. The FPC levies a fine of Rs. 5/- on an absentee member.

*Rules and Regulations:* Here again the underlying principle is that the forest can be used for consumptive purposes and are not meant for any commercial use. The important rules evolved are:

1. Rights to collect fuel wood and NTFP
2. Rights to grazing in the forest
3. Felling of trees prohibited without the permit from FPC
4. Trees required for purposes like making agricultural implements, cattle shed and house building are allowed. But the member has to apply to the committee, who after

verification of the genuineness of the need earmarks tree for felling.

5. A differential cess rate has been evolved for forest products, which the members have to pay to the committee for meeting their requirements. The money is kept as Village Development Fund (VDF). The VDF is used for giving credit to members at 5% interest. A sprayer for agricultural purposes has also been brought from the VDF.
6. Different species are preferentially earmarked for various uses and only those species are allowed to be felled.

**Table 8.1 :** Various Activities wise Use of Tree Species

| *Items* | *Tree Species* |
|---|---|
| Ploughs | Kuruma |
| House Construction | Kumbhi, Bahada, Ankula |
| Wooden Plants | Sal, Siris, Gambhari |
| Bullock Cart Beams | Bandhana Seedha |

Forest area lies at the periphery of the village. The FD has issued a map clearly demarcating the boundary. A *dhandi* (foot path) has been made all along the boundary to demarcate the boundary on the ground. Everyday a four members protection squad patrols the forest. A baton (*Thenga*) is used to rotate the duty among the members. Bows and arrows are carried along. Bania FPC also cooperates with other FPCs for protection. Deogarh and Bania FPC had caught some smugglers in one such operation and fined Rs. 800/- and split the fine equally. In another incident, Bania FPC and the FD confiscated nine bicycles two of which, were given as a reward to the FPC by the FD. The members narrate such instances with pride as examples of their strict vigil.

*Recognition of the FPC*

The FD has accorded recognition of the FPC by formalizing the committee as per government order. They have issued a map to the FPC demarcating the forest area under protection. While Bania FPC and such others provide effective protection to their forests, some pilferages continue in patches of forests under FD jurisdiction. Teak trees account for most of the pilferages. Teak trees were planted by the FD a decade ago. But FPC resent any attempt to plant teak in their forest. FPCs are firmly of the view that teak being of commercial value brings in outside interest and there by clashes. Local forest staffs also agree to the sentiments of FPC members. For the FPCs, teak plantation is an attack against consumption use norm.

## Forests Protection Movement of Madhya Pradesh and Chattisgrah

Madhya Pradesh and Chattisgarh forest area accounts for nearly 23% of India's total forest area; per capita forest area is 0.4 hectare, the highest in India. However, the area under productive forest is only around 44% compared to 82.3% in Kerala, 60% in Jammu and Kashmir, 66.8% in Maharashtra, 65.3% in Tamil Nadu, 67.7% in U.P. and an all India average of 46.7%. This shows the poor status and performance of forestry in these two states.

The total growing stock is around 410 million cubic meters, which is nearly 24% of the total national stock. Though in terms of forest area, erstwhile M.P. used to rank number one, there are large tracts in the Chattisgarh and Malwa regions which are treeless and sizeable blank shave appeared within forest belts. Today the forests of these two states are facing a multitude of problems due to following reasons:

1. Increasing demand pressure due to population growth even in areas where forest resources appear to be plenty;
2. Depletion of forest resources due to indiscriminate felling of trees under 'Nishtar' rights - a long term commitment of government to accept the people's right over the forests;
3. Increasing imbalances between demand and supply, in terms of availability of forest resources to meet the local needs of fuel, construction timber, wood for agricultural use, fencing and protection material and grazing lands.

According to official records, there are 9 districts having less than 15% of their area under forests, 16 districts with 15% to 32% and 20 districts with more than 33% forest cover. However, this macro view ignores the fact that even within forest rich area problems exist. The long blank tracts in the forest rich districts of Bilaspur and Raipur are the vivid examples of such aberrations. The forest department has estimated that failure to raise a minimum of 80,000 hectares of fuel wood plantations each year till 2000 A.D., have caused serious problems to the state forests.

Several forest protection movements have taken place in M.P and Chattisgarh to counter the rapid depletion of forest resources. Some of those cases are depicted here.

*Forest protection movement of Rajgarh district*

This section covers a few cases which deal with a cross-section of 'people-tree' relationship. A careful reading of these cases would highlight that each case has an important contribution to make.

In the absence of social forestry programmes, essentially based on the principle of joint management and decision-making, the only lead for field investigation available was the 'Panch-Vans' scheme in Rajgarh district, and to some extent in Bilaspur-Raipur districts.

*1. Forest village*

Dharampur is a forest village located in Rajgarh district. The population of the village is around 300. There are some 200 cattle. The land is not fertile, but mainly stony. There are no irrigation facilities. Even for drinking water, villagers have to travel a distance of 3 to 4 kms.

The inhabitants of Dharampur are mainly Banjaras (Gypsies). There are, however, 3 Muslim families and 4 Thakur families. Legally owned land is very small but by means of encroachments on public lands, villagers have increased their holdings. About 10 acres of the forestland, towards the hillside, has sandalwood trees. The main occupation of the villagers has been, working in a nearby stone quarry; selling of fuel-wood mainly collected through illegal felling of trees, and temporary employment in ad hoc-projects of road building or in plantations.

The forest guard affirmed the criminal bent of mind of the villagers. The reported murder of a forest guard in 1973 being an instance. The fight took place when forest guards tried to prevent villagers from stealing the sandalwood. On an average, a family sells nearly 25 to 30 kg of the fuel wood per day. The main buyers are the buses and trucks running between Bhopal and Narshinghgarh for the respective markets. It is believed that the village community is probable not hardworking and has always been interested in earning easy money through thefts of forest resources. Describing their problems, the villagers, on their side, spared no efforts to express their strong reactions against the forest officials; probably in defence of their own conduct. The reasons for this hostile attitude towards the forest officials could be:

a. the creation of a game sanctuary in an area where villagers were quarrying stone. This has deprived them of their regular employment and has also put an end to the use of the water pond much needed for their livestock. Similarly a large space, customarily used for a village fair, has been impounded for the sanctuary thus depriving the communities of their meeting place,
b. another decision to fence 65 hectare of forestland adjacent to the village for a 'Panch-Vans' programme, has created problem of grazing for the livestock. Though grass as high as 2 to 2 ½ feet could be seen all along the field, villagers could not use it, as the forest department has yet not decided on the systems of grazing-rights distribution. This 'Panch-Vans' scheme is in operation since July, 1978. Recently 1000 '*poolas* (Bundle)' of grass is sold for Rs. 70 for which, earlier, the local community had to pay nothing. Perhaps latter this right could be accommodated under the schemes, but it has created a crisis at this point of time with an assurance of solution in the future,

c. villagers complained of getting different rates for work in the forests e.g., in one situation they were employed directly on a job-order (trench digging) basis by the department, and in another situation they were employed by a contractor of the forest department who usually paid them lower rates.

Further probing revealed that the community was not consulted in any of the decision taken, like the creation of the sanctuary, the use of the water pond in the sanctuary area. Villagers were apparently not aware of the benefits that would accrue to them through the 'Panch-Vans'. They never knew that Panch-vans were meant to provide free grass for livestock and fuel wood, in difficult time. Obviously, the scheme was bound to restrict the free movement of cattle all over the place. It was, however, learnt that even this quarrying operation was illegal. In spite of checks and closures, one could see head loads of fuel wood lying on the road, and on the roofs of the huts.

*2. Mr. Hukum Singh: A tree lover in Rajgarh District*

Mr. Hukum Singh on his own initiatives was able to convince villagers to fence nearly 100 acres of village land belonging to the farmers of the village, to grow more trees and raise grass in a more systematic manner. It is extremely important to capture and record such experiences of 'people-tree' relationships, in remote areas, where the initiative did not come from the forest department.

Dhabla is a small village with nearly 100 people. The soil condition is bad and in the absence of any irrigation, yield from electrified, the villagers still face drinking water problems. There are nearly 100 to 120 animals (cattle and goats) belonging to the villagers. The quality of cattle is very poor. Since the land yield is extremely low, the entire life of the villagers is centred around their livestock. They use mainly 'cow dung' as fuel for cooking purposes. Miles and miles of area around this village is barren. The land is unfertile. Dialogue with the old villagers brought back the memory of forests that existed around them. However, felling and burning of trees as fuel has completely denuded the area.

Dhabla village must be considered as fortunate in having a tree-lover like Mr. Hukum Singh. Narrating his experiences, he stated he had been able to convince the villagers to grow more trees with reasons like:

a. tree would make their village look more beautiful
b. trees would provide privacy to the villagers, especially to the women who otherwise are forced to defecate in the open
c. trees would improve the rain-fall in this area.

Initially he faced resistance from villagers owing to (i) livestock's grazing problems; (ii) extra expenditure on cattle feed, because earlier they were allowing the livestock to graze. Being a lover of trees and an enthusiast, Hukum Singh overcame this resistance by paying out from his pocket to compensate for the nominal losses and, also by planning the restricted grazing for livestock. He has thus tried to raise plantations that would meet village needs and help in strengthening the village economy based on sheep-farming and dairying, along with farming.

Talking to him revealed that he hopes to spread this movement to the nearby villagers. He felt that assistance in supplying and planting tree saplings would be sufficient to involve and motivate people for the present. He also felt that the reasons given above would convince the villagers to protect and maintain the forests in future. He expressed a desire to equip his village with a Gobar Gas Plant, and hoped that the forest department would help in installing it.

### 3. *Rajgarh Cases Revisited*

The fresh review of these cases draws attention to the followings:

a. Vast tracts of unused and under-used land is awaiting economical use. So far no assessment is available about the land capability, but the facts remain : viz., that long back forests existed and that private initiatives have now been taken to develop a link between economic needs, land use and forest development. These, however, remain isolated instances and have passed unobserved.

b. The Panch-Van scheme, a centrally sponsored programme of forest development for the community's welfare, seems to have been enforced in this region. Probably Rajgarh was selected due to the fact that barren land exists in abundance. As indicated by the people, their involvement in this programme is missing since it conferred on them at best the status of wage - earners in trench digging. Some attempts claimed that villagers were involved in choosing the species to be planted. Probably the villagers' preference for fruit trees did not receive acceptance. No feedback is available about the fate of six lakh plants distributed to nearly 1,60,000 farmers in the district. The possibilities are that most of these have perished.

c. The experiences reflected by these cases suggest that the region is well-set to receive a dynamic programme like community forestry, provided it exploit the activity mix best suited to the environment, and avoids the pitfalls that the Panch-Van scheme has encountered. For example, forest farming should be linked to livestock farming programmes; species should be selected with care; negative consequences like displacing existing avocations without providing alternatives and, enclosing *mela* areas as sanctuaries need to be avoided. It is necessary to build-up public awareness and opinion, before taking - up large plantation programmes. Failure to be economically relevant and socially acceptable will cause widespread discontent.

*Cases from Bilaspur District*

*1. The Van-Premi sangh : Forest lover's club*

It was around 1976 a 'Van Premi Sangh' was formed in the forest rich area of Bilaspur. Since involvement of the people in the management of trees is the king-pin in community forestry, it was assured that such clubs could be a means to motivate people and involve them in implementing social forestry programmes.

This club located in a large town is essentially a club of forest contractors. It has about 12 members and the local ex-range officer had initially played an active part in generating enthusiasm for the club. Currently, the club is completely non-functional and members have no idea about its affairs.

Keenness to revitalize the club was singularly missing. Two of the members, who made constructive suggestions, wanted to broad base it with participation from people having different backgrounds. Some of the forest officials were of the view that the club is an 'eye-wash' to shift the focus of activities to certain plantations. Contractor-members expected favour from the Forest Department. It was realized that the formation of this club was a political activity, removed from the concept of social forestry for the dominant members had no true interest in trees of forests. Such selfish interests and attitudes cast doubts on the utility of these clubs in forest management.

### 2. *Case of an 'Adarsh' (Model) village*

This is a description of an 'Adarsh village' in Bilaspur. It is a large village with a population of 3500 people and a middle school for 80 students. Nearly one third of the village population is educated and 75% of the families have very small land holding. The maximum extent of land, owned by 3 or 4 families, is of the order of 20 to 30 acres. The minimum land holding would be around half an acre. The cattle population is around 1000. The caste structure is : Brahmins 20, families; Thakurs 25, families; Sahu, 90 families; Harijan 100, families; Tribal 30, families; and Yadav 40 families.

The village has no irrigation facility and only one crop is grown a year. Even the earthen dam under construction nearby, will be of no avail to this village. The village has no drinking water facility in spite of an overhead tank and an electrified tube existing since 1962. Almost all the houses have a water connection and in spite of spending Rs. 12,500/- on a drinking water scheme, the villagers are deprived of this facility. According to the villagers, wrong specifications of the pump-set, with no corrective measures for the past 15 years, have made the scheme a failure.

Despite being an Adarsh (model) village, some of the urgent problems it faces are the increasing number of unemployed youth, absence of land for cattle, illegal encroachments on land by village influential, absence of a fuel wood depot, non-availability of electricity and recurring shortage of kerosene or other fuel.

The 'Panch-Van' scheme is located on a 35 hectare piece of forestland. The trees (mixed plantation) were planted in 1977. Among the species grown are Jackfruit, Mango, Cashew, Acacia, Bamboo, Eucalyptus. The plantation appeared to be in good shape. The grass had not been cut. A local guard is stationed to protect the plantation.

Enquiries regarding the location of a 'Panch-Van' near the village revealed, that owing to this programme the villagers were having grazing problems and fodder shortage persisted. None of the villagers could describe the probable benefit of the 'Panch-Van' as none were aware of the forest Department's intentions for distributing free fodder or grass. All they could describe as a benefit was the temporary employment they got under the 'Panch-Van' programme.

### 3. *Reserve forest near Bilaspur Railway Station*

Nearly three kilometers east of Bilaspur Railway Station there is a 500 hectare plot of reserve forest, which is now completely tree-less and full of '*Palas* (Flame of the forest)' bushes. Opposite to this is another 50 to 60 hectares of Reserve forestland suffering a similar fate as the bigger plot. One year back, the '*Sarpanch*' (an elected village leader) of a nearby Hardi Tona village was approached by the forest department with the request to look to the stray cattle, numbering a few hundred, living in the degraded forest land. These stray cattle were becoming a nuisance to the villagers. This complaint resulted in digging trenches and planting Sesame and Bamboo along the entire plot of 500 hectares. After six months, except for self-growing '*Palas*' bushes nothing survived on this plot. The forest department is however hopeful of Sesame (a good coppicing species) coming up again after the rains. Meanwhile the plot has become a living place for the driven-out stray cattle as certain trenches have been filled up. Probably this place is also a regular haunt of all kinds of anti-social elements, ranging from bootleggers to other indulging in more socially unacceptable activities.

Around this vacant land and the forest blank in the reserve forest, some eight villages are situated with a total population of about 10,050 persons. The availability of such a large fertile area in a somewhat densely populated region is a matter of public interest. Discussion with a cross-section of the population (including the *Sarpanch*) regarding alternative uses of the land proved quite informative. This gathering gave an indication of the villagers' aspirations. It was suggested that :

a. the entire area be fenced by bamboo plantation,
b. suitable patches be developed for crop farming, which would further require irrigation facilities, and
c. the patch of government owned '*murram*' land along-side this forest department land be developed for grazing purposes and for raising forage-fodder crops.

In total the suggestions are: (a) development of a mixed plantation capable of enriching agriculture and livestock enterprises (b) land use should meet the villager's forest basic needs for fuel-fodder. Near unanimity prevailed regarding the growing of Bamboo, and *Babool* trees. It appears that, any programme of tree plantation by itself will not be acceptable to the villagers, unless its backward linkages are integrated and a benefit sharing system is envisaged. From villages around this case, some 1,000 people or so migrate to Allahabad during the off-seasons, and an equally large number are engaged in selling wood in Bilaspur. In the absence of developed woodlots and alternative jobs, continued depletion of reserve forest stock is the natural out-come.

*4. Case of people managed forests: A successful project*

This case is located in Marwali forest range, in a place called 'Samer Darri', in Bilaspur District. The village is 160 kilometers north of Bilaspur. Its population is around 2000. The *Panchayat* van (forest belonging to the village *Panchayat*) is on a 1500 acre plot. The forest has mixed plantation and is very rich in bamboos. This plantation is in a better condition than the degraded forests of the forest department. The good condition of the plantation can be ascribed to one or more of the following reasons:

a. it is located on a somewhat fertile soil,
b. the villagers have extended cooperation in supervising the works,
c. a sense of belongingness between the people and the programme is apparent,
d. the earning capacity of the forest is better and that benefits the village.

A similar story can be told about another plantation in Sarguja district. Around 1976-77, under the land distribution scheme to the landless, some villagers were given land in the forest area, instead of the revenue area. A majority of the landowners agitated when they were refused possession by the forest department, which had plans to rehabilitate the degraded forests. As a result, the villagers who wanted the land to be allotted to them in the forest zone resisted the plantation programme. To avoid a confrontation, a joint committee re-examined the whole affair. Records established the ownership of the forest department. Ultimately the village leadership yielded to this claim, but demanded that the department plant fruit trees on the land allotted to them even though the ownership remained with the department. In return, they assured the protection of the forest. Since the conflict was resolved through mutual understanding, action was taken to prevent the indiscriminate felling of trees by refugees from Bangladesh, who were earning their living by consequent on the convergence of interests of the people and the forest department.

*5. Case of people's managed forests : A project that failed*

This case is located in Hoshangabad district. Some 50 years back, forestland of approximately 100 acres planted with teak was given to the village *panchayat*. For the last three years, this *panchayat* is pressing the forest department to take back the ownership and management of the plantation, as it is unable to maintain and protect the forest resources. Some of the reasons behind the situation are: (a) the *panchayat* and the community are almost unaware of the commercial value of the plantations, probably its gestation period being too long; (b) the *panchayat* is unable to protect the forest, as it has no legal force nor any facility to take action against violators; (c) lack of technical expertise to manage such a plantation.

The above cases revealed at least three facets relevant to a dynamic programme of community forestry:

1. land-use planning and choice of species have to address the immediate needs and aspirations of the local community;
2. whether the forest department has the appropriate technology, to harmonies these conflicting claims, is an issue of vital importance;
3. preparedness of the local community and identity of interests are vital, before the community assumes partnership role in management and/or ownership of a forest.

We are aware that these and other such cases deserve to be studied in greater depth. Thus economic costs and social gains should be listed for analysis. A detailed review of such experiments can yield valuable knowledge about social dynamics, village aspirations, site capability and the organizational structures best suited, to the management o such projects.

## The Ralegaon Siddhi Project Experience

Ralegaon Siddhi is perhaps the India's most popularly known model of micro-watershed development initiated and fostered by local people under the guidance of an enlightened and benevolent local leader. The Ralegaon Siddhi project was launched in 1975. The major force behind the project is Padma Shri Anna Hazare who after retirement from the Indian army in 1975, returned to his native village- Ralegaon Siddhi and started village reconstruction and development work. The project is well-known all over the country and well-documented. Ralegaon Siddhi is a village of about 2,100 people located in the drought-prone Parnal tehsil of Ahmednagar district of Maharashtra. The village receives scanty rainfall of only 250-300 mm annually. Hence, the highest priority in the project was given to harvesting and conservation of rainwater. The project covered four watersheds and a total geographical area of about 962 ha of which about 651 ha was cultivable, 137 ha forest land, 123 ha revenue wasteland, and 51 ha village pasture land. The total expenditure incurred on the project from 1975-76 to 1985-86 was about Rs. 11.42 million of which Rs. 4.74 million (about 42%) was granted by the Government of Maharashtra, Rs. 4.08 million borrowed from the bank of Maharashtra, Rs. 1.34 million contributed by the local people mainly through *shramdan* (voluntary contribution of about). Rs. 1 million granted by various nongovernmental organizations (NGOs), and the remainder by other sources including Anna Hazare who donated Rs. 87,000. The average cost of the project per ha of the total geographical area covered was about Rs. 11,761 which included the cost of a hostel building (Rs. 16 lakhs) and veterinary hospital (Rs. 1 lakh).

A series of 31 check dams and nala bunds constructed under the project, have created about 282,000 cubic metre water storage capacity. This has resulted in increased availability of ground water. This has facilitated sinking of community wells. Water from these wells supplied at a moderate rate has enabled the farmers to grow two or three crops every year including fruits and vegetables which are now exported even to Dubai. As a result of increased availability of water for irrigation, the total cropped area in the watershed increased from 619 ha in the pre-project period to 859 ha in 1985-86. The project had a significant positive impact on crop, milk yield, fodder production, employment, and incomes. It has been observed that after the implementation of the project, no villager goes out of the village in search of work as they used to before.

The villagers have participated whole-heartedly in the project and have contributed through both *shramdan* and cash. All the soil and water conservation structures were built through community action. The villagers have completely stopped grazing their animals on common property lands and have switched to stall-feeding which has become possible as a result of increased grass production from the common property land after stoppage of grazing. They have stopped illicit lopping and felling of common property trees and planted more than two lakh trees mostly on the common property lands including hill slopes. This has prevented soil erosion besides providing a variety of products such as fuel wood, fodder, fruits etc. To enlist people's participation in the village development work including the project activities, Anna Hazare has organized the villagers into some ten different associations of which six are engaged in development and management of land, water, and forests. Equitable distribution of water among the eligible farmers is ensured through various *Pani Puravatha Mandals* (Water Supply Association). Anna Hazare uses the forum of *Gram Sabha* (village body meeting) to introduce new ideas and seek people's involvement in refining and implementing them. He makes sure that the final decisions taken in such meetings are considered by the majority of the villagers as their own.

The Ralegaon Siddhi experience shows that the rural people under the guidance and leadership of good, enlightened and honest persons could develop and manage their CPR and distribute the benefits equitably. Given proper leadership, the Relegaon Siddhi model can be replicated in other villages in India. Anna Hazare is now trying to institutionalise the model by training youth who have volunteered to follow in his footsteps.

When villagers are well-informed about the various rural development programmes launched by the government for their benefit and when they are organized and have the support and guidance of good local leaders, they can demand from the government officials what is meant for them and thus achieve their common goal of development through their own resources supplemented by funds earmarked by various governmental and non-governmental organizations for rural development.

## NGO Initiated Forest Movement : Case of National Tree Growers Cooperative Federation Limited (NTGCF)

It started as a project of the National Dairy Development Board (NDDB) in 1986, when at a request from the National Wastelands Development Board, a pilot project on Tree Growers' Cooperatives was initiated in selected districts in five states. It was an attempt to apply the institutional template of cooperative at the village level (a) to bring together village communities in an efforts to promote vegetation on degraded lands, (b) to help villagers to create and govern village wood-lots to meet their requirements of fuel wood and fodder. Two years later, in 1988, an apex federation the National Tree Growers' Cooperative Federation (NTGCF) was created, and the implementation of a full scale project handed over to it. The project was supported by the Swedish international Development Authority (SIDA) from 1991 to 2002, and continues to be supported by the Canadian international Development Agency from 1993 onwards. The project is now working in 23 districts in the seven states of India viz. Andhra Pradesh, Karnataka, Rajasthan, Gujarat, Orissa, Madhya Pradesh and Uttaranchal. Recently NTGCF has been re-christened as Foundation for Ecological Security (FES) to focus on broader issue of ecology at wider dimension. However, here we will continue to address them as NTGCF.

It became clearer to NTGCF that a single institutional template, the cooperative structure, would not suffice as its project grew and exposed to the complex and varied historical contexts, the differing policy and tenurial environments, and the diverse physical settings. It also realised that the cooperative's legal framework in its existing form in various states would be inept to integrate with the many tenure options existing in the various states, especially the dynamics of village commons. Simultaneously, organisation became also conscious that the conservation of nature and improving dependent rural livelihoods are two sides of the same coin. Here we would discuss the various options they tried in their quest for appropriate village institution, mapping the strategy for livelihood promotion, designing institutional framework, and strengthening communications across the village.

*Appropriate village institutions*

As a pilot project of the National Dairy Development Board, the Tree Grower's Cooperatives Project, opted for a cooperative framework which had been successful in the field of dairying. State Governments were approached to lease revenue wastelands to cooperative societies registered under the State Cooperative Society Acts for the purpose of developing wood lots to meet fuel wood and fodder needs of the locals. However, the difference between milk cooperatives and cooperatives to govern and manage common lands soon became apparent.

A fundamental difference was that while in the case of milk, individual owners of cattle pool milk for collective bargaining, in the case of the tree growers' cooperatives, the very resources are commonly held. This critical distinction raised further questions regarding the compatibility of cooperatives as an institutional design when the lands were *de facto* and in some cases *de jure* commonly held. Moreover, in rural communities that are characterized by inequalities, an institutional design that ensures equitable access rights to the less articulate is necessary. Another concern was the very cooperative design. The cooperatives tended to signal commercialisation and marketing of the various benefits accruing from the natural surroundings. Such signal was not in harmony with what rural communities seem to see as their coexistence with commons. It was desirable that work be done at a scale and in a contiguous manner that would revitalize the hydrological system and build on the socio cultural linkages in a given area. But it became apparent that by working on scattered patches of land, only some short-term needs would be met. This would not have a long-term and cumulative impact on both the livelihoods of rural communities as well as on the ecological health of the environments on which they are dependent. Depending upon the various administrative categories of land and the institutions, it was felt that tree growers association or body should be allowed to be work with a variety of institutional forms such as the *van panchayats*, *panchayats*, *gram sabhas*, watershed associations, village forest committees, etc.

Over the years, the organization has worked with various institutions in protecting and managing land resources, providing its resources to strengthen the work of such bodies. For example, in Uttaranchal *van panchayats*, which have a proven record of successful community participation and governance of natural resources, were clearly a better institutional option than the tree cooperatives. The institution of the *Van Panchayat* is recognized by the government as having a permanent legal right and control over the village forest. However, some recent policy changes concerning forest management may affect the autonomy of the *Van Panchayat* institutions and could weaken their existing management systems and their ability to adapt. It is clear that a community which has a longer or permanent tenure over a forest and autonomy in governance would have a greater sense of accountability and ownership and would therefore be more prudent in the use and management of such lands.

Village committees, which traditionally protect and govern *gramya* (village) jungle lands and forestlands adjacent to their villages, are being supported in Orissa. The effort was to assist traditional institutions in recording, in the form of written bye laws, the principles that had evolved over many years. This would contribute to a more coherent understanding and dialogue on the patterns of resource use by the constituent villages. In Karnatak the process was tried with village *panchayat*s. NTGCF obtained permission from the Department of *Panchayati* Raj and Rural Development to fund the *panchayats* directly. This has paved the way for greater autonomy of the hamlet level sub-committees of the *panchayats* in formulating site- specific natural resource management plans and to carry out the requisite interventions. The choice of hamlet level committees has helped in decentralizing decision making to those most closely associated with and dependent on the common lands. At the same time representatives of the *panchayats* are taking a keen interest in the activities of the constituent hamlets.

In Madhya Pradesh, the government has devolved powers to the *gram sabha* at the level of hamlet or revenue village. It is noteworthy that by an amendment of the Constitution, *panchayats* which are enshrined as the local governance institutions have also been mandated the responsibility of managing their natural surroundings. In difficult times when rights over resources may be contested, such constitutional arrangements can safeguard interests of the concerned communities.

Considering the topography and the physical scope of work, NTGCF has striven to remain abreast of changing policies and dynamics and work with institutional forms which would have the widest possible mandate and that could, wherever possible, govern and protect all the land categories in a given watershed. However in states like Andhra Pradesh, Madhya Pradesh and Rajasthan multiple institutions in the same watershed is the available option. This duplication often results in the registration of the same group or village community under different committees because the land they are protecting and regenerating are under various departments.

### *Livelihoods and commons*

While pursuing ecological conservation, organisation realised that even after years of degradation and neglect, forests, grazing land, community ponds, and water holes for cattle and other domestic animals continue to play an crucial role in rural livelihoods. Communities depend significantly on those resources for a variety of benefits. In degraded areas, in the absence or limited availability of alternate sources of livelihoods or agriculturally productive land, communities are all the more dependent on these common natural resources. Such dependence is higher in the case of the poor, and become more imperative during times of stress, such as droughts or crop failures. The link between conservation of nature and improved rural livelihoods is clear.

Degradation of land and depletion of water resources are among the most serious problems being faced in many parts of the world including India. Such a trend is all the more severe on lands that are customarily held as commons or owned by the government. Conventional development initiatives have for several years, failed to realize the importance of and the need to protect and nurture these lands. A perspective that could appreciate the positive interdependencies that exist among various resources and production systems in a physical context is imperative. Besides providing many benefits to the surrounding communities, such lands serve the critical purpose of maintaining biodiversity and act as sinks for recharging ground water. In many areas these are the only places that remain as habitats for a variety of plants and animals.

Organisation also experienced that the failing ecological health of the commons has led to a complex spiral of adverse economic and ecological consequences. While farmers with larger land holdings can adapt to meeting their grazing, fuel wood and water needs from their own private resources, the poor, particularly women, are significantly affected by the crises, as the commons remain their own private resources, the poor, particularly women, are significantly affected by the crises, as the commons remain their last physical and political space. Often, as we have experienced in the semi and areas of the country, following continuous years of drought, the poor communities do not have any recourse but to continue to extract whatever biomass is available down to the last blade of grass from the commons, for their animals. It is also observed that deeper aquifers are tapped by those who can afford to at such times. This overuse of the land results in an ecologically and economically detrimental cycle. As things get worse poor communities are forced to migrate.

Hence NTGCF started working through various physical and institutional interventions to halt and reverse ecological degradation by revegetating fragile lands and reducing soil, nutrient and water run off. Such efforts are beginning to yield results and in many villages in Andhra Pradesh, Rajasthan and Madhya Pradesh water and fodder were available for the animals even during the critical periods of drought. The increased employment opportunities have provided succour to the poor who would have otherwise migrated. In areas where the geo-hydrology permits small streams also flow during some parts of the year. Apart from the seeding and planting interventions, many of the native species are regenerating, perhaps from the existing rootstock.

Amidst such developments NTGCF became involved in increased discussion on the mechanisms of resource use. Such debate was necessity as it apprehended that efforts which had gone into conservation might come to naught unless there is active debate on the principles underlying appropriation within the community as well as across communities.

### *Institutional design*

NTGCF since the beginning emphasized that local institutions for self-governance supported by the programme interventions remain accountable to the local people. By design and focus, the interventions aim at centring the poor and their interests in the management and governance of the resources. The critical elements of such a design are the inclusion of every resident in the habitation; inclusion of habitations if the resources are shared across communities; representation of their interests in the decision making equal wages for men and women; payment of wages as stipulated by the Government; and emphasis on conservation and local use rather than commercialisation of the benefits.

In day-to-day manifestation of such design principles, communities engage in dialogues within themselves and with their neighbouring communities and strive to arrive at decisions that are just and acceptable. In inequitable settings the discussions are more protracted and various interest groups strive to find spaces either as a compromise or tend to assert their positions. This engagement is dynamic and is manifested in activities such as deciding the species, the location of a water harvesting structure, regulation of grazing, norms of work behaviour and responsibilities, and importantly, on the domination of decision making and in the distribution of benefits.

In recent times NTGCF teams were also involved in building discussions around crucial matters of exclusion of the more needy within a village. In villages which have attained a stage where matters concerning distribution of grasses have come to the fore, discussions are centred around the mechanisms for distribution rather than an inferior arrangement of auctioning the produce to the disadvantage of the poor. In places where it is difficult to introduce fair wages as stipulated by the government, tactical arrangements that would not compromise the wage standards were arrived at. In Orissa and Andhra Pradesh, norms of regulations across villages are being negotiated as the resources are commonly held, and in some cases accessed, by villages that are situated away from the resources.

*Strengthening communications across the village*

At the village level, NTGCF ensured regular meetings involving the entire village assembly is the common forum for planning and implementation. Issues of importance are discussed at various levels so that there is a larger consultation and concurrence. Periodically, representatives across villages meet to arrive at area specific regulations. Inter village disputes concerning boundaries, access and collective responsibilities are discussed. In a logical progression, such meetings also discuss other matters concerning the area.

In Ajmer, while the distance between the villages did not offer much scope for strengthening such collectives, the adjacent areas in Bhilwara built on their existing systems of inter village forums. Such fora were even instrumental in lobbying for a secure tenure over their land with the local politicians and administration. In Madhya Pradesh, such forums negotiated with nomadic pastoralists and the district administration in charting out a path for the migrant cattle. In Andhra Pradesh, such conglomerates are interacting with adjacent semi urban centers to arrive at measures that cater to their firewood needs. In Orissa, Andhra Pradesh and Gujarat, local newsletters highlighting issues concerning natural resources, policies and developments in the area are periodically published.

As the work of the organization and its experience has grown, the NTGCF has begun to increase its participation at various regional, national and international forums. It is important that policy and perspectives at various levels all contribute harmoniously to the goal of eco-restoration and ecological security.

*A state-wise summary*

NTGCF is working with 879 village institutions involving 1,05,598 members. Of these, 507 are Tree Growers' Cooperatives and 372 are other forms of village level institutions. Of the 63,462 hectares of common land made available to them, these institutions have brought 21,772 hectares under regeneration activities and planted nearly 14.2 million trees on their common lands, as well as their private lands. This work has generated about 3.6 million workdays of employment in these villages (FES Annual Report, 2002).

During past few years, work was initiated in 60 village institutions. Of which 7 are Tree Growers' Cooperatives, 4 van *panchayats*, 19 village under the Joint Forest Management 12 *panchayats* and 18 village committees.

One of the foremost concerns of the project in each state has been to ensure an improved status of tenure and ownership of village communities over the commons. Experience informed by theory validates that commons are best protected and governed by the local communities. Both ecological goals as well as livelihood concerns can find a sustainable match when tenure is clear and rights and responsibilities of the communities is commonly understood. Growing from efforts to develop the natural surroundings in a contiguous patch defined by topographical and socio-cultural domains, the process of assessing the biomass, water diversity and energy capacities of the areas are being initiated. Community needs and present patterns of production, use and the sustainability of various options would gradually follow.

In another area of strategic importance, NTGCF is also assessing the need to integrate activities to support livelihoods so as to sustain its efforts in crafting institutions around commons. In transition village economies where the livelihoods are not solely dependent on the commons, singular attempts to build institutions around the commons may prove to be tenuous. On the other hand diversification into other livelihood support activities may diffuse the focus of the NTGCF and stretch the village institutions' capacities. While these issues are to be fully understood in the coming years, immediate efforts was to integrate the activities with the development programmes of other organizations in the area.

### *1. The Papagni river uplands project*

Originating in the southeast of Karnataka in the Kundalagurki hill ranges of Kolar district, the Papagani flows eastwards into southwest Andhra Pradesh, joining the Pennar river before draining into the Bay of Bengal. The Papagni river uplands project area, which spreads across the state borders of Karnataka and Andhra Pradesh, is also the region where two major geographical regions of the peninsula the Deccan plateau and the Eastern Ghats meet. Papagani flows seasonally through a semiarid landscape of red soil and granite outcrops, thorny scrub and mixed dry-deciduous, degraded forest. The region receives 600-800 mm of rain annually but the devastated hill slopes with sparse vegetation cannot hold this precipitation long enough for it to percolate and recharge water tables. The loss is compounded by the fact that top soil too gets rapidly washed away in the rush of water.

The communities here practice rain-fed agriculture supported by the large number of tanks which abound in the region. However, increasing siltation leading to reduced capacity and the breakdown of institutional mechanisms of repair and maintenance has now become a major problem. The project stepped in 15 years ago building a partnership with the communities to begin the process of protection, regeneration and revegetation on their commons and revitalizing systems of management and governance of their natural resources.

In Andhra Pradesh, fifty-five thousand hectares comprising a total of 264 hamlets in the districts of Chittoor and Anantapur were delineated for the NTGCF to carry out its intervention in the catchment of Chinneru and Pedderu tributaries of the Papagani, and Pedderu tributaries of the Papagani, and the main Papagani river itself.

Since the start of the project, the intervention has progressed from the ridges of the hills in Cuddapah and Chittoor to the adjacent ridges of Anantapur district, extending financial assistance to 146 habitations in the protection and management of natural resources in about 5,200 hectares.

Interventions on land and other natural resources have been carried out by the community under the framework of Tree Growers' Cooperatives registered under the Mutually-Aided Co-operative Societies Act, to work on revenue lands, and village Forest Committees (VFC) for interventions on forest lands.

The revival of small cattle ponds, locally called Chalamu, the construction and repairing of rock filled dams and earthen bunds, and revegetation of ridges through plantation and seeding has had a significant impact on the retention of moisture and increased availability of water and fodder for cattle in the project villages.

As vast stretches of land are being brought under local governance, the team has seen the need for villages which have begun taking initiatives on their commons, to include neighbouring communities that have not yet begun such efforts. Involving them fully in the early stages in such mutually beneficial decisions would preclude future conflicts in institutional and ecological processes. The traditional Burrakatha and Malliahgarikukkalu street play forms were used with great effect for the third year in succession to spread the massage of reviving protection and governance systems to improve the commons.

While federating for a of village communities have been maturing into bodies that mediate successfully in serious conflicts on resources and boundaries, they need to arrive at arrangements of transaction in responding to conflicts arising from fuel wood demands of semi-urban settlements.

Discussions with the Government resulted in it agreeing in principle to extend the lease periods from the present arrangement of 20 years to 50 years. With more villages coming under the joint Forest Management arrangements and also a few cases where the same village residents are registered as separate institutions to manage the revenue lands and forest lands, efforts are being made to have a common institution that could manage the two categories of land avoiding the duplication.

*2. Lessons from Anand*

The work is spread over 72 villages in the districts of Anand, Kheda, Pachmahals and Vadodara. Initiated in 1968, the project has focused primarily on areas such as the highly degraded ravines on the banks of the river Mahi and pockets of extremely difficult areas like the saline mud flats of Khambhat (Gulf of Cambay) on the Western limits.

While institutional designs such as the supremacy of the general body, transparent mechanisms in fund distribution and accounting etc. were incorporated, the cooperatives were organized with only a section of the village households in most of the villages, alienating the actual user groups inadvertently.

To undo such mistakes, NTGCF team has been assisting the cooperatives in including all user groups and ensuring universal membership, and building up communication among the users on issues of common concern.

The scattered and limited availability of revenue wastelands, forest lands or gazing lands offers little scope for working in a contiguous area. Communities here are less dependent on the commons, viewing such lands as additional sources for monetary incomes rather than primary sources for their livelihoods, which are based on cash crop cultivation, dairy and other occupations.

In 2002, the team began to explore the possibilities of expanding its work in the western extremes of the project area. The benefit from plantations of *Prosopis juliflora* in the saline mud flats of the Khambhat area has been substantial in acting as a salt-wind-break to the adjacent lands that were hitherto unproductive. In one village, 30 hectares of land was reclaimed for agriculture, as a result of the windbreak, besides improving the productivity in another 60 hectares. Though there are vast stretches of such land along the coastline, the team has identified 19 villages having 1,900 hectares in Khambhat and Dhanduka areas, for further exploration on socio-economic aspects.

Efforts to increase the membership in the cooperatives and bring previously excluded or alienated customary users of the commons back into the decision-making and sharing process has continued, with positive results in 23 villages. As the lease period of 15 years to a cooperative is considerably short and some cooperatives formed earlier are to reach the end of the term, the team has had discussions with the government to renew and increase the period of lease as is set down by the other State Governments. The issue is under consideration.

### 3. *Dahod project*

Located in the undulating topography of Dahod, the project was careful to take larger ecological goals into consideration, and so contiguous land masses which would enable a watershed approach, in the catchments of the Kali and Khand rivers, were selected Working on forests and grazing lands, the project here is attempting to work under the institutional templates of joint forest management and the *panchayats*.

The two river systems Kali and Khan, having their catchments in Dahod and Garboda talukas comprise 107 villages, spread over an area of 90,000 hectares. Initiated in 1998, the project works with 66 hamlets on over 1,700 hectares of common land of which forest land is around 1.250 hectares and grazing land 430 hectares.

The district of Dahod, designated a schedule-V area, was created in 1997 by reorganizing the predominantly tribal areas of

Panchmahal district. The community once dependent on forest subsists now on maize farming and heavy seasonal out migration as labour to various parts of Gujarat, Madhya Pradesh and Rajasthan.

Conflicts over encroachments of commons intensive drought relief operations and the time taken in permission form different department of the government has affected the pace of work till now, especially with respect to physical activities such as soil and moisture conservation and water harvesting structures, contour bunding, trenching and fencing.

The team's effort has been to support the various institutional options and nest these within the framework of the *panchayat* body. The local *panchayat* administration has permitted the NTGCF to directly fund the *panchayat*s for regeneration and protection activities. Recurrent deficits in rainfall have had a detrimental effect on the potential of intensive seeding efforts conducted over the past three years. The withdrawing of permission to two village institutions from working on forest land and the delay in getting permissions for seven other village institutions under JFM arrangement has been somewhat of a setback in the project's progress this year.

In the meantime, the team started working within the provisions of a sate Government resolution granting legal status to the practice of communities using forest lands for grass production where the communities commit themselves to protect the forests. Falling within Schedule-V areas, *panchayat*s prove to be an institutional option to manage natural resources because of the provisions vested by the 73rd constitutional amendment.

One of the important lessons experienced by the project during the year was that the period of funding, the construction of water harvesting structures and other wage employing activities is a critical time for putting in place institutional guidelines and practices. It is desirable to utilize available funds over a longer period of time and sequence the funding of major constructions until appropriate management systems are worked out in the course of supporting several other preliminary activities.

*4. Orissa experience*

The project is located in Angul and Dhenkanal districts. The Mahanadi and the Brahamani rivers flow through the region, with several streams and rivulets crisscrossing the undulating landscape. The main occupation of people here is rain-fed agriculture, paddy being the principal crop with forests providing a critical livelihood and resource support. The dry tropical mixed deciduous forest is predominated by natural stands of Sal (*Shorea robusta*) and bamboo groves. Strong relationships of protection, management and use by the communities have evolved due to the dependence, need and proximity of the communities to these forests and the practice and Community-based Forest Management (CBFM) is common.

Because of this and the high regeneration from existing rootstock due to protection alone, the team has been emphasizing enrichment plantation and seeding of native and endemic species primarily. This is being complemented by the construction of water harvesting structures in order to increase the availability of water. The area is rich in biodiversity with 141 species of trees, 59 shrubs, 33 grasses, and several animals including 42 mammal and 54 bird species.

In the context of persistent problems pertaining to leasing of revenue wastelands, the team began to work with the existing traditional village institutions on *Gramya Jungle* lands lying within the revenue boundaries of villages. It also began to link up with forest protecting communities in the area to support institution building and tenurial rights. The NTGCF has felt it relevant that the rich history of protection of natural resources by communities in this region by recognized and the future challenges for the project lie in effectively dealing with these issues.

Of the 59 cooperatives that have so far carried out physical activities on revenue wastelands through plantation permissions, only six have been leased land since the project began in 1987. The team, meanwhile, began working with existing village institutions on *gramya jungle* lands adjacent to the villages, where tenure is clear and more established. Recently, the district administration has given permission to work on grazing lands, which provides the opportunity to work with 30 more villages. The specific arrangements and the nature of development activities that are to be designed for work on grazing lands is being discussed before commencing any activities.

Since 2001, the project has been working with the self initiated forest-protecting communities in a predominantly forested region of Athamallik. NTGCF has continued the process of helping communities document their oral rules and regulations in 18 villages. Besides being critical documents of record for the future this process also help the village community to question the status quo and restate the rules. Given the rich history of communities coming together for the protection and management of forests and water bodies, the recognition of their role and the legitimatisation of their rights over these resources is critical.

*Sabuja Barta*, the quarterly Oriya newsletter, was published for the sixth consecutive year focusing on issues of natural resource management and governance. Another series of issue papers, meant to support the team's work with the forest protecting communities in Athamallik, has been published since 2000. So far four issue papers have been brought out.

The team has been working with seven regional for a comprising 45 village institutions that are involved in protecting common stretches of land belonging to more than a village. Some of these for a also play an active role in addressing issues like forest fires, collection and trade of forest produce and policy development.

### 5. *Lessons from Madhya Pradesh*

The project was initiated in the year 1997 after the signing of a Memorandum of Understanding with the government of Madhya Pradesh. The Government has delineated 13,000 hectares of revenue land in Shajapur and Rajgarh districts for the implementation of the project. For the first phase of the project interventions, 60 villages in the Lakhunder river basin, Agar block in Shajapur and 161 villages in the Gadganga river basin in Khilchipur block in Rajgarh, were identified. These river basins are part of the Malwa plateau which is characterized by narrow drainage fissures amidst scattered mounds and hillocks of Trappean rocks. In the living memory of the people, the area used to have dense forests. Eventually it became completely denuded and only less than one per cent of the total geographical area is still classified as forests. With barren hillocks supporting little or no vegetation, the surface runoff takes invaluable topsoil with it, draining it into the Lakhunder and Gadgnaga Rivers. Agriculture and animal husbandry are the two major sources of livelihood for the people. Wage labour is one of major source of income for the marginal and landless people in Agar area.

The local communities, who inhabit in the project area, practice open grazing on the common lands to supplement their fodder requirements. Such common lands constitute 40 per cent of the geographical area. Increased cattle and human population coupled with the absence of any appropriate local institution has led to over exploitation and has severely degraded the commons. It has also resulted into large-scale encroachments on the common land. The project focused on two interlinked components-common land regeneration and water recharge and retention. It provided appropriate impetus to on modifying the existing practices of open, unregulated resource use towards a carefully managed, regulated use of the resources. Gradually as the dialogue and physical work progressed, issues of encroachment were brought in the common forum for discussion. In many villages institutional processes have created conditions where encroachments have been relinquished and the total area available as commons has increased substantially. During the dialogue and discussions the NTGCF team has made a constant attempt to differentiate between the encroachments by the powerful and that by the poor. The project processes have facilitated decisions where the poor are not forced to relinquish their critical source for survival.

Scarcity of drinking water for cattle following years of successive droughts has been a cause of major concern in the project area. In the last few years' extensive soil and moisture conservation activities such as contour bunds and digging of trenches were taken up, followed by the construction of several water harvesting structures. These proved to be extremely beneficial both in making surface water available for drinking as well as in substantially increasing the water-table in the area. In the absence of regulatory mechanisms on groundwater use, the potential for conflicts over water is evident and the team is initiating a dialogue within the communities on the matter.

Till recently, cooperatives were being registered under the more flexible and autonomous Madhya Pradesh Swayattata Adhiniyam Act 1999. The conversion of cooperatives registered under the previous Act to the new Act is also in progress. NTGCF is now trying to transfer the lease from the erstwhile cooperatives to the *gram sabha* (the 4th tier of *Panchayati Raj* Institution), under the *Madhya Pradesh Panchayati Raj (Sansodhan) Adhiniyam 2001.* Regulated grazing mechanisms are being put in place in several areas. However, because of the consecutive three years drought and scarcity during 2001-03, animals could not be kept off land set aside for regeneration even during the critical monsoon period.

### 6. *Bhilwara (Rajasthan) experience*

Situated in the south-eastern part of Rajsthan, the project covers parts of Mandalgarh, Mandal and Raipur Tehsils in Bhilwara and parts of the Pisangan and Masuda Tehsils in Ajmer districts. Kinship settlements of mostly Gujjars are to be found with Rajput, Meena, Dankad, Merat, and Rawat forming the other dominated castes. The hamlets on average consist of 60-70 households. Initiated in 1995, the project is working within a geo-hydrological context to address the entire natural resources base in four major watersheds of Lilry and Burha in Beawar and Menalil and Mej watersheds in Mandalgarh. It is now associated with 121 village institutions including 76 cooperatives, 30 Grazing Land Development Committees and 15 Watershed Associations. The total potential area of land which can be worked upon is around 16,000 hectares with about 2,500 hectares of land under secure tenure. Approximately 1,100 hectares of grazing land and 13,000 of other commons are available to the project, under permission from the

Government.

Because of the continuing drought in recent years, highly drought resistant species which can withstand the moisture-scarce conditions during the critical period of germination are planted. Maintenance and appropriate use of the resources is given high priority by reviving old community rules that used to promote conservation in the past. As a result communities have come forward to conserve biomass. Impact of such effort have become quite visible with regenerated vegetative patch. NTGCF team has been making efforts to align local initiatives in resource management and working out agreements on boundaries for resource use and grazing rights of different villages in the watersheds. Representatives across villages are beginning to assume the long-term responsibility of maintaining the water harvesting structures.

Despite the two years consecutive drought, the water levels in the wells in some of the project villages showed an increase while groundwater levels have reportedly dropped in general. The communities ascribe this to the soil and moisture conservation activities that were undertaken, and without being conclusive, the geo-hydrological studies undertaken by the NTGCF also support this.

Some of the villages have taken a decision on their own to protect, and in some cases dibble grass seed on those forest lands which are adjacent to their villages and which form the upper ridges of watersheds on which they are working. Village Forest Committees are being formed in order to work on these lands under the joint Forest Management arrangements, in rather unusual circumstances, after two years of follow-up approvals were accorded for five proposals while five other proposals submitted later are still pending.

Having categorized the various village institutions according to the period of association and extent of work completed, the NTGCF team channelled its energies either on resource maintenance and sharing, developing institutional aspects of governing and protecting the commons or on developing a perspective plan and building appropriate institutions in the villages, in different areas.

Experiencing the versatility of traditional federating bodies in providing a platform for taking decisions on resource regulation, the NTGCF team has encouraged such federation to take up the maintenance of water harvesting structures. The visible results of the project have helped village institutions to tap the resources of governmental development schemes and to establish a working link with local bureaucracy.

### 7. *The Gori river valley project (Uttaranchal)*

The Gori river valley is in Pithoragarh district of Uttaranchal, bordering Tibet and Nepal. The Gori originates from the Milam glacier and also fed by several other glacial rivers till it joins river Kali, the biggest trunk river of Kumaon, Falling in the overlapping transition zone of the flora and fauna of the eastern and western Himalayas, the region has rich biodiversity with more than 2,000 plant, 35 mammal and more than 120 bird species. There are 136 villages in the valley with a total population of 41,763. Living in climatic extremes of severe winters and monsoon downpours averaging 2,500 mm annually, the communities are dependent on subsistence agriculture and livestock (nomadic sheep and goat) herding, supplemented by wool work, extraction of valuable medical and aromatic plants and cash flows from non-residents.

The project began in 1992 and spread into the three blocks of Munsiari, Dharchula and Didihat of Pithoragarh district, to work on protective and regenerative measures on their commons. Lower down in the valley work has continued beyond the low dividing ridge lines into a neighbouring river valley in a few villages of the Bhoj Patri Gad valley, a tributary of the Ram Ganga. The project is currently supporting 88 villages, 27 through the institution of TGCs and the remaining 61 through Village Forest Councils called the *Van Panchayats Van Panchayats* are chosen as the primary institutional choice because of their cultural antecedents and history of secure tenure over village forests. The *Van Panchayats* took up the bulk of protection and revegetation work on village forestland.

Beginning in the highest villages of the Gori river valley, the project in Uttaranchal has progressed downwards, covering the three blocks of Munsiari, Dharchula, and Didihat of Pithoragarh district.

The NTGCF team continued its work with *Van Panchayats*. The new *Van Panchayats* Rules' passed by the State Cabinet of Uttaranchal in April 2001, giving the Forest Department a significant say in the management of *Van Panchayats* has been received with scepticisms as the *Van Panchayats* members apprehend a loss of their autonomy.

A total of 1.8 lakhs saplings of about 41 species were planted during the monsoons. Saplings of four difficult to grow species, *Rhododendron arboreum*, *Ficus Roxburghii, Ficus nerifolii and Syringa emodi,* were provided by the central as well as village nurseries. Extensive hedgerow plantations of agaves, locally called *Rambaans,* acted as a good long term protective fence along the boundaries of protected plots. Under very difficult climatic conditions 50,000 saplings of 13 different species were also planted during the winter months. *Van Panchayats* with the help of NTGCF are fast learning new techniques of protection and revegetation and becoming strengthened in the process.

## Conclusion

Management of village commons for sustainable production of forest resources with the help of village forest committees for overall development of the village is possible, provided the members of the committee are trained in forest management principles and practices on scientific lines. They are to be supported in preparation of management plans and guided at the initial stage. In addition, legal backing to make the committee functional is also required. Clear-cut policies, giving powers to the committee, for creation, protection, management, harvesting and for utilization usufructs are also required to be framed. Motivational and technical support is required to be given by appropriate agencies. Involvement of local youth clubs and other voluntary agencies will certainly help in making the approach a fruitful one.

Blue print approach hardly works under varied social, politico-institutional, economic and ecological context. NTGCF although works in several states of India never tried to simplify its modus operandi by working through standard model. It tried to adapt to the local situations and as a result could raise sustainable institutions for forest management under different social, political, economic, and ecological situations. Government organisations and NGOs need to be responsive to such adaptations if they wish to elicit people's participation in commons in general and CBFM in particular.

# 9

# EPILOGUE : ELICTING PEOPLE'S PARTICIPATION

Having discussed the aspects of centralised and non-centralised approaches towards forest management, we have daunting task of compiling our findings that contribute to enhancing people's involvement in forest management in rational as well as realistic manner. We have seen be it India or South East Asia, centralised forest management not only made estranged people from forest but also caused mass degradation of forest resources. From late seventies various governments started taking corrective measures to involve people in forest management by partially recognising their rights over such resources. Such efforts resulted in emergence of CBFM in different forms. At the same time we have also discussed non-governmental initiatives towards CBFM either as self-initiated or indigenous effort or as an external facilitation of NGO. Book primarily dealt with the question, ' Do the members (people) of different CBFMs participate in forest management activities with same degree of zeal and enthusiasm?' The answer we got was an emphatic 'no'. It was on this backdrop we ventured to discover the factors that were responsible for such variance. Our task is to put all these factors together and to construct a participation framework. Before constructing the comprehensive framework for people's participation, we would like to summarise all our findings.

## People's Participation: A Comprehensive Understanding

Sustained participation in community-based forest management helps in maintaining the resource base and the flow of accrued benefit over time. People's participation in planning (rule making, species selection, conflict resolution, etc.) phase enhances shared knowledgc about forest management. During implementation phase, collective tasks like plantation, post-plantation care (or protecting coppice growth in case of regeneration), monitoring and patrolling, etc. are executed. These activities foster mutual trust, reciprocity, identification with the collectivists' norms, intra-group communication on forest and allied livelihood problems, and reduce apprehension and anxiety among villagers. With the effective participation in planning and execution phases, willingness to cooperate and stay in FPC becomes stronger. Direct participation entails the voluntary, committed, and sustained support of individual appropriators. Indirect participation incorporates just, fair, and right behaviour of appropriators, and support of family members and fellow villagers towards forest protection.

Tribal communities had higher participation than non-tribal because of their historical identification with forest and ethno-religious beliefs (Guha, 1983). Tribal economy was found more dependent on forest and its resources than others. Agriculturists, who perceived short- and long-term benefits from forest, participated more readily. Carpenters and grazers whose livelihood was affected adversely by forest protection, and service-holders and businessmen who had very little dependence on forest registered lower participation in forest management. Villages/FPCs with homogenous population faced less economic and social conflicts (Vedeld, 2000) due to their commonality and mutual confidence that promoted their participation. Single village FPCs had inherent commonality, mutual understanding, and reciprocity compared to multiple village FPCs and accordingly participation was higher in former than in latter.

Forest dependent communities treated forest as assets, savings, and insurance both in short- and long-terms (Chambers and Leach, 1987; Foley and Barnard, 1984). Evidence suggested that for eliciting participation, communities and individual choices had to be given appropriate importance (Pimbert and Pretty, 1998; Shah, 1987; Shepherd, 1987). People would participate in a half-hearted manner if external intervention or state legislation undermined local choices (Chopra and Chatterjee, 1990; Pimbert and Pretty, 1998; Shah, 1987). ICFM elicited more people's participation than CCFM and JFM because of the absence of external interference, single village-based management unit with fairly homogenous population. Members of ICFM had full freedom in framing their organisation and its rules as per their priorities, which enhanced their social solidarity and sense of ownership. External interference hampered these and thereby reduced participation in CCFM and JFM. Though CCFM follow ICFM pattern, it had relatively lower participation because of partial acceptance of externally imposed rules and values by crafting agencies. In JFM, too much state interference worked against people's sense of belongingness and decreased participation in forest management.

People's participation in forest management also depends on how a particular institutional evolution and other character help each individual member in embracing social identity, group based identity, and organisational citizenship. Institutional process which ensures individual freedom of choice, local self governance, pre-eminence of local rights and knowledge system, participatory leadership, and federation opportunity found conducive in building social identity and organisational citizenship thereby elicited more participation. Evaluation of institutional rules for general administration, personal stakeholding, and inclusion of non-members in FPC was influenced by the extent of freedom the communities enjoyed in making such rules. Under full freedom in making rules as in ICFM, the evaluation of such rules was most favourable, when the freedom was restricted as in CCFM, the evaluation of rules was less favourable, and when the freedom was still restricted as in JFM, the evaluation of rules was least favourable. When the constituents of FPCs perceived the institutional rules favourably, their participation increased accordingly. If communities do not have the freedom in framing the institutional rules, appropriators' participation in forest management would be lower and grassroots organization would be fragile.

Managing Committee was the governor of institutional rules and the forest resources. To win the FPC members' trust and support, the governor was expected to be transparent and accountable. Depending on the interaction between managing committee and members of FPC in the forms of formal or informal meetings, ICFM's managing committee was most transparent and accountable, followed by CCFM and JFM. The interaction occurred weekly in ICFM, and monthly or bimonthly in CCFM (Poffenberger, 1990; Sen and Das, 1987; Sarin, 1996), and was usually brief, formal, and irregular due to the nonavailability of forest officials and political nominees (Raju, 1998) in JFM. When members of FPCs perceived the managing committee as transparent and accountable, their participation increased commensurately.

Conflicts cannot be avoided in collective venture. Conflicts were relatively less in ICFM and CCFM than JFM. Conflicts occurred primarily due to theft in JFM that destroyed forest wealth. ICFM and CCFM were successful in not letting the conflicts to cause damage to forest. Conflicts were best resolved when it motivated conflicting parties to fix things by adopting a mutually agreed change to achieve the goal. Conflict resolution through mutual agreement was the strength of ICFM and CCFM. The process not only resolved the problem but also motivated conflicting parties to adopt changed behaviour. Other modes of resolution as practised in JFM failed to initiate such positive change and caused reoccurrence of problems in JFM. Although CCFM had much similarity with ICFM, it was not free from certain pitfalls. Weaknesses in some cases were resolving conflicts through the opinion of dominant group or by the intervention of crafting agencies/NGOs. CCFM would have done better if such incidences were reduced.

Satisfaction with and gain from conflict resolution in any collective action had two implications. First, it reduced the scope of violation of agreed norms, and second, it encouraged spontaneous participation. In ICFM and CCFM conflicts were resolved by consensus/mutual agreement rather than majority opinion, whereas conflicts were resolved primarily through majority opinion in JFM.

In addition, roles played by crafting agencies in CCFM, and forest department and local political members in JFM could not be avoided. Hence, satisfaction with and gain from conflict resolution were more in ICFM followed by CCFM and JFM. Satisfaction with conflict resolution increased participation. However, gain from conflict resolution could only influence the direct participation in ICFM and CCFM. This happened because any benefit accrued through conflict resolution boosted the immediate moral than long-term conviction. Following statement would clarify the fact:

*" Forest protection is our cultural duty, but when there is conflict, I get demoralised and simply stop cooperating until the dispute is amicably solved" (Tribal from Semra village of Jharkhand).*

*" Look when people work together, conflicts, disputes are but natural. When disputes occur I too get carried away for some time but not for too long because forest is another God to me" (Inhabitant of Pada village of Orissa).*

In contrast, JFM presented a different case. In JFM both types of participation were not affected by feeling of gain. This might be due to the fact that when share of timber yield was distributed among the members, it was mere Rs. 250 (US$ 5) to Rs. 300 (US$ 6) per household. This might have dampened people's hope of getting substantial profit from timber sells after years of hard labour. Besides this, people had a suspicion that forest officials did have some conspicuous nexus with timber contractors. When conflicts persisted for long-time, as it happened in some JFM, gain from conflict resolutions failed to solicit direct participation.

Forest institution acted as a collection of individuals, which tried promoting a collective cause. For making collective choice, appropriators needed to sacrifice immediate smaller gains in order to have larger collective gains in future by accommodating individual choices for forest management through negotiations. Such process instilled collective self-confidence, geared coordinated collective action, and promoted collectivists' identity with forest institutions. It also induced (a) greater loyalty to the forest institution, (b) higher obedience to institutional rules, and (c) extra-role behaviour like motivating others for the cause. Any form of external intervention as in CCFM and JFM undermined local choices and priorities, decreased collectivists' identity with the forest institutions, and accordingly dwindled loyalty to forest institutions, acquiescence with institutional rules, citizenship behaviour, and finally group-based activity for forest management. Hence, greater freedom to the constituents would increase collectivists' identity with the forest institution, ensure effective governance of the institution, and elicit more participation in forest management. People's participation would be facilitated if the forest institutions were confined to single village, forest-dependent people, and tribal or homogenous communities.

Governance of forest management institutions depended also on intangible attributes of emotional attachment and loyalty to the institution, in-group feelings, and interpersonal sensitivity. Unlike Corporate Sectors, these institutions did not enjoy any direct economic transaction between governing authority and other members. In such institutions, individual's decision to cooperate with governing authority depended also on how leaders exert influence on constituents. With the spread of literacy and awareness among forest communities, demand for transparency and democracy was on the rise. Involvement of members in goal-setting, problem solving, and decision-making ensures transparency and accountability, enhances mutual trust, and instilled a sense of ownership (Raju, 1998). Leaders in ICFM and CCFM were predominantly participative because such institutions provided more freedom to the constituents in organisational goal-setting, rule- and decision-making, and conflict resolution. Leaders in JFM were perceived manipulative and authoritarian because of the dominance of forest department in all rule- and decision- making, irregular meeting between managing committee and general members because of the absence of forest officials, and lack of leaders' concern for members.

Members' direct and indirect participation was enhanced under participatory leader because such leaders promoted collective decision-making, in-group feelings, and administered reward or sanction objectively. Though few members perceived their leaders to be charismatic, this style evoked only higher direct participation than participatory style. Compared to participative leaders, manipulative and authoritarian leaders inhibited participation because of their non-transparent working styles, favouritism, and self-centred decision-making. Hence, irrespective of forest management institutions, charismatic or participatory style can enhance peoples' participation (Shah, 1994a).

Regardless of the types of forest and styles of leadership, leader's character enhanced participation while leader's ethics reduced participation. Hence, leader's character associated with charismatic or participatory style was the predominant predictor of people's participation. This agreed with the earlier conclusion that too much of charisma fostered dependency syndrome rather than nurtured the rational participation (Nandy and Kakar, 1980) among forest communities.

Irrespective of forest types and leadership styles, more the members were close to their leaders, more was the members' participation in forest management. ICFM and participatory or charismatic style induced higher leader-member closeness because they promoted collective decision, democratic participation, mutual trust, and ensured individual rights. Indeed, lesser power distance in grassroots organisation ensured higher individual support and cooperation in forest management (Triandis, 1994, 1995, 1996).

Value prioritisation demonstrated an act of balancing between intra- and inter-generational needs. Values like 'livelihood security from forest', 'sacrificing the present benefit', 'avoidance of free riding', and 'strict sanction' were given more importance. For poverty-stricken forest dependent communities, sacrificing any present benefit can be considered as the most difficult task. Members of ICFM and CCFM showed more sensitivity to this task of balancing than their counterparts in JFM. In JFM, people's deprived desire of 'self-governance' was vividly expressed in their most important value. Practice of regular interaction, collective decision-making, and self-governance helped in imbibing common values within the organisation. As these practices were more prevalent in CCFM and ICFM, they succeeded in developing higher value congruence than JFM. When the values of the members matched with the values espoused by forest institution, it found expression in desirable activities for forest conservation and induced greater involvement of members in forest management.

For forest communities, protection of forest is a religious duty (Guha, 1983) and source of meeting livelihood demand in short- and long-run. ICFM and CCFM offered greater benefits to their members and assured more rights over forest compared to JFM. JFM offered lesser short- and long-term benefits to its members that dispirited them to uphold the religious value of forest as a God to them. Irrespective of forest types, as individual valued forest more central to their personal lives, more they assisted in forest protection.

Regardless of forest types, participatory and charismatic styles along with the leader's character and lower power distance between leaders and members induced greater participation whereas too much of charisma dwindled participation. When the values of forest institution and its members were identical, and members considered the forest central to their lives, they participated more in the forest conservation. If the leadership styles and character otherwise do not conformed to the above styles and character, this can be changed by providing training, coaching, and counselling to the leaders of grassroots forest institutions. The value identification and centrality to forest can be enhanced through conducting regular meetings, nurturing interpersonal relationship and exhibiting participatory and charismatic leadership styles. By doing so, power distance can also be reduced. Finally, participation of members can be assured if the leaders carry the responsibility to change the mindset of the constituents of forest institutions and help them to re-identify with their eco-friendly cultural heritage.

Furthermore, we have also seen from the above case studies that social capital of rural communities *inter alia* can play crucial role in managing natural resources judiciously for economic development. Social capital encompasses all factors that facilitate people's involvement in collective action. Internal or external leadership play pivotal role in unleashing the power of social capital. In Chichkali village, Khaksi Toli and Traditional Khuls local level leadership facilitated in harnessing the benefit of mutual trust, reciprocity and institutional arrangement for economic use of natural resources without impairing the microenvironment. But such local initiatives may not prop up everywhere naturally. It requires certain external assistance. Furthermore, it is evident that people should not confine themselves only to intra-group network. It fosters a narrow outlook. Community that look beyond has better chance of development. Therefore, it is important while nurturing the intra-group network each community should develop liaison with external agencies for accessing to various benefit flow. Spread of social network enhances the magnitude of social capital. Ralegaon Siddhi and community based river water parliament are two successful evidences of amplified social capital. External assistance played pivotal role both in reviving and preserving social capital. NTGCF and Sambandh facilitated the villagers to rediscover their social capital and thereby usher them into new era of development. NTGCF tried reviving forgotten or submissive local resource management system by building on the social capital. Villages that suffer from trauma of resource degradation need such intervention to regain their old vitality. Similarly vested interest some time threatens to jeopardise a well functioning social system as happened in Ratnakiri case. Such attack need to nipped at the bud. But only local protest may be adequate to block such encroachment. NGO and government need to come forward protect and preserve such system.

## Conceptual Framework

Forest institutions acted as a collection of self (appropriators) which tried promoting a collective cause. Forest communities accommodating individual choices, and sacrificing immediate smaller gains in order to have larger collective gains in future, made collective choices for forest management through negotiations and collective decisions. It instilled collective self-confidence, geared collective action, and promoted collectivists' participation in forest conservation. It also fostered (a) greater loyalty to the grassroots forest institution, (b) higher obedience to institutional rules,

(c) transparency and accountability of managing committee, (d) reciprocal problem-solving style of conflict handling, (e) participatory leadership, and (f) members' identification with institutional values. Any form of external intervention as in CCFM and JFM when undermined such outcomes, dwindled collectivists' loyalty to forest institutions, acquiescence with institutional rules, value identification and finally group-based activity for forest management. Hence, greater freedom of constituents ensured effective governance in forest management and increased collectivists' participation. People's participation was facilitated when the forest institution was confined to single village, forest-dependent people, and homogeneous communities.

Based on the above findings Figure 9.1 depicts that where social capital that includes mutual trust and reciprocity within community, pre-eminence of local priorities, self-governance, community homogeneity and long-term economic dependencies, is given due importance, they lead to higher (a) obedience to institutional rules, (b) transparency and accountability of managing committee, (c) reciprocal style of conflict resolution, (d) participatory leadership, (e) identification with institutional values, and (f) social identity. All these outcomes enhance the participation. ICFM enjoys higher members' participation owing to social and economic homogeneity, freedom of rule-making, better access rights, people's friendly management, graduated sanction, sincere patrolling, resolving the conflicts through consensus, participatory leadership and identification with institutional values. Such features generated higher participation among members of ICFM than CCFM and JFM. However, CCFM had higher participation than JFM because many of the above features were also nurtured in CCFM units. Inadequacy of above features disheartened people in JFM and thereby evoked lesser participation.

## Conclusion and Policy Implications

Notwithstanding the difference among three different forms of forest and the differences in the study area, people's participation in forest management was influenced by composition of FPC, institutional

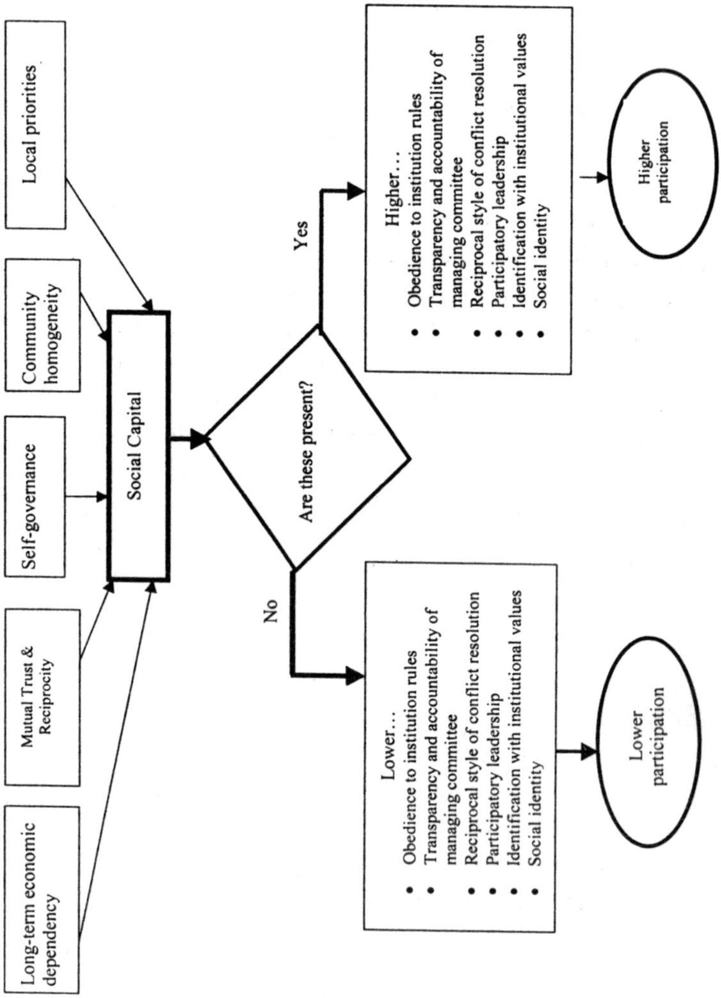


Figure 9.1 Conceptual Framework Explaining People's Participation

governance, mode of conflict resolution, leadership styles, traits, leader-member closeness, congruence between individual and organisational values, and centrality of forest in one's life. Study has revealed that higher people's participation occurred in (i) smaller FPC with higher social and economic homogeneity, (ii) forest type offering greater scope for self-governance, (iii) FPC having participatory leadership promoting decentralised decision-making, (iv) FPC having higher congruence between organisational and individual values.

Empirical evidences showed that ICFM and CCFM were more successful in promoting in-group feelings, group based pride and respect, and thereby evoking higher participation than JFM. But ICFM and CCFM control only a small fragment of Indian forest resources. Even today, around eighty five percent of official forest resources are under FD's control. More so, while establishing the legitimacy of local people's stake on forest, it would be unjustified to deny the stake of nation state. Therefore, JFM umbrella is an essential pre-requisite for making forest protection a mass movement across the country. For making JFM a more viable alternative to ICFM, and CCFM, JFM need to enhance the level of assurances to win people's confidence by conforming to the ICFM system. In JFM, the level of assurances, in-group feelings, and group based pride and respect, can be increased by adopting following set of institutional measures:

1. FD ought to recognise the legitimacy of local rights over forest resources. JFM, therefore, should try to establish a system of equitable distribution of benefits between FD and JFM members.
2. FD needs to appreciate that in-group feelings, and group based pride and respect are promoted when people have greater freedom in all category of rule- and decision-making process. Therefore, JFM should allow full power to people to work out their institutional framework and thereby reduce the dominance of FD in decision-making process.
3. As social and economic homogeneity promotes in-group feelings more spontaneously, JFM units should be formed

at relatively smaller level (village or hamlet). This will help in harnessing intra-community cohesion and close interaction among members.

4. JFM should try to embrace the principle of graduated sanction and resolving conflict through consensus decision in all intra-village/FPC matters as practised by ICFM. For inter village/FPC conflict resolution, JFM should promote Federation of JFM units and empower it to take decision in such conflicts in a democratic manner.
5. The role of gram panchayat in forest management is found to be less satisfactory and disappointing in many places. Although exclusion of gram panchayat particularly in government owned forestland might not be possible, their presence in JFM committee should be limited to an advisor.
6. JFM should promote locally accepted leadership rotation practice. JFM should also train the leaders to act in participatory manner. Close association between leader and other members should be encouraged.
7. Institutional management for forest institutions needs to be more liberal in accommodating the views of weaker sections, minority groups, and women. Building consensus in each decision-making process sometime requires longer negotiation. However, such approaches give more stability to institutional structures as well as enhanced people's adherence to the institutional resolution.

## Research Agenda

People's participation in collective action is a complex issue that changes with both time and space. Although several researchers identified the characteristics of long enduring institutions, less emphasis was given in finding out the link between participation and the institutional characters. Interaction between behaviour of resource users and resource use system is an important predictor of sustainable resource management. Factors complementary to people's participation for optimum resource utilisation need to be understood more precisely. Since spatial-temporal dynamics often influences the above interaction, empirical evidences from different locality can be emancipating and enriching.

Role of leaders in collective action arena is another less addressed aspect. In the era of globalisation socio-economic homogeneity is likely to be replaced by heterogeneity over time. In such situation leaders will have to play more crucial role for sustainable collective actions. These roles need to be identified more distinctly and how participation can be ascertained among heterogeneous communities needs to be understood.

Process of building value congruence between organisation and individuals has not been studied. This process assumes greater importance in rural Indian context. Considering the unorganised varied social dynamics of rural areas, understanding of various process of value congruence will strengthen collective action like forest management.

# APPENDICES

*APPENDIX-I*

**Unrotated and Rotated Factor Loadings on Participation and Institutional Governance**

| Variable[a] | | Unrotated Loadings I | II | III | Rotated Loadings I | II | III | Communality |
|---|---|---|---|---|---|---|---|---|
| PR | 1 | .85 | -.31 | | .90f | .11 | | .816 |
| | 2 | .85 | -.17 | | .83 | .23 | | .743 |
| | 3 | .56 | -.51 | | .73 | -.20 | | .574 |
| | 4 | .48 | .43 | | .24 | .60 | | .420 |
| | 5 | .82 | .02 | | .73 | .39 | | .676 |
| | 6 | .87 | .02 | | .77 | .40 | | .752 |
| | 7 | .76 | -.14 | | .74 | .21 | | .593 |
| | 8 | .51 | .64 | | .18 | .81 | | .679 |
| | 9 | .26 | .62 | | -.04 | .67 | | .447 |
| | 10 | .65 | -.13 | | .64 | .17 | | .433 |
| | 11 | .74 | .02 | | .66 | .35 | | .552 |
| | 12 | .53 | .25 | | .36 | .46 | | .339 |
| Explained variance | | 5.57 | 1.46 | | 4.75 | 2.27 | | |
| Explained variance (%) | | 46.4 | 12.2 | | 39.6 | 18.9 | | |
| IR | 1 | .80 | .06 | -.42 | .27 | .86 | -.02 | .816 |
| | 2 | .75 | .22 | -.47 | .20 | .88 | .14 | .830 |
| | 3 | .82 | -.01 | -.35 | .13 | .81 | -.09 | .786 |
| | 4 | .86 | -.01 | -.01 | .61 | .61 | -.05 | .745 |
| | 5 | .90 | -.00 | .01 | .71 | .56 | -.03 | .818 |

*(Appendix-I Contd...)*

*(Appendix-I Contd...)*

| | | | | | | | | |
|---|---|---|---|---|---|---|---|---|
| | 6 | .85 | -.03 | .30 | .82 | .38 | -.04 | .815 |
| | 7 | .85 | -.09 | .32 | .84 | .35 | -.09 | .832 |
| | 8 | .64 | .08 | .53 | .82 | .08 | .11 | .691 |
| | 9 | .08 | .80 | .27 | .15 | -.09 | .82 | .711 |
| | 10 | -.10 | .83 | -.11 | -.19 | .09 | .81 | .708 |
| | 11 | .55 | -.09 | .02 | .41 | .36 | -.11 | .311 |
| Explained variance | | 5.58 | 1.40 | 1.08 | 3.37 | 3.28 | 1.40 | |
| Explained variance (%) | | 50.8 | 12.7 | 9.8 | 30.7 | 29.9 | 12.8 | |
| MCTA | 1 | .52 | -.05 | | .44 | .29 | | .274 |
| | 2 | .65 | -.49 | | .81 | .03 | | .661 |
| | 3 | .79 | -.37 | | .84 | .21 | | .756 |
| | 4 | .86 | -.19 | | .78 | .40 | | .768 |
| | 5 | .76 | .02 | | .58 | .50 | | .581 |
| | 6 | .75 | .35 | | .36 | .74 | | .681 |
| | 7 | .76 | .23 | | .44 | .66 | | .635 |
| | 8 | .53 | .64 | | .01 | .84 | | .697 |
| Explained variance | | 4.05 | 1.00 | | 2.83 | 2.22 | | |
| Explained variance (%) | | 50.7 | 12.5 | | 35.4 | 27.8 | | |
| CR | 1 | .54 | -.64 | | .47 | -.69 | | .701 |
| | 2 | .98 | .06 | | .98 | -.04 | | .960 |
| | 3 | .98 | .06 | | .98 | -.04 | | .960 |
| | 4 | .93 | .16 | | .94 | .07 | | .886 |
| | 5 | -.15 | .95 | | -.05 | .96 | | .933 |
| | 6 | .26 | .86 | | .34 | .83 | | .809 |
| Explained variance | | 3.15 | 2.10 | | 3.14 | 2.11 | | |
| Explained variance (%) | | 52.5 | 34.9 | | 52.4 | 35.2 | | |

[a] PR = Participation; IR = Institutional Rules; MCTA = Managing committee's transparency; and accountability;
CR = Conflict resolution.

*APPENDIX-II*

**Unrotated and Rotated Factor Loadings on Participation and Leadership Qualities**

| Variables[a] | | Factor Loadings | | | | | | |
|---|---|---|---|---|---|---|---|---|
| | | Unrotated Loadings | | | Rotated Loadings | | | Communality |
| | | I | II | III | I | II | III | |
| LT | 1 | .61 | -.24 | -.23 | .57 | .31 | -.24 | .48 |
| | 2 | .57 | .20 | -.54 | .80 | -.12 | -..02 | .65 |
| | 3 | .71 | .10 | -.29 | .75 | .18 | .04 | .60 |
| | 4 | .22 | .45 | .39 | .40 | .18 | .61 | .40 |
| | 5 | .69 | .12 | -.05 | .60 | .32 | .17 | .49 |
| | 6 | .34 | .63 | .19 | .28 | .04 | .68 | .55 |
| | 7 | -.13 | .63 | .22 | -.10 | -.21 | .63 | .45 |
| | 8 | .63 | .27 | -.15 | .56 | .24 | .31 | .47 |
| | 9 | .73 | -.38 | .38 | .29 | .86 | -.05 | .83 |
| | 10 | .77 | -.36 | .32 | .36 | .83 | -.06 | .83 |
| | 11 | .73 | -.05 | -.14 | .65 | .37 | -.02 | .56 |
| | 12 | .56 | .25 | -.07 | .54 | .17 | .26 | .39 |
| | 13 | .42 | -.16 | .45 | .04 | .62 | .13 | .40 |
| Explained variance | | 4.40 | 1.55 | 1.14 | 3.23 | 2.36 | 1.51 | |
| (%) Explained variance | | 33.85 | 11.93 | 8.80 | 24.83 | 18.18 | 11.57 | |
| Cumulative variance (%) | | 33.85 | 45.78 | 54.58 | 24.83 | 43.01 | 54.58 | |

[a]LT = Leadership Traits.

## *APPENDIX-III*

**1.00 Items for measuring people's participation in the affair of forest management**

1.1 Did you participate in any meeting called by forest protection committee?
(Always/ Sometimes/ Never)

1.2 Do you take part in discussion besides mere attendance?
(Always/ Sometimes/ Never)

1.3 Did you participate in the rule making process?
(Yes/No)

1.4 Do you abide by the norms and regulations of CFM/JFM?
(Always/ Sometimes /Never)

1.5 Did you contribute any labour towards FOREST activities of common interest?
(Always/ Sometimes/ Never)

1.6 Did you take part in selecting/ electing the members of managing committee?
(Always/ Sometimes/ Never)

1.7 Did you ever take part in selecting/ electing the president / chairman of forest protection committee?
(Always/ Sometimes/ Never)

1.8 Do you encourage others to abide by the rules and regulations of forest protection committee?
(Always/ Sometimes/ Never)

1.9 Did you ever report to managing committee about any violation of rules by any members?
(Always/ Sometimes/ Never)

1.10 Do you help the forest protection committee in monitoring/patrolling the forest?
(Always/ Sometimes/ Never)

1.11 Do you co-operate with managing committee for ensuring equitable distribution of benefits from forest?
(Always/ Sometimes/ Never)

1.12 Do you encourage your spouse to abide by forest protection rules? (Always/ Sometimes/ Never)

**2.00 Evaluation of institutional rules** (Tick the response against each question)

(**Response:** F= Fair; NFUF= Neither fair nor unfair; UF= Unfair; A=Acceptable; NAUA= Neither acceptable nor unacceptable; UA= Unacceptable; D= Desirable; NDUD= Neither desirable nor undesirable; UD= Undesirable.)

How do you assess...

2.1 the eligibility criteria for membership of every household of the village in the FPC general body? (F/NFUF/UF) (A/NAUA/UA) (D/NDUD/UD)

2.2 existing women's rights to take part in general body? (F/NFUF/UF) (A/NAUA/UA) (D/NDUD/UD)

2.3 the share of benefits you get from forest? (F/NFUF/UF) (A/NAUA/UA) (D/NDUD/UD)

2.4 the existing forest monitoring/ patrolling system? (F/NFUF/UF) (A/NAUA/UA) (D/NDUD/UD)

2.5 the system of sanction/punishment for the offenders who violate rules of FPC? (F/NFUF/UF) (A/NAUA/UA) (D/NDUD/UD)

2.6 the rights of every villager to choose the members of managing committee ? (F/NFUF/UF) (A/NAUA/UA) (D/NDUD/UD)

2.7 the representation of each sub-group in managing committee ? (F/NFUF/UF) (A/NAUA/UA) (D/NDUD/UD)

2.8 the system of selection/election of president/chairman? (F/NFUF/UF) (A/NAUA/UA) (D/NDUD/UD)

2.9 the sharing of benefits to non-members? (F/NFUF/UF) (A/NAUA/UA) (D/NDUD/UD)

2.10 the inclusion of panchayat members/ political persons in the managing committee? (F/NFUF/UF) (A/NAUA/UA) (D/NDUD/UD)

2.11 the scope to modify rules of FPC by general body? (F/NFUF/UF) (A/NAUA/UA) (D/NDUD/UD)

**3.0 Perception of managing committee**

Fill the response number on the left-side provided space.

Always = 2, Sometimes = 1, Never = 0

3.1 Did you feel neglect by the attitude of MC?

3.2 Did the MC maintain proper financial account?

3.3 Did the MC share the information with general body?

3.4 Did the MC consult general body before revising the rules?

3.5 Did the MC distribute all benefits equally?

3.6 Did the MC sincere in protecting and managing the forest?

3.7 Did the MC motivate general members for forest protection?

3.8 Was the MC sympathetic to members' need at the time of difficulties/ emergency?

**4.0 Satisfaction with conflict resolution**

4.1 What are major issues of conflict within your forest protection unit? (a. membership, b. formation of managing committee; c. planning of activities, d. distribution of duties and responsibilities, e. distribution of employment, f. financial accounting, g. distribution of benefits, h. theft and sanction, i. Others specify............)

§ Within the FPC:

§ Between adjacent villages:

4.2 Number of such conflicts occurred during last two years (from records):

§ Within the FPC:

§ Between adjacent villages:

§ With Panchayat administration:

4.3 How such conflicts were resolved? (a. mutual agreement and discussion, b. majority opinion, c opinion of dominant group, d. arbitration of Panchayat, e. arbitration of Forest staff / NGO staff, f. Others (specify) ........................

§ Within the FPC:

§ Between adjacent villages:

Fill the response number on the left-side provided space.

Highly satisfied = 2, Satisfied = 1, Not satisfied = 0

In the last two years, have you been...

4.4 satisfied with conflict resolution within the village?

4.5 satisfied with conflict resolution between the villages/FPCs?

4.7 satisfied with conflict resolution between non FPC villages?

4.8 satisfied with conflict resolution between Panchayat and your FPC?

Fill the response number on the left-side provided space.

Fully = 2, Partially = 1, Not at all = 0

In the last two years, to what extent...

4.9 did conflict de-motivate you for forest protection?

4.10 did conflict resolution cause any loss to you ?

**5.00 Evaluation of Leadership Styles, Qualities, and Individual Closeness with the Leader.**

5.1 Four situations are described below. Which situation matches with your leader / chairperson / president best?

A. She/He patiently listens to everyone's views and suggestions. She/He although often agrees to act according to the group decision, changes her/his words/ decisions later on. She/He favours people of her/his choice. She/He shows sympathy/favour to those who support her/his action. She/He maintains a good rapport with influential people/bodies like panchayat, forest staff, political leaders etc. She/He wants to continue as leader as long as she/he can.

B. She/He herself/himself decides all policies and strategies for forest protection. She/He emphasises obedience to her/his decision and respect to him. She/He cares for her/his village/unit reputation. She/He likes those who are loyal to her/him. She/He tries to be father figure but very strict. She/He puts herself/ himself first always.

C. She/He is people oriented. She/He along with villagers determine the policies and strategies for forest protection. Though she/he is concerned with efficient management, she/he cares a lot for forest protection unit members. She/He praises appropriate activities of the members and criticises the inappropriate activities. She/He takes part in all activities equally with the members. She/He sympathetic to others needs at the time of difficulties. She/He encourages in-group feeling.

D. She/He is a visionary. She/He tries to motivate members with future prospect. She/He is a good speaker. She/He is much concerned about forest conservation. c often takes personal risk in order pursue group activities. She/He brings out new ideas. She/He is also sensitive to the needs and feelings of other members but tries to develop mutual liking and respect.

**A. Manipulative. B. Authoritarian. C. Participatory. D. Charismatic.**

5.2 How do you rank your leader's on following traits: (Place a pebble on appropriate step of the given ladder against each trait)

a. Eco-conservationist
b. Good organiser
c. Sacrificing
d. Impartial
e. Honest (Sincere)
f. Ability to deal with external agencies
g. Sympathetic to others need
h. Visionary
i. Collective decision maker
j. Tolerant to others view
k. Respect to others (villagers)
l. Trustworthy
m. Self discipline

5.3 A line is given below. Your leader is standing at one side. Indicate your position on this line on the basis of your relation with her/him.

**6.0. Assessment of protection values in individual life**

6.1 Arrange the following guiding principle for forest protection in order of priority (Separate cards indicating each items were given to the respondent).

| VALUES | RANK |
|---|---|
| Sacrificing the present benefit | ................................ |
| Avoidance of Free Riding | ................................ |
| Livelihood security from forest | ................................ |
| Communal sharing | ................................ |
| Equal rights | ................................ |
| Dutiful | ................................ |
| Obeying collective decisions | ................................ |
| Eco-conservation | ................................ |
| Self Governance | ................................ |
| Strict Sanction | ................................ |

6.2 Suppose the circle below is your life space. Where do you place the forest protection activities in this circle?

**Score**..................

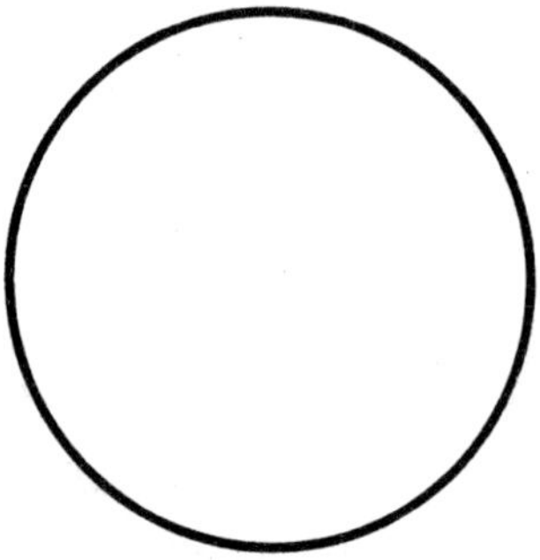

# BIBLIOGRAPHY


Agarwal, A. (1987). Between need and greed: The wasting of India, the greening of India. In A. Agarwal, D. D'Monte & U. Samarth (Ed), *The fight for survival*. New Delhi: Centre for Sceince and Environment.

Agarwal, A., & Narain, S. (1990). Strategies for the involvement of the landless and women in afforestation: Five case studies from India. *A Technical Cooperation Report: World Employment Programme*. Geneva: International Labour Office.

Agrawal, C., & Saigal, S. (1996). *Joint forest management in India: A brief review* (Working Paper, May 16). New Delhi: Society for Promotion of Wasteland Development.

Anderson, R., & Huber, W. (1988). *The hour of the fox: Tropical forests, the World Bank and indigenous people in central India.*New Delhi: Vistaar.

Appadurai, A. (1995). The production of locality. In R. Fardon (Ed.), *Counterworks* (pp. 204-225). London: Routledge.

Aquino, R.M., Castillo, R.A. del, & Payuan, E.V. (1987). *Mounting a national social forestry program: lessons learned from Philippine experience*. Working paper, Environment and Policy Institute, East-West Center, Honolulu, Hawaii, 72.

Arnold, J.E.M. (1987). Community forestry. *Ambio, 16*(2/3),122-128.

Arnold, J.E.M. (1991). *Community forestry, ten years in review* (FAO Community Forestry Note, No. 7). Geneva: FAO.

Arnold, J.E.M. (1993). Management of forest resources as common property. *Commonwealth Forestry Review 72* (3), 157-161.

Arnold, J.E.M., & Stewart, W.C. (1991). *Common property resource management* (Tropical Forestry Paper No. 24). Oxford: Oxford Forestry Institute, University of Oxford.

Attwood, D.W., & Baviskar, B. S. (1987). Why do some cooperatives work but not others? A comparative analysis of sugar cooperatives in India. *Economic and Political Weekly, 22*(26), A38 - A56.

Attwood, D.W. (1988). Social and political preconditions for successful cooperatives: The cooperative sugar factories of western India. In D.W. Attwood & B.S. Baviskar (Ed.), *Who shares? Cooperatives and rural* development. New Delhi: Oxford University Press.

Bajaj, M.1990. An examination of the potential for investment in natural regeneration of degraded forest with community participation. *Wastelands News 6*(1), 7-21.

Ballabh, V., & Singh, K. (1988). *Van (forest) panchayats in Uttar Pradesh hills: A critical analysis*. Research paper. Gujarat, Anand: Institute of Rural Management.

Balland, J.M., & Platteau, J.P. (1996). *Halting degradation of natural resources: Is there a role for rural communities?* Oxford: FAO and Claredon Press.

Bandyopadhyay, J. (1983). The challenge of social forestry. In W. Fernandes & S. Kulkarni (Eds.). *Towards a new policy*. New Delhi: Indian Social Institute.

Banki, E.S. (1981). *Dictionary of administration and management*. Los Angeles: Systems Research Institute.

Bardhan, P. (1993). Managing the village commons. *Journal of Economic Perspectives, 7*(4), 87-92.

Barkow, J. H., Cosmides, L., & Tooby, J. (Eds.), (1992). *The adapted mind*. New York: Oxford University Press.

Barnes, D.F., Olivares, J. (1988). *Sustainable resource management in agriculture and rural development projects: policies, procedures and results* (Working paper No. 5). Environment Department, Policy planning and Research, World Bank.

Bene, J.G., Beall, H.W. & Cote, A. (1977). *Trees, food and people: Land management in the tropics*. Ottawa, Canada: IDRC.

Berkes, F. (1986). Local-level management and the common problem: A comparative study of Turkish coastal fisheries. *Marine Policy, 10*, 215-229.

Blair, H.W. (1986). Social forestry: Time to modify goals? *Economic and Political Weekly 21*(30), 1317-1321.

Breman, J. (1997). The village in focus. In J.Breman, P. Kloos & A. Seth (Eds.), *The village in Asia revisited*. Delhi: Oxford University Press.

Britt-Kapoor, C. (1994). *A tale of two committees: Village perspectives on local institutions, forest management and resource use in two central Himalayan Indian villages* (Rural Development Forestry Network Paper No. 17a). London: ODI.

Bromley, D. (1993). Common property as a metaphor: Systems of knowledge, resources and the decline of individualism. *The Common Property Digest, 27* (1), 1-8.

Bromley, D.W. (1986). The common property challenge. *Proceedings of the conference on common property resource management* (pp. 1-5). Washington: National Academy Press.

Bromley, D.W., Fenny,D., McKean, M., Peters, P., Gilles, J., Oakerson, R., Runge, C.F., & Thomson, J. (Eds.)(1992). *Making the commons work: Theory, practice, and policy*. San Francisco: ICS Press.

Bruce, J.W. (1999). *Legal bases for the management of forest resources as common property* (Vol. 14). Rome: Food and Agriculture Organisation.

Bruner. J.S. (1957). On perceptual readiness. *Psychological Review, 64*, 123-152.

Brunstein, J.C., & Collwitzer, P.M. (1969). Effects of failure on subsequent Performance: The importance of self-defining goals. *Journal of Personality and Social Psychology, 70*,395-407.

Buchy, M. (1996). *Teak and Arecanut: Colonial state, forest, and people in the Western Ghats 1800-1947*. Pondicherry: Indira Gandhi National Centre for the Arts.

Cernea, M.M. (1985). Alternative units of social organization sustaining afforestation strategies. In M.M. Cernea (Ed), *Putting people first: Sociological variables in rural development* (pp.276-293). Oxford, UK: Oxford University Press.

Cernea, M.M. (1987). Farmer organisation and institution building for sustainable development. *Regional Development Dialogue, 8*, 1-24.

Cernea, M.M. (1989). *User groups as producers in participatory afforestation strategies* (World Bank Discussion Papers, No. 70). World Bank

Chakravorty- Kaul, M. (1993). Durability in diversity: Two centuries of co-management in the Punjub forests, an institutional analysis, draft paper.

Chambers, R. (1983). *Rural development: Putting the last first.* London: Longman.

Chambers, R., & Leach, M. (1987). *Trees to meet contingencies: Savings and security for the rural poor* (Social Forestry Network Paper, 5a). ODI, 3-29.

Chambers, R., Saxena, N.C., & Shah, T. (1989). *To the hands of the poor: Water and trees.* New Delhi: Oxford-IBH.

Chattopadhya, G.P. (1975). Dependency in Indian culture: From mud huts to company boardrooms. *Economic and Political Weekly, 10*(22), M30 - M38.

Chopra, K., Kadekodi, G.K., & Murty, M.N. (1990). *Participatory development: People and common property resource.* New Delhi: Sage.

Chopra, S., & Chatterjee, D. (1990). Integrating conservation and development: A case study of the socio-economic forestry complex at Arabari, West Bengal. *The International Tree Crops Journal, 6*, 193-204.

Cloe, D.H. (1999). Clearing the air: Four propositions about property rights and environmental protection. *Duke Environmental Law and Policy Forum, 10*(1), 103-130.

Coleman, J.S. (1988). Social capital and creation of human capital. *American Journal of Sociology 94*, S95-S120.

Coleman, J.S. (1990). *Foundation of social theory.* Boston, MA: Harvard University Press.

Collier, P. (1998). *Social capital and poverty* (Working Paper, No. 4). The World Bank Social Capital Initiative.

Conger, J.A., & Kanungo, R.N. (1987). Toward a behavioural theory of charismatic leadership in organisational settings. *Academic of Management Review, 12*, 637-647.

Costanja, R., d'Arge, R., de Groot, R., Farber, S., Grasso, M., Hannon, B., Limburg, K., Naeem, S., O'Neil, R., Parvelo, J.,

Raskin, R.G., Sutton, P., & de van den Belt, M. (1997). The value of the world's ecosystem services and natural capital. *Nature*, 387, 253-260.

CSE (1985). *The state of India's environment 1984-85: The second citizen's report*. New Delhi: Centre for Science and Environment.

Deb, D., & Malhotra, K.C. (1993). People's participation: The evolution of Joint Forest Management in south West Bengal. In S. B. Roy & A. K. Ghosh (eds.), *People of India: Biological and cultural dimensions* (pp. 329-342). New Delhi: Inter India Publications.

Denslow, J.S., & Padoch, C. (1988). *People of the tropical rain forest* (p. 232). University of Barkely, USA: California Press.

Doosje, B., Ellemers, N., & Spears, R. (1995). Perceived intra-group variability as a function of group status and identification. *Journal of Experimental Social Psychology, 31*, 410-436.

Dove, M. (1993). A revisionist view of tropical deforestation and development. *Environmental Conservation, 20*(1), 17-56.

Durgaprasad, P. & Rajendran, V. (2001) development partnerships and networking for sustainable rural development: Perspectives, successes and challenges. *Journal of Rural Development, 20*(4),587-607.

Eckholm, E. (1979). *Planting for the future: Forestry for human needs*. Washington: Worldwatch Institute.

FAO (1978). *Forestry for local community development* (Forestry Paper, No. 7). FAO.

FAO (1985). *Tree growing by rural people* (Forestry Paper, No. 64). FAO.

Femconsult (1995). *Study of the incentives for Joint Forest Management* (Report to World Bank May 1995). New Delhi: World Bank.

Fisher, R.J. (1989). *Indigenous systems of common property forest management in Nepal*. Working Paper No. 18, Environment and Policy Institute, East-West Center, Honolulu, Hawaii, USA.

Foley, G., & Barnard, G. (1984). *Farm and community forestry* (Technical Report, No.3). Earthscan.

FES (2002). *Annual Report 2001-2002*. Anand, Gujrat: Foundation For Ecological Security

FSI (1998). *The state of forest report*. Dehradoon: Forest Survey of India.

Fukuyama, F. (1995). *Trust: The social values and the creation of prosperity*. New York: Free Press.

Gadgil, M. (1989). Deforestation: Problems and prospect. *Foundation day lecture*, Society for Promotion of Wasteland Development, New Delhi.

Gadgil, M. (1998). Grassroots conservation practices: Revitalising the traditions. In A. Kothari, N. Pathak, R. V. Anuradha, & B. Taneja (Ed.), *Communities and conservation* (pp. 219-238). New Delhi: Sage.

Gadgil, M., & Guha, R. (1992). *The fissured land: An ecological history of India*. New Delhi: Oxford University press.

Gadgil, M., & Rao, P. R. S. (1994). A system of positive incentives to conserve biodiversity. *Economic and Political Weekly, 29*(32), 2103-2107.

Gasgonia, D.Z. (1991). *Development assistance and property rights in the Philippine uplands*. Paper presented in East-West Centre Programme on environment, Bali, Indonesia.

Gibbs, C.J.N., & Bromley, D.W., (1989). Institutional arrangements for sustainable managements of rural resources: Common property regimes and conservation. In F. Berkes (Ed), *Common property resources, ecology and community-based sustainable development* (pp. 22-32). London: Belhaven Press.

Gilmour, D.A., & Fisher, R.J. (1991). *Villagers, forests and foresters, the philosophy, process and practices of community forestry in Nepal* (p.212). Kathamandu, Nepal: Sahayogi Press.

GOI (1976). *Report of the National Commission on Agriculture, Part IX, Forestry*. New Delhi: Department of Agriculture and Cooperation, Government of India.

Granovetter, M. (1985). Economic action and social structure. *American Journal of Sociology. 91*, 481-510.

Gregersen, H.M. (1982). Village forestry development in the Republic of Korea: A case study. *Forestry for local community development programme series, FAO*, Rome, Italy, 104 p.

Grootaert, C. (1998). Social capital: the missing link? (Working Paper, No. 3). The World Bank, Social Capital Initiative.

Guha, R. (1983) Forestry in British and post-British India: An historical analysis. *Economic and Political Weekly, 18*(44), 1882-1896.

Guha, R. (1989). *The unquiet woods: Ecological change and peasant resistance in the Himalayas*. Delhi: Oxford University Press.

Gupta, A. (1985). Socio-ecological paradigm to analyse the problem of poor in dry regions. *Eco-Development News, 32*, 71-75.

Hall, J.B., & Rodgers, W.A. (1992). Buffers at the boundary. *Rural Development Forestry Network Paper,* No. 13A, Overseas Development Institute, London, UK.

Handy, C.B. (1976). *Understanding organizations*. Harmondsworth, UK : Penguin.

Hardcastle, P.D. (1987). *Micro-planning for social forestry: A description of the system designed for Karnataka Social Forestry Project, India* (Social Forestry Network Paper, 4c). ODI, 24.

Hardin, G. (1968). Tragedy of commons. *Science, 162*, 1243-1248.

Haslam, S.A., & Turner, J.C. (1992). Context-dependent variation in social stereotyping 2. the relationship between frame of reference, self-categorization and accentuation. *European Journal of Social Psychology , 22*, 251-277.

Haslam, S.A., McGarty, C., & Turner, J.C. (1999). Salient group membership and persuasion: The role of social identity in the validation of beliefs. In J. Nye & A. Brower (Eds.), *What's social about social cognition? Research on socially shared cognition in small groups* (pp.29-56). Newbury Park CA:Sage.

Haslam, S.A., McGarty, C., & Turner, J.C. (1999). Social identity salience and the emergence of stereotype consensus. *Personality and social Psychology Bulletin, 25*, 809-818.

Haslem, S.A., Powell, C., & Turner, J.C. (2000). Social identity, self-categorization, and work motivation: Rethinking the contribution of the group to positive and sustainable organisational outcomes. *Applied Psychology: An International Review, 2000, 49* (3), 319-339.

Heiner, R.A. (1983). The origin of predictable behaviour. *American Economic Review, 73*, 560-595.

Herzberg, F. (1966). *Work and the nature of man*. Cleveland, OH : World Publishing Co.

Herzberg, F., Mausner, B., & Snyderman, B. (1959). *The motivation to work*. New York: Wiley.

Herzverg, F., Mausner, B., & Snyderman, B. (1959). *The motivation to work*. New York: Wiley.

Hiermath, S.R., Kanwalli, S., & Kulkarni, S. (1994). *All about draft forest bill and forest lands*. Dharwad: Samaj Parivarthan Samudaya.

Hobley, M. (1987). Involving the poor in forest management: Can it be done? The Nepal - Australia project experience (Social Forestry Network Paper, 5c). ODI, 1-16.

Hobley, M. (1996). Participatory forestry: The process of change in India and Nepal. *ODI Rural Development Forestry Study Guide 3*. London: Agriculture Administration Unit.

Hobley, M., Jeffrey, Y., Campbell, R., & Bhatia A. (1995). Community forestry in India and Nepal: Learning from each other. *Himalayan Paryavaran*, 78-97.

Hoffman, E., McCabe, K.A., & Smith, V.L. (1998). Behavioural foundations of reciprocity: experimental economics and evolutionary psychology. *Economic Inquiry, 36*, 335-352.

Huxley, E. (1960). *A new earth: An experiment in colonialism*. London: Chatto and Windus.

Hyman, E. L. (1985). Monitoring and evaluation of forestry projects for local community development. *Agricultural Administration, 19*, 139-160.

Hyman, E.L. (1983). Pulpwood farming in the Philippines from the viewpoint of the smallholder: An ex post evaluation of the PICOP PROJECT. *Agricultural Administration* 14,23-49.

Jeffery, R., & Sundar, N. (Ed). (1999). *A new moral economy for India's forests?* (pp. 16-54). New Delhi: Sage.

Jewitt, S. (1996). *Agro-ecological knowledge and forest management in the Jharkhand, India: Tribal development or populist impasse?* Unpublished doctoral dissertation, Newham College: University of Cambridge.

Jodha, N.S. (1986). Common property resources and rural poor in dry regions of India. *Economic and Political Weekly, 21*(27), 1169-1181.

Jodha, N.S. (1989). *Management of common property resources in selected areas of India*. Nepal: ICIMOD.

Jodha, N.S. (1990). Common property resources and rural poor in dry regions of India. *Economic and Political Weekly, 21*, 1169-1181.

Jodha, N.S. (1994). Common property resources and the rural poor. In R. Guha (ed.), *Social Ecology.* Delhi: Oxford University Press..

*Joint Forest Management Update 1998.* Society for Promotion of Wasteland development, New Delhi.

Kant, S., Singh, N.M., & Singh, K.K. (1991). Community based forest management systems: Case studies from Orissa. In *Swedforest*, New Delhi.

Katz, D., & Kahn, R.L. (1978). *The social psychology of organisations* (2nd Eds.). New York: John Wiley.

Khare, A. (1998). Community based conservation in India. In A. Kothari, N. Pathak, R.V. Anuradha, & B. Taneja (ed.), *Communities and conservation (pp. 81-101).* New Delhi: Sage.

Korten, D. C. (1986). *Community management: Asian experience and perspectives*. West Hartford, CT: Kumarian Press.

Kothari, A., Anuradha, R.V., & Pathak, N. (1998). Community-based conservation: Issues and prospects. In A. Kothari, N. Pathak, R.V. Anuradha, & B. Taneja (Ed.), *Communities and conservation* (pp. 25-57). New Delhi: Sage.

Kramer, R.M. (1993). Co-operation and organizational identification. In J.K. Murnigham (Ed.), *Social psychology in organizations: Advances in theory and research*. Englewood Cliffs, NJ: Prentice Hall.

Lal, J.B. (1994). Economic value of India's forest stock. In A. Agrawal (Ed.), *The price of forest* (p. 44). New Delhi: Centre for Science and Environment.

Lam, W.F. (1998). *Governing irrigation systems in Nepal: Institutions, infrastructure, and collective action*. Oakland, CA: ICS Press.

Landy, F.J. (1989). *Psychology of work behaviour* (4th edn.). Pacific Grove, CA : Brooks Cole.

Lele, S., & Rao, R.J. (1996). Whose cooperatives and whose produce? The case of LAMPS in Karnataka. In R. Rajagopalan (Ed.), *Rediscovering cooperation* (pp. 53-91). Gujarat, Anand: Institute of Rural Management.

Locke, C. (1995). *Planning for the participation of vulnerable groups in communal management of forest resources: The case of Western Ghats forestry projects*. Doctoral thesis, Centre of Development Studies, University of Wales.

Lynch, O.J. & Talbot, K. (1995). *Balancing acts: Community based forest management and national law in Asia and the Pacific.* Washington, D.C: World Resources Institute.

Lynch, O.J. (1992). Securing community based tenurial rights in the tropical forests of Asia. *World Resource Institute, Issues in Development,* (November).

Mackean, M. (1987). *Success on the çommon: A comparative examination of institution for the common property resource management.* Paper presented at a conference on 'Advances in comparative institutional analysis' at the Inter-university Centre of Postgraduate Studies at Dubrovnik, 19-23 October. Durham: Duke University.

Malhotra, K. C. (1995). Linkages between biodiversity, conservation and development: Lessons emerging from India. In P. Kumani (Ed.), *Empowering Society* (pp. 224-235). Madras: The Gurukul Lutheran Theological College

McCay, B.J., & Acheson, J.M. (1987). *The question of the commons: The culture and ecology of communal resources.* Tuscon: University of Arizona Press.

McClelland, D.C. (1987). *Human motivation*. New York : Cambridge University Press.

Meglino, B.M., Ravlin, E.C., & Adkins, C.L. (1989). A work values approach to corporate culture: A field test of the value congruence process and its relationship to individual outcomes. *Journal of Applied Psychology, 74*(3), 424-432.

Ministry of Environment and Forests (1990). *Circular on involvement of village communities and voluntary agencies for regeneration of degraded forest lands*. MoEF No. 6-21/89-F.P.

Mol. P.W., & Wiersum, K.F. (1993). Asia. In D.A. Messerschmidt (Ed), Common forest resource management: Annotated bibliography on Asia, Africa and Latin America. *Community Forestry Note*, No. 11, FAO, Rome, Italy, 25-52.

Molinas, J. (1998). The impact of equality, gender, external assistance and social capital on local level cooperation. *World Development, 26* (3), 413-431.

Nadkarni, M.V., Pasha, S.A., & Prabhakar, L.S. (1989). *The political economy of forest use and management*. New Delhi: Sage Publications.

Nair, C.T.S. (1985). Crisis in forest resource management. In J. Bandyopadhyaya (Ed.), *India environment:Crisis and responses*. Dehradoon: Natraj Publishers.

Nandy, A., & Kakar, S. (1980). Culture and personality. In U. Pareek (Ed.), *A survey of research in psychology*, 1971-1976, (Part 1, pp. 136-167). Bombay: Popular Prakashan.

Narayan, D. (1996). *The contribution of people's participation: Evidence from 21 rural water supply projects* (Occasional Paper Series No. 1). Environmentally Sustainable Development, World Bank.

NCHSE (1987). *Documentation on forest and rights* (Vol. I). New Delhi: Centre for Human Settlements and Environment.

Nelson, N., & Wright, S. (1995). Participation and power. In N. Nelson, & S. Wright (Eds.), *Power and participatory development* (pp. 1-20). London: Intermediate Technology Publications.

North, D.C. (1990). *Institutions, institutional change and economic performance*. Cambridge, UK: Cambridge University Press.

North, D.C. (1998). Economic performance through time. In M. C. Brinton, & V. Nee (Ed.), *The new institutionalism in sociology* (pp. 247-257). New York: Russell Sage Foundation.

Nuitjen, M. (1992). Local organisation as organising practices: Rethinking rural institutions. In N. Long & A. Long (Ed.), *Battlefields of knowledge* (pp. 47-84), London: Routledge.

Oakerson, R.J. (1986). A model for the analysis of common property problem. *Proceedings of the conference on common property resource management* (pp. 13-29). Washington: National Academy Press.

Oakes, P.J. (1987). The salience of social categories. In J.C. Turner, M.A. Hogg, P.J. Oakes, S.D. Reicher, & M.S. Wetherell, *Rediscovering the social group: A self-categorization theory* (pp. 117-141). Oxford: Blackwell.

Oakes, P.J. (1987). The salience of social categories. In J.C. Turner, M.A. Hogg, P.J. Oakes, S.D. Reicher, & M.S. Wetherell, *Rediscovering the social group: A self-categorization theory* (pp. 117-141). Oxford: Blackwell.

Oakes, P.J., Haslam, S.A., & Turner, J.C. (1949). *Stereotyping and social reality*. Oxford: Blackwell.

Oakes, P.J., Haslam, S.A., & Turner, J.C. (1949). *Stereotyping and social reality*. Oxford:Blackwell.

Oakes, P.J., Turner, J.C., & Haslam, S.A. (1991). Perceiving people as group members : The role of fit in the salience of social categorizations. *British Journal of Social Psychology, 30*, 125-144.

Oakley, P., & Marsden, D.(1984). *Approaches to participation in rural development.* Geneva: International Labour Office.

Olofson, H. 1980. An ancient social forestry. *Sylvatrop Philippine Forestry Journal, 5*(4), 255-262.

Ostrom, E. (1986). Issues of definition and theory: Some conclusions and hypotheses. *Proceedings of the conference on common property resource management* (pp. 597-615). Washington: National Academy Press.

Ostrom, E. (1990). *Governing the commons: The evolution of institutions for collective action* (pp. 182-212). Cambridge: Cambridge University Press.

Ostrom, E. (1998). A behaviorial approach to the rational choice theory of collective action. *American Political Science Review, 92*, 1-22.

Ostrom, E. (1998). A behaviourial approach to the rational choice theory of collective action. *American Political Science Review, 92*, 1-22.

Ostrom, E. (1999). Coping with tragedies of the commons. *Annual Review of Political Science, 2*, 493-535.

Ostrom, E., Dietz, T., Dolsak, N., Stern, P.C., Stonich, S. & Weber, E. (eds.)(2002). *The drama of commons*. Washington, DC: National Research Council, National Academy Press.

Ostrom, E., Gardner, R., & Walker, J. (1994). *Rules, games, and common pool* resources. Ann Arbor: University of Michigan Press.

Ouwerkerk, J.W., Ellemers, N., & de Gilder, D. (1999). Social identification, affective commitment, and individual effort on behalf of the group. In N. Ellemers, R. Spears, & B. J. Doosje (Ed.), *Social identity: Context, commitment, content*. Oxford: Blackwell.

OXFAM (1998). *Joint Forest management in Andhra Pradesh*. Hyderabad: OXFAM Trust.

Padoch. C. & Vayda, A.P. (1983). Patterns of resource use and human settlements in tropical forests. In F.B. Golley & H. Lieth (Eds), *Tropical rain forest ecosystems, structure and function* (301-313). Amsterdam, Netherlans: Elsevier.

Palit, S. (1993). *The future of Indian forest management: Into the twenty-first century*. Unpublished manuscript.

Palmer, I. (1976). *The new rice in Asia: Conclusions from four country studies*. Geneva: UNRISD.

Pathak, A. (1994). *Contested domains: The state, peasants and forests in contemporary India*. New Delhi: Sage.

Peluso, N.L. (1992). *Rich forests, poor people-resource control and resistance in Java*. Berkely, USA: University of California Press.

Peluso, N.L., & Poffemberger, M. (1989). Social forestry in Java: Reorienting management systems. *Human Organization, 48* (4), 333-344.

Persoon, G.A., & Wiersum, K.F. (1991). Anthroplogy in a forest environment. In P. Kloss & H.J.M. Claessen (Eds), *Contemporary anthropology in the Netherlands: The use of antroplogical ideas* (pp. 85-104). Amsterdam, Netherlands: VU University Press.

Pimbert, M. (1994). *Training workshop on joint forest management, West Bengal, India*. Switzerland: WWF.

Pimbert, M., & Pretty, J. (1998). Diversity and sustainability in community-based conservation. In A. Kothari, N. Pathak, R. V. Anuradha, & B. Taneja (Ed.), *Communities and conservation* (pp. 58-80). New Delhi: Sage.

Poffenberger, M. (1990). *Forest management partnership: Regenerating India's forests*. New Delhi: Ford Foundations.

Poffenberger, M., McGean, B. & Khare, A. (1996). Communities sustaining India's forest in the twenty-first century. In M. Poffenberger & B. McGean (eds.),*Village voices, forest choices: Joint forest management in India* (pp. 17-55). Delhi: Oxford University Press.

Poffenberger, M., & McGean, B. (Ed). (1996). *Village voice, forest choices: Joint forest management in India* (pp. 1-13). New Delhi: Oxford-IBH.

Poffenberger, M., & Singh, C. (1993). The legal framework for Joint Forest management of forestlands in India. In J. Fox (Ed.), *Legal frameworks for forest management in Asia: Case studies of community/state relations*. Honolulu: East West Centre.

Poffenberger, M., & Singh, C. (1996). Communities and the state: Re-establishing the balance in Indian forest policy. In M. Poffenberger, & B. McGean (Ed.), *Village voices, forest choices: Joint forest management in India* (pp. 56-85). New Delhi: Oxford-IBH.

Pretty, J. (1995). *Regenerating agriculture: Policies and practice for sustainable and self-reliance*. London: Earthscan Publications.

Pretty, J. & Ward, H., (2000). Social capital and the environment. *World Development, 29*(2), 209-227.

Putnam, R. (1993). *Making democracy work: Civic traditions in modern Italy*. Princeton, N. J.: Princeton University Press.

Raju, G. (1998). Institutional structures for community based conservation. In A. Kothari, N. Pathak, R.V. Anuradha, & B. Taneja (Ed.), *Communities and conservation* (pp. 303-322). New Delhi: Sage.

Raju, G., Vaghela, R. and Raju, M.S. (1993). Development of people's institutions for management of forests. In A*nnual report: VIKSAT*. Ahmedabad: Nehru Foundation for Development.

Redfort, K.H., & Padoch, C. (Eds) (1992). *Conservation of neo-tropical forests: Working from experience.* New York, USA: Columbia University Press.

Regan, J.F., Rokeach, M., & Grube, J.W. (1982). Personal and corporate values and corporate identification of managers from several levels of an organisation. *Academic Psychology Bulletin, 4*, 345 - 355.

Reidenbach, R.E., & Robin, D.P. (1990). Toward the development of a multidimensional scale for improving evaluations of business ethics. *Journal of Business Ethics, 9*, 639-653.

Ritchie, D. (1992). *A strategy for Asian forestry development.* Washington D. C.: World Bank.

Rockeach, M. (1973). *The nature of human values.* NY: Free Press.

Rokeach, M. (1971), Long-range experimental modification of values, attitudes, and behaviour. *American Psychologist, 26*, 453-459.

Rokeach, M. (1971). Long range experimental modification of values, attitudes, and behaviour. *American Psychologist*, 26, 453-459

Roy, S.B. (1992). Bilateral matching institution: An illustration in forest conservation. *Journal of Indian Anthropology Society, 27*, 253-262.

Roy, S.B. (1993). Forest protection committees in West Bengal. *Economic and Political Weekly, 27* (29), 1528 -1530.

Roy, S.B. (1995). Social interaction towards institutionalisation of development programme: Case study from joint forest management. In S. B. Roy (Ed.), *Enabling environment for joint forest management* (pp. 35-46). New Delhi: Inter-India Publications.

Roy, S.B. (1995). Social interaction towards institutionalisation of development programme: Case study from joint forest management. In S.B.Roy (ed.), *Enabling environment for joint forest management* (pp. 35-46). New Delhi: Inter-India Publications.

Roy, S.B., & Chatterjee, M. (1994). *Joint Forest Management: A training manual.* New Delhi: Inter-India Publications.

Rudd, M.A. (2000). Live long and prosper: Collective action, social capital and social vision. *Ecological Economics, 34*, 131-144.

Sally, D. (2000). I, too, sail past: Odysseus and the logic of self-control. *Kyklos, 53*(2), 173-200.

Sarin, M. (1996). From conflict to collaboration: Institutional issues in community management. In M. Poffenberger, & B. MacGean (Ed.), *Village voices, forest choices: Joint forest management in India* (pp. 165-209). Delhi: Oxford University Press.

Saxena, N.C. (1987). Commons, trees and the poor in the Uttar Pradesh hills. *ODI Social Forestry Network Paper, 5*(f), 1-43.

Saxena, N.C., & Sarin, M. (1999). The Western Ghats forestry and environmental project in Karnataka: A preliminary assessment. In R. Jeffery, & N. Sundar (Ed.), *A new moral economy for India's forest?* (pp. 181-215). New Delhi: Sage.

Sayer, J. 1991. *Rainforest buffer Zones: guidelines for protected area managers* (p.94). Gland: International Union for Conservation of Nature and Natural Resources.

Schalger, E., & Ostrom, E. (1992). Property rights regimes and natural resources: A conceptual analysis. *Land Economics, 68*(3), 249-262.

Schalger, E., Blomquist, W., & Tang, Y.S. (1994). Mobile flows storage, and self-organised institutions for governing common pool resources. *Land Economics, 70*(3), 294-317.

Sen, D., & Das, P.K. (1987). The management of people's participation in community forestry: Some Issues. *ODI Social Forestry Network Paper, 4*(d), 1.30.

Seymour, F.J. (1991). Social forestry on public lands in Indonesia: a blurring of ends and means. In D. Challinor & M.H. Frondorf (Eds), *Social forestry: Communal and private management strategies compared* (pp. 23-24). Washington D.C.: School of advanced International Studies, John Hopkins University.

Shah, T. (1987). Gains from social forestry: Lessons from West Bengal. *ODI Social Forestry Network Paper, 5*(e), 1-20.

Shah, T. (1991). *The dynamism of India's village cooperatives:*

*A survey of issues and new agenda for research.* Anand: Institute of Rural management.

Shah, T. (1994 a). *Design for democracy: Building energetic farmer organisations.* Anand: Institute of Rural Management.

Shah, T. (1994 b). *Seeking salience: Governance and management in Indian village cooperatives.* Anand: Institute of Rural Management.

Shamir, B. (1991). Meaning, self and motivation in organizations. *Organizational studies, 12*, 405-424.

Shepherd, G. (1987). Workshop synthesis: Discussion and outcome. *ODI Social Forestry Network 'Paper, 5*(g), 1-13.

Shepherd, G. (1989). *Putting trees into the farming systems: Land adjudication and agro-forestry on the lower slopes of Mount Kenya* (Social forestry Network Paper, 8a). London: ODI

Shiva, V., Sharatchandra, H.C., & Banyapadhyag, J. (1992). Social forestry - no solution within the market. *The Ecologist, 12* (14), 158-168.

Shyamsundar, S., & Parameshwarappa, S. (1987). Forestry in India: The forester's view. *AMBIO, .26* (6).

Silwal, U.K. (1986). Attitude, awareness, and level of people's participation in community forestry development programme. *Nepal Forestry Research Paper Series,* No. 3.

Simon , H.A. (1996). *The sciences of the artificial* (3rd Ed.). Cambridge, MA.: MIT Press.

Singh Neera M. & Singh Kundan K. (1993). Forest protection by communities in Orissa: A new green revolution. *Forest, Trees, and People, Newsletter* no. 19.

Singh, C. (1986). *Common property and common poverty: India's forests, forest dwellers and the law.* New Delhi: Oxford University Press.

Singh, K. (1992). *People's participation in natural resource management* (Workshop report No. 8). Gujarat, Anand: Institute of Rural Management.

Singh, K. & Ballabh, V. (1997). *Co-operative management of natural resources.* New Delhi: Sage.

Singh, K., & Ballábh, V. (1996). Introduction and overview. In K.

Singh, & V. Ballabh (Ed.), *Cooperative management of natural resources* (pp. 13-38). New Delhi: Sage.

Sinha, J.B.P. (1990). A model of effective leadership styles in India. In A.M. Jaeger, & R.N. Kanungo (Ed.), *Management in developing countries* (pp. 252-263). London & New York: Routledge.

Sinha, J.B. P. (1995). *The cultural context of leadership and power*. New Delhi: Sage.

Sinha, J.B.P., & Sinha, M. (1974). Middleclass values in organisational perspective. *Journal of Social and Economic Studies*, 1, 243-252.

Sinha, S. (2000). *Water management systems of Himachal Pradesh: Case study of Khuls*. Unpublished Post Graduation Diploma in Rural Development Dissertation, Xavier Institute of Social Services, Ranchi.

Skutsch, M.M. (1994). *Social forestry as sustainable development, comparative strategies in Sri Lanka*. Thesis, University of Enschede, Netherlands.

Smith, H.J., & Tyler, T.R. (1997). Choosing the right pond: The influence of the status of one's group and one's status in that group on self-esteem and group oriented behaviours. *Journal of Experimental Social Psychology, 33*, 146-170.

Smity, H.J., & Tyler, T.R. (1997). Choosing the right pond: The influence of the status of one's group and one's status in that group on self-esteem and group oriented behaviours. *Journal of Experimental Social Psychology, 33*, 146-170.

Spears, J.S. (1983). Tropical reforestation: An achievable goal? *Commonwealth Forestry Review, 62*(3), 201-217.

Spurr, S.H. & Barnes, B.V. (1980). *Forest ecology* (3rd Eds.). NY: John Wiley and Sons.

SPWD (1998). *Annual report*. New Delhi: Society for Promotion of Wasteland Development.

Suar, D., Panda, B., & Sharan, M.B. (1989). Value comparison, organisational identification and job satisfaction among hospital employees. *The Creative Psychologist, 1*, 69-80.

Swallow, B. & Bromley, D.W. (1994). Co-management or no

management: The prospects for internal governance of common property regimes through dynamic contracts. *Oxford Agrarian Studies, 22*(1), 3-16.

Tajfel, H., & Turner, J.C. (1079). An integrative theory of intergroup conflict. In W.G. Austin & S. Worchel (Eds.), *The social psychology of inter-group relations* (pp.33 47). Monterey, CA: Brooks/Cole.

Tajfel, H., & Turner, J.C. (1979). An integrative theory of inter-group conflict. In W.G. Austin & S. Worchel (Eds.), *The social psychology of inter-group relations* (pp.33 47). Monterey, CA: Brooks/Cole.

Triandis, C. Harry (1996, April). The Psychological Measurement of Cultural Syndromes. *American Psychologist, 51*, 407-415.

Triandis, H.C. (1994). *Culture and social behaviour*. New York: McGraw-Hill.

Triandis, H.C. (1995). *Individualism and collectivism*. Boulder, CO: West View Press.

Turner, J.C. (1982). Towards a congnitive redefinition of the social group. In H. Tajfel (Ed.), *Social identity and inter-group relations* (pp. 15-40). Cambridge, UK: Cambridge University Press.

Turner, J.C. (1985). Social categorization and the self-concept: A social cognitive theory of group behaviour. In E.J. Lawler (Ed.), *Advances in group processes* (Vol. 2, pp. 77-122) Greenwich, CT: JAI Press

Turner, J.C. (1991). *Social influence*. Buckingham, UK: Open University Press & Pacific Grove, CA: Brooks/Cole.

Turner, J.C. (1999). Some current themes in research on social identity and self-categorization theories. In N. Ellemers, R. Spears, & B. Doosje (Eds.), *Social identity: Context, commitment, content* (pp. 6-34). Oxford: Blackwell.

Turner, J.C., & Onorato, R. (1999). Social identity, personality and the self-concept: A self-categorization perspective. In T.R. Tyler, R. Kramer, & O. John (Eds.), *The psychology of the social self* (pp. 11-46). Hillsdale, NJ: Erlbaum.

Turner, J.C., Hogg, M.A., Oakes, P.J., Reicher, S.D., & Wetherell,

M.S. (1987). *Rediscovering the social group: A self-categorization theory*. Oxford: Blackwell

Tyler, T.R. (1999). Why people co-operate with organizations: An identity-based perspective. In B.M. Staw & R. Sutton (Eds.), *Research in organizational behaviour* (Vol. 21, pp. 201-246). Greenwich, CT: JAI Press.

Tyler, T.R. (1999). Why people co-operate with organizations: An identity -based perspective. In B.M. Staw & R. Sutton (Eds.), *Research in organizational behaviour* (Vol. 21, pp. 201-246). Greenwich, CT : JAI Press.

Van der Bliek, J. (1991). Environmental management in rural development in Ratnapura, Sri Lanka. In H. Savenije & A. Huijsman (Eds), *Making haste slowly: Strengthening local environmental management in agricultural development* (pp. 207-224). Amsterdam, Netherlands: Royal Tropical Institute.

Van der Hoek, A. (1991). Local level planning in the uplands of East Java, Indonesia. In H. Savenjiji & A. Huijsman (Eds), In H. Savenije & A. Huijsman (Eds), *Making haste slowly: Strengthening local environmental management in agricultural development* (pp. 189-206). Amsterdam, Netherlands: Royal Tropical Institute.

Vedeld, T. (1997). Village politics: Heterogeneity, leadership and collective action. The *Journal of Development Studies, 36* (5), 105-134.

Verma, R.C. (1990). *Indian tribes through the ages* (pp. 225-28). New Delhi: Ministry of Information and Broadcasting, Government of India.

VIKSAT (1995). *Annual report*. Ahmedabad, Gujarat: VIKSAT.

Vira, B. (1999). Implementing joint forest management in the field: Towards an understanding of the community-bureaucracy interface. In R. Jeffery, & N. Sundar (Ed.), *A new moral economy for India's forests?* (pp. 254-275). New Delhi: Sage.

Wade, R. (1982). *Village republics: Economic conditions for collective action in south India*. Cambridge: Cambridge University Press.

Wade, R. (1985). *Common property resource management in South Indian villages* (Monograph). Washington: IBRD.

Wade, R. (1988). Why some Indian villages cooperate? *Economic and Political Weekly*, April 16.

White, S. (1996). Depoliticising development: The uses and abuses of participation. *Development in Practice, 6* (1), 6-15.

Wiersum, K.F. (1990). International experience in social forestry. In *Report of Workshop on Social forestry in Indonesia* (pp. 135-143), held at Forestry Faculty, Gadjah Mada University, Yogyakarta. Regional Wood Energy Development Programme in Asia, FAO, Bangkok, Thailand.

Woolcock, M. (1998). Social capital and economic development: Towards a theoretical synthesis and policy framework. *Theory and Society, 27*, 151-208.

Woolcock, M. & Narayan, D. (2000). Social capital: Implications for development theory, research, and policy. *The World Bank Research Observer, 15*(2), 225-49.

World Bank (1987). *Forestry sector policy paper*. Washington D.C. USA.

World Bank (1996). World Bank participation source book. New York: Oxford University Press.

World Bank (1998). *World development report: Knowledge for development.* Oxford: Oxford University Press.

Young, O. (1999). *Governance in world affairs*. Ithaca: Cornell University Press.

Zuhair, M. (1998). Conservation by local communities in the Maldives. In A. Kothari, N. Pathak, R.V. Anuradha, & B. Taneja (Ed.), *Communities and conservation* (pp. 81-101). New Delhi: Sage.

# INDEX